AT HOME IN IRELAND

Kathleen Peddicord

Published by Lahardan Books

Published by Lahardan Books

Copyright © Kathleen Peddicord, 2022
All rights reserved

ISBN 978-1-958583-00-5

Book and Cover Design by Cristian Landero

No part of this publication may be reproduced, stored in, or introduced into a retrieval system, or transmitted, in any form, or by any means (electronic, mechanical, photocopying, recording, or otherwise), without the prior written permission of both the copyright owner and the publisher of this book.

The scanning, uploading, and distribution of this book via the Internet or via any other means without the permission of the publisher is illegal and punishable by law. Please purchase only authorized electronic editions, and do not participate in or encourage electronic piracy of copyrighted materials. Your support of the author's rights is appreciated.

For Dad,
who, like Ireland,
I carry in my heart

Acknowledgements

This book is a memoir. It reflects my present recollections of experiences over time. I've changed some names and characteristics, compressed some events, and recreated some dialogue.

This book would not exist if not for Ireland and is offered as a thank-you to the Emerald Isle and her friendly Irish who welcomed us when we landed on their shores and did their best to show us what was what.

I owe a great thanks, as well, to Rebecca Cole, my editor, without whom this story would have remained in my memory only. Whatever is worthwhile in the pages to follow is down to her efforts.

Finally, I thank my father for his unconditional support, not only in Ireland but throughout my life, and my husband Lief for suggesting that we seek our new starts in Ireland together. How different this story would have been had I gone it alone.

Contents

	Prologue 11
I	Baltimore 14
II	Rick 19
III	Lief 33
IV	First Date 48
V	Pouldrew House 61
VI	Honeymoon 72
VII	Waterford 81
VIII	The Granville Hotel 88
IX	Saturdays 106
X	You Say Potatoes 119
XI	All Mod Cons 129
XII	Your Man Mark Breen 134
XIII	Yes, I'm From America 145
XIV	Staffing Up 157
XV	Lahardan House 172
XVI	Rising Damp 180

XVII	Dinner With Morette	193
XVIII	Waterford Regional Hospital	200
XIX	Jackson	208
XX	Dad	219
XXI	Thom	228
XXII	Agora Ireland	245
XXIII	The Most Legendary Mystery In Irish History	255
XXIV	Rody Keighery's Auction Rooms	262
XXV	An Irish Cottage Garden	273
XXVI	Stone Walls	282
XXVII	Dead Bats And A Friendly Ghost	288
XXVIII	Weekend In Bantry	297
XXIX	Irish Pubs	307
XXX	Family Vacation	314
XXXI	Shell-shocked	329
XXXII	One Nice Young Couple From New York	334
XXXIII	Settled	345

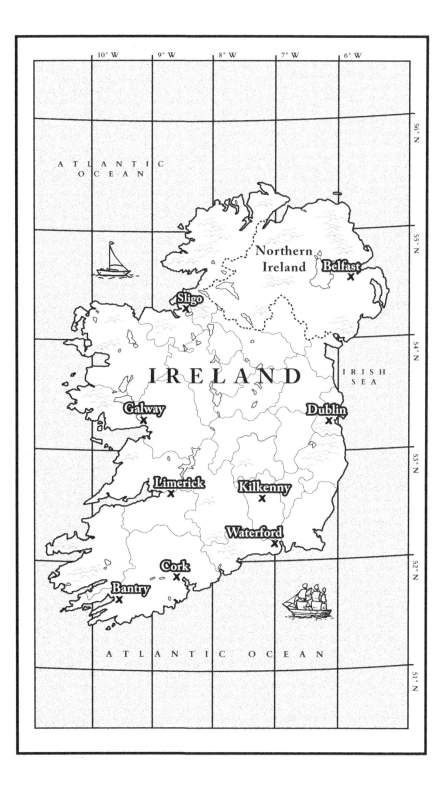

Prologue

"Does it ever bother you that your life is over?"

My daughter, Kaitlin, didn't break stride as she looked over her shoulder to ask her question. We were making our way back to the hotel after lunch. Kaitlin and her friend Jules led my husband, Lief, our four-year-old son, Jackson, and me slowly along the bayside promenade in Galway. Lief and I strolled arm in arm, smiling as Jackson darted off after another seagull only to return a minute later disappointed that he still couldn't catch one. To our left, beyond a low stone wall, the ice-green Atlantic churned. On our right was the city's eight-hundred-year-old cobblestoned central square, where we'd spent the morning poking around antique shops. For me, it was a day as good as days get. What was Kaitlin talking about?

"What in the world do you mean?" I called out over the stiff ocean breeze. Maybe I was kidding myself, but I wasn't afraid of my looming fortieth birthday. As far as I was concerned, I was just getting started.

Kaitlin turned to face me.

"Well, you know," she said with a grin, "you're married. You have two kids. You've had the same job forever. Your life is what it's going to be. Everything for you is figured out. And now you're about to be forty years old. What more could there be?" Ouch. My fourteen-year-old daughter was putting things into harsh perspective.

On one hand, she was right. I'd found the man I intended to spend the rest of my life with. I had two children. I'd been working at the same company since before Kaitlin was born—from her point of view, forever.

On the other hand, my life on this eve of my fortieth birthday was unrecognizable compared with what it had been not that many years before. Kaitlin didn't remember our days in New Freedom, Pennsylvania—a time when my preoccupation with climbing the corporate ladder I'd set myself on left little time for anything else, least of all leisurely seaside strolls—but, as hard as I'd tried to put it all behind me, I sure did. My life had been reinvented since then, and, taking in the scene surrounding me, I could only imagine more renaissance ahead, both for me and for Ireland, the country I called home.

I'd been an inadvertent immigrant to the Emerald Isle in the age of the Celtic Tiger, a time when great amounts of wealth were being generated, more money than this island had ever known. Since I'd arrived six years earlier with my new husband,

PROLOGUE

my eight-year-old daughter, and my business plan, the Irish had been busy covering their ancient green land with suburban track homes, shopping malls, and fast-food franchises. Local pubs were being replaced by multi-story dance clubs, and discount mortgage brokers were opening offices in every town and village across the land.

Ireland, like me, had a deep yearning for acknowledgement. She, like me, ached to compete in the global business arena. Over the seven years I lived in this country, I watched it race enthusiastically in the direction of its own demise, speeding toward an economic cliff.

But I'm getting ahead of my story.

How did I end up in Ireland in the first place? As is too often the case, the answer to that question had to do with a man.

I

Baltimore

I had forty-five minutes to get on the road. I let our dog, Sammy, out the back door so I could keep an eye on him in the backyard from the kitchen window while I packed Kaitlin's lunch—sandwich, applesauce, cookies, yogurt, and juice box. The staff at her daycare told me I sent too much food, but I liked for her to have options. I filled Sammy's bowls with food and water, then went upstairs to finish dressing for my big day. Rick was asleep and probably wouldn't wake up before Kaitlin and I left. He'd worked until closing at the restaurant the night before, as he had every night that week. I didn't know what time he'd gotten home and I couldn't remember the last time we'd had a conversation. I glanced at my watch—forty minutes until I needed to leave. Talking to Rick would have to wait.

I ran my presentation in my head as I slid on my new navy shift and pumps, no tights. I could never get through the day without snags, and I couldn't risk snags today. One of the doctors we were hoping would sign on as an editor for the health publishing division I was launching was coming to the Agora offices. I would spend the afternoon pitching my business plan and then take him to dinner. My bosses, Bill and Mark, and I had invested more than a year preparing for this day. The new division was my chance to step up to a next level of leadership and responsibility and to prove myself not only to Bill and Mark but to all Agora management. If Dr. Willix didn't sign today, I'd be back at square one, looking for a new doctor interested in working with us. Worse, I'd be giving Agora's Executive Committee reason to wonder if I were the right person for this job.

Thirty minutes. I headed to Kaitlin's room.

"Time to get up, Doodlebug," I said. When she opened her eyes and smiled up at me, I thought for an instant how nice it would be to get into bed alongside her and cuddle for a minute, but we didn't have time for that. Instead, I helped her from beneath the blanket and led her into the bathroom so we could wash her face and brush her teeth. Back in her room, I pulled her pink sundress over her head and combed her hair.

"Cereal or eggs?"

"Eggs and toast," she said. "With ketchup."

Downstairs, in the kitchen, she sat in her booster seat while I scrambled her eggs. My father had introduced her to the idea of ketchup on her scrambled eggs. Now, as with many things in

Kaitlin's world, only Poppy's way would do, and that was okay with me. He'd set most of my standards, too.

While Kaitlin ate, I ran downstairs to switch over the laundry from the washer to the dryer and to pick up her toys from the night before. Back upstairs I checked the stove clock again. Ten minutes. "Come on, Doodlebug, we've got to get going." When she'd finally finished, I wiped down the stove and the table, grabbed my sunglasses and keys, and led Kaitlin by the hand out the side door to my car.

Five minutes later we pulled into the parking lot at Touch Of Country Daycare, Main Street, New Freedom, Pennsylvania. Walking through the front door, I saw the poster for the book drive. Today was the last day to donate. I'd forgotten again. Of course I had. I'd also forgotten to bring cupcakes for the bake sale last month. And to sign her permission slip yesterday. I wanted to remember those kinds of things, but my work to-do lists always ended up taking priority. I didn't have time to worry again about what that meant about me as a mother right now. I walked Kaitlin to her three-year-old class, kissed her good-bye, and reminded her that Poppy and Gammy would be picking her up that afternoon and she'd be spending the night at their house.

"Okay, Mommy!" she called out as she ran off in the direction of the pretend kitchen.

I knew I should stop to speak with her teachers, but the clock hands were racing forward inside my head. I'd call later to tell them Kaitlin's grandparents would be picking her up. It was 6:45 a.m. If I was lucky, I'd be to the office by 7:30, but I knew I wouldn't be that lucky.

At my desk at last, I booted up my laptop and saw the time flash on the screen. 7:55. Just an hour until the marketing meeting, which would last the morning. I opened the file for the spreadsheet I'd been creating to share with the doctor. He needed to find my projected potential earnings sexy enough to sign a contract.

I made each of the next sixty minutes matter, blocking out everything but the task at hand and focusing in the way I've always been able to do when I needed to. I reviewed my projections, satisfied myself that the data made a respectable case, then saved the file, just in time to make it to my marketing meeting. After that meeting, I had lunch with a pair of new writers. Then I spent the afternoon making my presentation and finalizing the contract. When the do-or-die moment came, Dr. Willix was on board. My bosses Bill and Mark were happy. I let myself relax just a little.

By the time Bill, Mark, and Dr. Willix walked me to my car after our celebratory dinner, I had been in perpetual motion for sixteen hours, and, when I pulled up alongside my dark house in New Freedom, it was nearly midnight. As I turned the key, feet aching in my pumps, Sammy barked and jumped on the other side of the door. He sprinted past me to the backyard as I walked inside. The house was silent. I was ready to collapse.

Rick, still at work I assumed, hadn't left a note, but the light on the answering machine was blinking. "Kath," my father's message said, "the lady at Kaitlin's daycare didn't know Mom and I were picking her up today. But don't worry. It was fine. Everyone there knows us well. We took Kaitlin to the diner for dinner. She wanted a hamburger but ate some of your mother's broccoli so we thought it was okay. She's here now, asleep upstairs. We'll get her to daycare in the morning. Don't worry about that. I hope your big meeting was a success. Speak with you tomorrow."

I hadn't remembered to call Kaitlin's daycare to tell them her grandparents would be picking her up. Like so many other little daily failures, I told myself this one didn't matter, though I was having more trouble believing myself all the time. I was pushing hard at work and reveling in the highs of my successes there, but lows followed, like right now. Returning to my empty house, I had no choice but to admit, because I was finally too tired to push the thought from my mind, that my work triumphs seemed to come at the direct cost of failures as a mom. For now, I'd hold on to the sense of elation I'd brought home with me after having finalized the deal with Dr. Willix. I'd count the day a win and apologize to Kaitlin's teachers tomorrow. Meantime, I'd go upstairs to bed and hope Rick didn't make it home before I fell asleep. My husband would likely have been drinking with his fellow waiters after work, and I didn't have it in me to face that situation tonight.

11
Rick

When I'd first met him, Rick was working in a dive bar called Bratwursthaus where my friends and I hung out three or four times a week. He was tall and handsome, with broad shoulders and a mustache that made him look like Tom Selleck. He was the head bartender and the life of the party. Everyone knew him or wanted to know him. I'd seen girls approach him nearly every night. One night, he came toward me carrying a pitcher of draft beer, smiling, and singing along to Phil Collins on the jukebox to ask if I'd like to have dinner with him sometime. I was a junior in college. Rick was seven years older but had finished his decade-long college education experience only the year before. For him to be asking me out was a triumph.

For our first date he took me to The Crease, another local hangout where everyone knew him by name. Sitting at the table with him, I felt like a celebrity.

After that first date we were together nearly every night. By the end of that school year, I was unofficially living with him and his roommate. I spent that summer waiting tables at Something Fishy in Fell's Point and with Rick on his parents' boat moored at Back River. Like Rick, his mother and father were big socializers, and I found myself in an exciting new world of sunset cruises and yacht club dinners. I'd always been an introvert. At cocktail parties, I was the one at the back of the room sipping my drink slowly and hoping no one noticed me because if they did they might try to talk to me and what would I say? With Rick, I didn't need to worry about coming up with cocktail chit-chat. He was full of stories. I could just stand alongside him watching him entertain the crowd and enjoy a little overflow from all the adoration he enjoyed wherever he went. He had interests beyond mine like boating and riding motorcycles and pushed me thrillingly beyond my comfort zone.

By the time I graduated college, I took it for granted that Rick and I would get married. "Will you take a chance on me?" was how he finally popped the question. He must have realized that a future with him wasn't a guaranteed dream come true. The impromptu proposal was private, the two of us alone in his apartment. Later, Rick staged a dinner with both families at Baltimore Country Club where he got down on one knee and presented a ring he'd had made with a diamond given to him by his grandmother. Both times I said yes.

RICK

When I finished school, I went almost immediately to work as a proofreader for a Baltimore City-based publishing company called Agora. Rick got a job selling Macintosh computers for Towson Computer. He was good at it and made top salesman every quarter. One year his boss gave him an all-expenses-paid trip for two to Cancun as a bonus. Rick and I swam with stingrays and giant sea turtles, and he won first prize in the karaoke contest on the day cruise to Isla Mujeres wearing a costume that featured a grass skirt and a bikini top he made by tying two half-coconut shells together. I knew the whole scene was silly and I wouldn't have dressed up similarly myself, but I laughed at Rick's antics along with everyone else that day. It was a release. I'd never been good at letting myself have fun. Rick showed me how, and I liked it.

Kaitlin came along our first year together. She was the greatest joy either of us had ever known, and now it was the three of us at the yacht club each weekend. On the surface, we had an ideal life, but, while I'd exchanged college drinking for wine with dinner, Rick's habits didn't change. Rum drinks fueled his weekends, and he brought home a six-pack of beer every night. I should have made an issue of it, but I didn't have time for a husband with a drinking problem so I didn't allow myself to acknowledge that I might have a husband with a drinking problem.

Instead, I threw myself into my work, where I was hard driven to succeed but always felt several steps behind. In school, I was the first to raise my hand, always did all the extra credit, and studied during recess. I liked learning. And I liked being number one. At school, I generally was, and I'd taken for granted that it'd be the same in business. I'd work hard, and I'd shine. But my first years at Agora I was out of my element, constantly fumbling and trying to prove myself. I went from being the smartest one in most rooms to feeling embarrassed by the end of almost every exchange.

At Agora, the people around me were better educated, better traveled, and better spoken. For sure they were more experienced. Vivian, my Editorial Director, had been a correspondent for The *New York Times* and the *International Herald Tribune*. She and Agora owner Bill Bonner bantered about where to go in London for the most authentic carvery and debated the global investing implications of U.S. debt. I'd never been in the company of people who spoke about such intriguing topics, and they did it off-handedly. I found this world irresistibly fascinating and almost paralyzingly challenging. But I pushed ahead blindly, suppressing the ineptitude I felt all the time. Showing up each morning meant setting aside how disappointed I'd been in my performance the day before, but I kept showing up. I'd always felt I was on my way somewhere and frustrated that I wasn't getting there quick enough. I was sure Agora was going to push me forward, and I wasn't going to let inexperience and self-doubt get in my way. My mind was being opened to the world. The more my new Agora colleagues showed me of life beyond Baltimore, the bigger my appetite grew for knowing life beyond Baltimore.

RICK

Six months after I'd started at Agora, my friend Bruce, who'd been editor of Agora's travel magazine, *International Living*, handed in his resignation. After he did, he walked out of Bill's office and straight over to me. "You should go in there and tell him you want the job," Bruce said. "There's no one else in-house for the position. They'll have to advertise and interview and that will take time. They'll want to avoid that if they can. Plus, I know you can do it." Bruce was always encouraging me, always trying to shore up my self-confidence.

I was self-aware enough to realize that if I thought too long about making such a bold suggestion to my boss, I'd never do it, so I took Bruce's idea as a direct command, walked away from him and directly over to Bill's office. Bill's door was never closed.

"Could I speak with you a minute, please? I started. Bill looked up from his computer, smiled, and nodded.

"I understand Bruce is leaving. I think I could do his job. I think I could be editor of *International Living*," I blurted out, more surprised by my audacity with every word that came out of my mouth. Even more shocking was Bill's response.

"Well, now, there's an idea," he said. "I think that would be great. In fact, you'd be doing me a big favor. It would save me having to try to find and train someone new."

That was the start of my corporate climb in earnest. I liked being part of this Agora conversation, and, finally, I was finding my voice. Bill noticed before I did that I had an interest in marketing and began drawing me further into the business side of the business.

One day he asked me if I'd like to try writing a sales letter. I didn't know what that meant but said yes, I would, thank you very much. I'd find other sales letters, I figured, and mimic those. That's what I did. Bill mailed my letter, and it brought on more new subscribers than the promotion they'd been mailing. Bill told me that wasn't easy to do and asked if I'd like to write another sales letter.

Before long, I was attending more meetings and taking on more responsibility. I put my head down and worked harder, showing up early, eating lunch at my desk, and staying late, and I didn't mind. I found the long hours and non-stop deadlines invigorating. The most difficult thing for me is standing still, and Agora allowed me to be in constant motion. Within three years, I went from proofreader to publisher, from employee to partner. I had found my stride.

But the more I worked, the less time I spent with Rick and Kaitlin. My father had just retired. He and my mother were happy for any chance to see their granddaughter, and I let myself rely on them to pick up the slack for me at home. It was a dangerous trade-off. I was missing time with Kaitlin I'd never get back, but I rarely slowed down long enough to give those thoughts time to register. I was moving and shaking.

My role as editor of *International Living* required travel. I planned a trip to Belize to research a feature article on the beach-

RICK

front property market on Ambergris Caye. I flew to Belize City then took an eight-seater puddle-jumper over to the island where I was met by the real estate agent who had offered to show me around. He showed up wearing a T-shirt, shorts, and no shoes. "Welcome to barefoot paradise," he said as he shook my hand.

Like me, Ambergris Caye was but a young girl. San Pedro town, the fishing village around which development was just beginning, consisted of three parallel roads, all unpaved. The hotel where I stayed was the best on the island. Amenities included towels in the bathroom, a telephone at the front desk that was often out of service, and a front-line position on the Caribbean Sea.

I was booked in for five days. Each morning I'd meet the barefoot real estate agent in the lobby, and he'd take me out to tour more of the island's coast in his small boat. That was the only way to get around. Shortly outside town, San Pedro's three dirt roads converged into one rutted thoroughfare that stopped short at the jungle's edge.

"You had a phone call today," the young man in reception told me my final night when I returned from dinner with my barefooted host. "Here's the number."

I stood in the tiny open-air lobby trying to get a call to go through to Rick but couldn't. Finally, I gave up and went to sleep. I was traveling home the next day anyway.

I pulled up to our house in New Freedom just after 8:00 p.m., but downstairs was dark. I found Rick upstairs in his recliner in the family room watching television and drinking. I walked toward him to kiss him hello, but the look in his eyes stopped me.

"Is everything okay?" I asked.

Rick didn't answer but stared in a way that made me reluctant to get closer. Then, finally, "I want to know who you were with in Belize," he said.

"What do you mean?"

"I called the hotel where you were staying. They told me you checked in with a man and were there with him the whole time." He was laying back but not relaxed. His body was rigid. He had his head titled hard to one side and was holding tight to the arms of the chair.

"Checked in with a man? What man?"

"You tell me what man." He said loudly as he began to raise himself up from the chair. He was unsteady, and I thought he might trip over his own feet as he started toward me.

"The real estate agent who was showing me around the island met me at the hotel each morning. I guess the guy at the front desk could have thought we were together…"

"Yes, he thought you were together. He said you were together the entire trip." He was slurring his words and swaying. I tensed. I'd seen him jealous and intoxicated before. He could get very angry.

"You're drunk," I said. "I'm not going to try to have this conversation now. Go to sleep, and we can talk more in the morning."

RICK

"No, we'll talk now. I want to know what you were really doing in Belize this week," he said even louder. He'd spoken to me in this tone before. What followed was never good.

"I've told you. I was working. That's all. There's nothing else to say."

Rick got up from the chair and came toward me. I backed out of the family room and into our bedroom where I picked up the phone and, almost without realizing what I was doing, began dialing his father, Bud. I hadn't been able to check on her yet, but Kaitlin would be asleep in the next room. I didn't want anything to happen that might wake her up, and I was worried I wouldn't be able to handle Rick on my own.

"I've just returned from Belize," I told his father on the phone, "and Rick is very drunk."

"I'll be right over," Bud said.

I went back downstairs and sat in the rocking chair in the kitchen to wait. Both of Rick's parents arrived an hour later. His mother stayed with me while his father went upstairs. Rick had finally passed out in bed. I heard Bud call his name over and over until Rick finally woke up, then I went upstairs to stand in the hall outside our bedroom to listen.

"What's going on, Rick?" his father asked him.

"She went to Belize with a man," Rick said. "She spent a week in Belize with another man. She says it was work and nothing happened, but I don't believe her."

"We trust Kathleen," I heard Bud say. "She wouldn't be unfaithful to you. You need to apologize to her and make things right."

Rick didn't respond, and, in a few minutes, he fell asleep again. Rick's father and I returned to the kitchen, where Rick's mother was boiling water for tea. They left an hour later, and I went upstairs to sleep on the sofa in the family room.

The next day, Rick was quiet and distant. He didn't apologize or even bring up the subject of the argument the night before and neither did I. We had practice at pretending things were all right when they weren't and that's what we did, but Rick never recovered.

His performance at work began to suffer. He went from top producer to enduring months with zero sales. While my professional life continued to expand, his was stagnant and shriveling. He was jealous of the new world I was becoming part of at work, of my travel, and of the money I was earning. The greater his resentment grew, the more he drank. The more he drank, the less he worked. He stopped going out on cold calls to drum up new clients, which had been key to his historic success. Co-workers who were his friends and worried about him told me that he'd spend whole days sitting at a computer in the Towson Computer showroom playing video games. Days when he was out of the office, presumably selling, he couldn't produce any evidence for which clients he'd seen. His boss Toby carried him as long as he could.

Finally, one Wednesday, Rick came home early and I knew what had happened before he told me. He walked into the kitch-

RICK

en where I was making spaghetti and said, "I lost my job. Toby fired me. I almost didn't come home. I didn't know how I would tell you."

I was sorry for him. I realized he must have been feeling embarrassed and probably panicked and had a momentary impulse to reach over and hug him. That thought passed quickly, though, and was replaced by dread. Rick had resented my promotions, raises, and friendships at Agora when he was employed. I was afraid to find out how out-of-work Rick would handle even greater imbalances in our marriage.

He started a job the next week at a restaurant in New Freedom. It was intended as a temporary gig while he looked for a new career path, but it meant he was seldom home before 3:00 a.m. and that he had easy access to a lot of liquor and bar staff to drink with. Friends tried to tell him he had a problem. His parents and I spoke with him about getting help. He only got angry and said we all were worried about nothing.

About six months later, early one Saturday morning, I heard pounding at our side door. I got out of bed and ran downstairs. Through the window I could see two police officers standing on our stoop. I hoped their knocking hadn't also woken Kaitlin.

"Is Rick Yent at home?" one asked.

I knew with that question that my marriage was over.

"No," I said, trying to appear calm. "He didn't come back from his shift at the restaurant where he works last night." I hadn't even realized that he hadn't come home until the banging at the door woke me up. Rick was never home before 3:00 or 4:00 in the morning. I went to bed without him almost every night then found him asleep next to me the next morning.

"A green Ford pick-up truck registered in his name was driven off a bridge and is in the river a few miles down the road," the officer said.

I didn't know what to say, so I didn't say anything, but I wasn't shocked to hear the news. I'd been waiting for something like this to happen. They hadn't said anything about a body at the scene. Kaitlin's father wasn't dead at least. The officer handed me a card and told me to call the number on it when I heard from Rick.

I closed the door behind the two policemen, then went upstairs to check on Kaitlin. She was still asleep. I grabbed an afghan from the family room and returned downstairs. I pulled the blanket over my shoulders and sat down in the rocking chair in the kitchen to try to process. I couldn't imagine where else Rick would go, so he'd be home eventually. But what would I say to him when he came through the door?

An hour later, Rick finally appeared, agitated and wet.

"Two policemen were here a while ago," I blurted out, "asking for you."

"What did you tell them?"

"I said you didn't come home from work last night."

"You shouldn't have told them that!" he shouted. "What's

RICK

wrong with you? You should have said I was here asleep!"

I stood there in my pajamas shivering, watching Rick's soaked jacket drip onto the pine wood floor of our kitchen. His hair was wild. His eyes were, too.

"I need you to call the police now and tell them I've been home since 2:00 a.m."

I wasn't going to lie to the police, of course. Plus, that ship had sailed. They'd been to the house. They knew Rick hadn't come home all night. But the police weren't my problem. More than two years of this reality had been enough. Without planning it, almost without comprehending it, I heard myself telling Rick to leave.

"You've got to go," I said. "You can't stay here any longer. This can't be my life. This can't be Kaitlin's life."

At first, he didn't respond. Maybe he didn't hear me. Maybe he didn't understand me. Maybe he didn't think I meant it. He sat down in the rocking chair where I'd been sitting just moments before waiting for him. I watched a puddle form on the floor underneath.

"I want you to call Storm to ask if you can stay with him for a while," I said. Storm was Rick's best friend. He'd stayed with us when he'd been between apartments a few years earlier. I knew he wouldn't mind having Rick as a house guest.

Still, Rick didn't say anything. He didn't seem to be able to process what was happening.

After a few minutes, I told him, "If you don't call Storm, I will."

Finally, Rick got up from the rocking chair, walked slowly over to the phone, and began dialing his friend.

"Hey, Storm," he said, "I was wondering if you'd be up for a roommate for a while?"

Storm didn't ask any questions. Everyone had known for a long while that this day was coming. Storm agreed to come pick him up, and Rick went upstairs to change his clothes and pack a suitcase.

Kaitlin had slept through everything, thank goodness. I woke her, made her scrambled eggs and toast, and sat down at the kitchen table with her, trying to act like it was just another Saturday morning. As I watched her eat, though, the reality of what was happening began to settle in. From here on out, it'd be just me and her.

After she'd finished her breakfast, I took her outside and pushed her on her swing until Storm drove up. I stopped pushing. Rick came out of the house with his suitcase and came over to the swing set. "I'll see you soon, Sweet Pea," he said kneeling down before Kaitlin on her swing so he could hug and kiss her. "I'm going to go stay with Mr. Storm for a little while." Kaitlin sat quiet and still and I stood alongside her as we watched her father and Storm drive away. I knew Rick wouldn't be coming back, but how would I help my four-year-old understand why?

III
Lief

In the four years following my divorce, my role at Agora continued to expand. Now I was publishing the *International Living* magazine, rather than editing it, and also managing the health division I'd launched. I'd put my marriage with Rick behind me and had fallen hard for a man at work. As my best friend, Beth, had warned me often throughout that relationship, "With a workplace romance, in the end, it's always the woman who has to leave." She was right. When I finally admitted to myself that I needed to move on, the only way I could imagine breaking things off was by going far away. "You need to pull a geographic," Beth agreed. How, though, could I start over somewhere new without giving up the career I'd been working hard and long to build?

By this time, Agora owner Bill Bonner was not only my boss and mentor but also like a second father. Bill was witty, charming, and gallant, a larger-than-life character who told a great story, loved to travel, and prioritized ideas, the more contrarian the better. Bill eschewed popular culture and anything trendy and prized the traditional but not the conventional. He thought big and outside any box I'd encountered. I, too, had a huge appetite for discovery, though I'd never known it. Bill liked architecture, another interest that, when he introduced me to it, I realized I shared. On a business trip to Santa Fe, for meetings with the managers of the book business Agora owned there, Bill rented a car and drove us to Albuquerque to see the first house he'd ever built, which, he seemed really happy to note, was still standing, perched on the side of the hill where he'd left it. Bill also played guitar, including at office get-togethers, and had made a living for a short time in his twenties as a busker in the Paris Metro. He wore a homburg hat and, in winter, a gray wool scarf that he tied the way the French do.

When I'd first applied for a job, Bill had hired me as proofreader based on my answer to a single question about the use of the Oxford comma. I was for it, he against. When I managed to persuade him of the value of that final mark of punctuation in a series, he asked when I could start work. I'd been at Agora thirteen years when my years-long office romance imploded. Bill had known about my relationship with my colleague all along, and, when I came to him to say I'd finally realized it had to end because it had no future, Bill responded immediately to make a recommendation, suggesting the situation had been weighing on his mind as much as mine.

"I'd say a big change of scenery is what the doctor ordered," he said. "You need a break from Baltimore." It was unanimous. Beth, Bill, and I all thought a move was in my future. But where to go?

Bill proposed two options. I could reposition to Santa Fe, New Mexico, to work with Agora's book business, or I could move to Ireland to run the EU base he wanted to establish.

Those might seem like dramatic options—moving as a single mom with a young daughter to the other side of the country or the other side of the Atlantic—but, as soon as Bill put them on the table, I knew right away that I was going to make one of those leaps. Though I hadn't lived anywhere else, Baltimore was not my destiny, and, until this point, especially since the end of my marriage, I'd been biding time until the path to where I was really meant to be presented itself. Bill's bold suggestions put me at the fork that would get me on that path. Or, at least, the exhilarating opportunities Bill had set forth would move me on from Baltimore. Finally I had the chance I'd craved to venture out and see more of the world.

The question now was how to choose which side of the fork to follow. Having been editor and then publisher of a magazine focused on options for Americans interested in living and investing overseas, the idea of moving to a new country wasn't nearly as big a deal for me as it might have been for most people. I'd been advising others on how to relocate overseas for a decade. It was time to take my own advice. Besides, I'd been to Santa Fe and could take it or leave it. Though I'd never seen Ireland, I'd been infatuated by storybook tales of Celtic castles and kings since I was a young girl. If I were making a big move, I'd make the biggest move possible. Ireland would be my new course.

Bill's assistant put an Irish flag in the center of the conference table in our main board room, and Agora's Executive Committee and I spent two nights a week around it for months conceiving a strategy to open our EU outpost. Our plan hinged on our application being accepted by Ireland's Investment and Development Agency (IDA), which was offering tax incentives to foreign companies that set up businesses in the country and hired Irish staff. That's why Agora was going to Ireland—for a better corporate tax rate. That and Bill's family was Irish.

The IDA approved our application and gave us three options for where to base our operation—Sligo, Galway, and Waterford. Another choice. I'd need to go have a look in person. Agora organized tours in places we identified as most appealing for Americans interested in going abroad. I'd plan one to Ireland and offer it to my *International Living* readers. Twenty-five of them signed up to visit the Emerald Isle with me, and I decided to bring Kaitlin and my parents along. Ireland would be Kaitlin's new home, too, and I wanted her and my parents to be part of the adventure from the start. The schedule I put together had us flying to Dublin then traveling for ten days in Waterford, Cork, Galway, Sligo, and Belfast before returning to the capital. My mother, father, and

Kaitlin were excited for the trip, but I'm not sure they believed it was the start of a trans-Atlantic move. That was okay. I'd bring them around.

The first morning of the tour, I sat at the head of the conference table in the meeting room of Dublin's Jury's Hotel, introducing myself and reviewing the day's program with the group. We'd hear that morning from a representative of the IDA, a banker, an attorney reviewing residency options, and a real estate agent for an overview of the Irish property market. After I adjourned the meeting and people began dispersing to the dining room for breakfast, I booted up my laptop to check emails. Nothing. No error message to indicate why not, but no emails in my in-box. Technology is not my friend. I felt a slight sense of panic rising in my stomach. I needed to be able to email to keep up with things back in the office in Baltimore. If I couldn't, I'd fall out of touch. Who knew what I'd miss.

"I'm having trouble accessing my email," I said to the man sitting next to me. "Have you been able to get yours to work?"

"I haven't tried," he said. "You should ask that fellow down at the end of the table to help you. His name is Lief Simon. I think he knows about computers."

With his shoulders tense and hunched, his face tight, and his eyes focused intensely on his laptop screen, this Lief character didn't look very friendly, but he was my only option, so I walked down to the other end of the table.

"Hello," I said. "I'm Kathleen Peddicord."

"Yes, I know," he said without looking up.

"Welcome to Ireland," I added cheerfully. "I'm sorry to interrupt you, but I understand you're something of a computer whiz. I'm having trouble getting my email to work. Would you mind taking a look to see if you can figure out what the problem might be before we start the morning meetings?"

"I'm on vacation," Lief replied, still barely glancing up from his laptop.

"Ah… uh… yes… ok… I understand. No problem," I said as I turned to go back to my seat.

Although he didn't seem to want to, Lief Simon got up and followed me to my computer. Then he sat down next to me, taking charge of the mouse. He clicked around a bit, and emails began downloading into my in-box. "Wow, that's great, thank you so much," I said as he stood up and walked away without a word. "What a knucklehead," I thought, smiling and shaking my head as I began responding to messages in my inbox.

After that first morning in the Jury's Hotel, I didn't have any other interaction with Lief Simon until we got to Sligo. It was late June, but, dressing that morning, I pulled on three layers, including a wool sweater I'd purchased in Waterford and a rain slicker I'd bought in Galway. I'd packed for June weather in Baltimore but by now I'd learned that June in Ireland isn't anything like June back home. Every day felt colder and damper than the day before.

This wasn't a sightseeing tour. We did a little of that, but we weren't tourists. We were a bunch of Americans thinking about moving to Ireland. Most were considering retiring here, some were shopping for real estate opportunities, trying to take a position in the expanding Celtic Tiger economy, and a few, like me, were looking to start businesses. In each city where we stopped, we met with attorneys and real estate agents to continue expanding our understanding of current opportunities for living and investing on the Emerald Isle, then we'd go scouting, seeing as many properties for sale as time in the place allowed. The viewings we'd had so far hadn't really connected with the specifications I'd outlined in my requests to the agents I'd contacted, and none of them had been able to explain why not. I'd asked for thatched-roof cottages and stone country houses, but we'd yet to see any of either. Instead, the agents kept showing us houses built no more than a decade before. In some cases, we were seeing houses still under construction. I didn't make an issue of it in front of the group, but, here in Sligo, the agents had done a better job of matching what we'd see to what I'd requested. Specifically, we were off to look at farms. Sligo is one of the least densely populated parts in Ireland. If you're moving to Sligo, you're probably looking for rural escape.

We met in the lobby of our hotel early that morning, boarded our waiting bus, then drove out of the city and into the barren, gray expanses of this wild, windy region. Ireland's northwestern coast is under constant assault from the raging Atlantic. Looking at Ireland on a map, the island appears to lean to the right, as though it's being pushed farther east or maybe drawing back to protect itself from the force of the waves and the gale. On the ground, the scene is otherworldly, almost lunar, the basalt cliffs fractured and fingered into dramatic landscapes that exist nowhere else on this planet.

The agent who'd scheduled our first viewing appointment was to meet us at a crossroads outside town. We arrived a few minutes before the appointed hour, and our driver pulled over to the side of the road to wait. Forty-five minutes later, no Irish estate agent. My tour-goers were growing restless.

"Perhaps we should return to the city?" one woman called out from a few rows back. "I don't want to spend the whole morning sitting on this bus."

"Let's give Sorcha fifteen more minutes," I suggested. "If she hasn't shown up by then, we'll return to town, and I'll try calling her from the hotel."

Twenty minutes later, just as I was thinking we had no choice but to abort, a young Irish woman drove up in a little red Nissan. "Another fine Irish morning," Sorcha said brightly after she'd parked and walked over to the open door of the bus. "A fine Irish mist we're having, isn't it. Shall I come aboard and introduce myself to all of ye'?"

I looked down at Sorcha, smiling up at me through the Irish drizzle, calmly cheerful and completely unconcerned that she was more than an hour late, then I looked back at my tour group. We had an appointment to meet another agent after lunch. I ran through the logistics of the rest of the day. Maybe we should bail on this first viewing?

"Tell her to lead us to the property," came Lief's deep baritone voice from his front-row seat. "We don't need to be introduced to the woman. We just need to get going. She's wasted enough of our time."

I looked down at Sorcha, and wondered if there was any chance she hadn't heard Lief's comments. What was with this guy? He hadn't said anything that I hadn't been thinking myself, but he'd actually said it all, out loud. He'd taken me by surprise, but I had to admit to myself that he'd done me a favor. Now I didn't have to be the heavy.

"Right," she said with a smile that was less convincingly bright. "Let's get going then. We're off, so." I guess she'd heard.

Twenty minutes later, we arrived at the twenty-five-acre farm. The property had a big stone house, a large barn, and six other outbuildings. The owner came out to greet us and show us around. Kaitlin and my parents followed him and the rest of the group over to the house. I wandered off on my own in the direction of the barn. Given an option, I'll always choose the path less traveled. I'd go see the house after the rest of the group had finished their tour.

The barn was empty inside and appeared as though it hadn't been used in years. There were no animals, no fresh hay or grain, only patches of mud on the floor under places where the Irish mist was falling through the holes in the roof. A wooden ladder at the other end led up to a second level. I'd been scouting property markets around the world for more than a decade, including many country ruins like this one. An old wooden ladder leading I didn't know where was irresistible. I walked over to climb this one.

When my head popped up above the floor of the upper level, to my surprise, I saw Lief. He was standing alone in the corner making notes in a journal. There was something about this guy I couldn't shake. In my few interactions with him, he'd been brusque or downright rude. But somehow I'd come away each time smiling.

I stood on the ladder taking him in for a moment. He was tall, even when leaning over as he was now to write in his journal, and broad shouldered. He was wearing a deep brown Mackintosh and a black felt Stetson. I wondered if he'd bought the rain coat somewhere along the way like I'd bought the one I was wearing. I knew he hadn't found the cowboy hat in Ireland. He'd brought that with him. I hadn't been able to figure out how old he was. When he was relaxed, like now, I wondered if he was even twenty-five.

"Hello," I called out. "I didn't expect anyone to be up here."

"This property might work for the corporate retreat I want to create," Lief said, not really looking up at me. "What do you think?"

"Corporate retreat?"

"Yes, that's why I'm moving to Ireland. To start a business. I have two ideas. I bought your 'How To Run An Irish Pub' report, and I'm considering buying one. My other idea is to buy a country property like this one to convert into a venue for executive retreats. It's a growing global market, and I think Ireland could be a competitive option."

"Is that your experience?" I asked. "Managing corporate retreats?"

"No, I'm a CFO for a hotel firm. But I'm bored with accounting. Plus, I've had enough of being an employee. The most important thing to me at this point is to get my own thing going. Since I got my MBA in international finance, I've lived and worked in Chad, Kazakhstan, and Salta, Argentina," Lief continued. Was he giving me his resume?

"I returned to the States because my wife didn't like Salta and said she'd had enough of living overseas. She and I divorced two months ago." And now he was offering his marital status? Suddenly this guy was open and forthcoming?

"Now that it's just me, I'd like to go offshore again. I've been reading *International Living* for five years. One of my professors in graduate school told the class about it. *So he must be older than he looks, I thought, maybe closer to my age than I realized.* It was your articles on Ireland over the past year that gave me the idea to consider this country. Really, you're the reason I'm here," Lief said, finally looking up and over at me directly. Suddenly, I felt self-conscious and shy, realizing he was sizing me up the way I'd been doing to him.

"I'm always worried when readers tell me that," I said. "Now I feel responsible for you!"

"Don't worry. I'll make up my own mind," Lief said, smiling in a way that was more sardonic than cheery. No, I certainly wouldn't call this guy cheerful. But he did keep taking me off guard in ways I was finding surprisingly attractive.

"But back to the point," he continued. "What do you think about this place for my corporate retreat idea?"

Developing the collection of tumbledown structures around us into an executive-worthy property would be a colossal undertaking, but it would be the kind of project that captures my imagination. Evidently, Lief wasn't daunted by the prospect either. Maybe there was more to him than I'd seen so far. He was a CFO with an MBA who was considering buying two-hundred-year-old ruins in Sligo, Ireland, to create a center for corporate retreats. I wasn't sure how all that added up, but unconventional wasn't a problem for me. Ordinary doesn't keep my interest, and, while most people would probably find the plan Lief was considering foolish or crazy, to me it was a tantalizing fantasy.

"It would be a lot of work," I said, "but what an adventure. I like old buildings the way some women like new shoes. For me, near ruins like these are seductive, oozing romance and charm. I barely register what they are. I see only what I imagine they could be. And, yes, this place could be amazing."

Lief didn't respond, but I could feel him smiling at me again, this time more warmly, as I made my way back down the ladder to join the group.

The final night of the tour, back in Dublin, I was sitting in the dining room of the Jury's Hotel with my parents and Kaitlin. We three girls were keeping my father company while he enjoyed a glass of after-dinner Jameson. Lief was in the pub, just beyond the dining room, sitting in front of the fireplace with two other tour-goers. He was in my line of sight through the open doorway, and I couldn't keep myself from glancing over. I had to look away quickly when he got up and started walking in our direction.

"Some of us are going across town to a pub later," he said when he reached our table. "Would you all like to come along?"

"No, no, not us," my parents replied together. "But you go, Kathleen," my father urged.

"Yes, you should go, Mom," Kaitlin said with a big, encouraging smile. She seemed to like the idea of her mother having a night out.

I thought about my encounter with Lief up among the rafters in the old barn in Sligo, him in his cowboy hat writing in a journal, and I nodded my head. "Yes, okay," I said. "That sounds fun."

Lief and I shared a taxi with two others from the group. It dropped us in the middle of a row of Georgian townhouses, one of which held the club the concierge at the hotel had recommended. We climbed down the stone stairs to the subterranean nightspot and pushed open the door. We could see straightaway that this wasn't going to be the authentic Irish experience we all had been hoping for. Strobe lights dangled from the ceiling, and the DJ was playing not Irish folk songs but American pop. Why were these Irish so interested in importing the American way of life, I wondered, as I'd done all throughout the tour. Everywhere we'd traveled we'd seen more new-built cookie-cutter suburban-style houses than thatched-roofed cottages or old stone houses and way more commercial construction than made sense to me in a place with a total population of just three million people. This country is at a crossroads, I thought. Just like me.

Some of the group danced in a circle, but I hung back, sitting with a few others, including Lief, at one of the old wooden tables. The music was so loud that conversation was almost impossible, but I was enjoying sitting beside Lief. Being near him felt surprisingly comfortable.

Just before closing time, he leaned into my ear to ask, "Would you like to dance?"

"I really only know how to two-step," he said. "I don't think that will work with this music, but I'll do the best I can." What a study in contradictions this guy was. For much of the tour, he'd been painfully direct. Then, in the barn in Sligo he was disarmingly open. Now he was self-deprecating, almost sheepish.

He had me feeling something I hadn't felt since my early days with Rick. In the years since the end of my marriage, I'd had a few forgettable dates, a couple of potential romances that had ended before they'd had a chance to take hold because, between work and Kaitlin, I just didn't have time for them. Then there was the one long relationship with the guy I'd fallen head over heels for at work but shouldn't have. Now, sitting alongside Lief, our shoulders brushing now and then, I was a young girl again, electrified. I was definitely drawn to this guy. Yes, I wanted to dance.

We bopped around in a group with the others, and, though we weren't touching, I felt very connected to this man I barely knew who seemed to be enjoying himself as much as I was. Minutes later, before my romantic imagination could run very far with the possibilities of the evening, the bartender rang the bell for last call. Lief and I shared another cab back to the hotel. The group of us Dublin nightclubbers posed for a photo in the hotel lobby then hugged good night and said good bye. I figured with a pang that was the last I'd see of any of them.

IV
First Date

The next morning, Kaitlin, my parents, and I flew back to Baltimore, to begin formulating next steps. Now that I'd toured parts of Ireland, I had opinions. Sligo had a *Wuthering Heights* appeal but didn't seem like a place to build a business or raise a daughter. I decided I'd focus my research on Galway and Waterford. I bought every guidebook to the Auld Sod on the shelves at my local Borders and Barnes and Noble and scheduled lunches with everyone at Agora who'd spent time in Ireland, starting with Beth who'd been there many times over the years. Beth had mainly joined pub tours, so her experience was limited and not necessarily relevant, but she knew my perspective and priorities better than anyone. I probably should have been focused on things like the cost of housing and the process for establishing residency, but I was more interested in Beth's funny stories about the characters she'd met during her pub crawls and her descrip-

FIRST DATE

tions of the great houses and castle gardens she'd seen. These were the reasons I was drawn in Ireland in the first place.

A few weeks later, the phone rang in my office one afternoon. It was Patti, the marketing assistant who'd helped organize the Ireland tour.

"A guy from our trip last month called to ask for your number," she said.

"Which guy?" I asked.

"Lief Simon. He called this morning to say he wanted to speak with you. I told him I'd have to check first."

"Lief Simon…"

"The one we went dancing with the final night in Dublin," Patti said.

She didn't need to explain. I'd known right away who Patti was talking about. As busy as I'd been, I hadn't been able to keep my mind from drifting to thoughts of that day I'd encountered Lief Simon in the rafters of the barn in Sligo. Hearing that he'd called, I felt excited. Yes, I'd be happy to speak with Lief Simon again.

"Okay, yes, go ahead and give him my number," I told Patti.

Two hours later, when I returned from a meeting, I had a voice mail:

"Hi. This is Lief Simon. We met in Ireland a few weeks ago. I'd like to take you to dinner. Give me a call…"

Lief left four phone numbers—apartment, work, cell, and weekend house. So much for playing it cool. I called the work number.

"Hi," Lief said. "Thanks for returning my call."

"No problem. I wasn't sure which of the four numbers you left to try first," I said, teasing to see his reaction.

"Well, I wanted to be sure you could reach me anytime," he said. This guy was disarmingly straightforward.

"I was hoping we could get together," Lief said.

"But you're in Chicago, and I'm in Baltimore."

"I'll come to Baltimore if you'll have dinner with me."

When an opportunity appeals, it's hard for me not to be all in. And, though I couldn't really identify why, I found the idea of seeing Lief Simon again hugely appealing. So, as I've always done, without considering potential implications too hard, I made my mind up in the moment. This guy didn't seem to think it was crazy to fly from one state to another for a dinner date, and neither did I. We were a match.

"That sounds great," I told Lief trying not to appear too eager.

"I'll check flights and get back to you with a date. Speak with you again soon," Lief said as he hung up. He called back an hour later to say he'd bought a ticket to Baltimore for two weeks from Friday. This guy didn't waste any time. Still, two weeks seemed a long time away. I'm not good at waiting.

The next day Beth and I went for lunch at the tearoom in The Woman's Industrial Exchange on Charles Street. We liked meeting there because nobody else from Agora did. We could speak openly without worrying about who might overhear what.

FIRST DATE

When I'd come to work for Agora, it was a small operation employing a dozen people, including Beth. She had enough experience to be a mentor but she was not so much older that we didn't enjoy doing the same things. She was always in good spirits and full of positive energy, and you couldn't help but have a good time when she was around. When we met, Beth was at the end of a messy divorce, though you'd never have known it because she was always in such good humor. The first night we two single girls went out together, the weekend after she'd officially left her husband, she ended up dancing on a tabletop in a Fell's Point bar. I stood across the room watching in wonder at the self-confidence required to let yourself go like that.

Beth knew every detail of my story—from becoming engaged to Rick and why I finally asked him to move out to my frantic climb up the Agora corporate ladder and my office romance that she'd cautioned me against from its start. I spent so much time in her office seeking her counsel—first about my troubled marriage, then about the twists and turns of my workplace love affair—that she bought a pillow for me that she kept on her couch that read, "Tell Me About Your Childhood." Beth never let me fool her or myself. She always told me what I needed to hear whether I wanted to hear it or not, and I loved her for it.

"That guy from the tour to Ireland who I told you about," I said as we were seated in the diner. "The one who was so rude. Remember? He called and invited me to dinner. He says he'll come to Baltimore or I could fly to Chicago. So I'm wondering… can you think of any reason we need to be in Chicago?"

Beth shook her head and smiled as if to say, "Oh, no, here we go again." Instead, what she actually said was, "In fact, I'm going to the Windy City this weekend for a publishing convention. You can come along if you want." She said the last three words—"if you want"—in a taunting sing-song tone.

"But I feel I must point out," Beth continued, "that you've made this mistake before. Jumping in with both feet before thinking things through. It doesn't always work out so well, does it? You're having to move to a new country to get over your last romance," Beth said looking directly at me with a big smile that was both mocking and supportive.

"I know, I know," I said. "That's why I want you to be there with me. To keep me from letting myself run away with myself."

"Fine," Beth said. "We can share a hotel room."

"Great," I said. "I'll let Lief know when he calls tonight."

"Do you think we have time to stop in that dress store by the harbor on our way back to the office after we eat?" I added. "I want to shop for something new to wear."

Beth shook her head again. "Don't you have work to do?" she asked. "I know I do. But, yes, fine. We can stop. Briefly." I never suggested time out of the office, so Beth realized this was important to me.

When we arrived at the hotel in Chicago Friday afternoon,

FIRST DATE

Beth wanted to take a nap. She turned out the lights in the room and laid down on her bed. I laid back on mine, too, and closed my eyes, but I knew I'd never be able to fall asleep. The butterflies in my stomach were doing summersaults. Finally, I gave up and got up to take a shower and dress in the new black knit skirt and matching sweater that Beth had helped me to pick out.

I woke Beth a half-hour before Lief was due to collect us. She changed her clothes, and we walked down to the lobby and out onto the street. No one but Beth knew I was in Chicago to meet this guy. Kaitlin was spending the weekend with my parents. I'd told them about the publishing conference but not about the first date with the fellow from Ireland. I suspected that most people would have thought flying to another city to meet up with a man I hardly knew was mad.

"You look nice," Beth said, as I fidgeted in my pumps and adjusted the buttons on my sweater. "You're not having second thoughts, are you?"

If I was, it was too late. Lief had just pulled up. He kept the engine running but got out to come around to where we were waiting. He was wearing a dark suit and tie and… cowboy boots. He'd told me he'd be coming straight from the office, meaning he'd worn cowboy boots to work. What kind of CFO wears cowboy boots?

"Hey," I said. "It's great to see you again. This is my friend Beth, the one I mentioned to you on the phone. I'm here with her for the conference. I really appreciate you inviting her to come along with us." When I'd called Lief to tell him that he didn't need to fly to Baltimore to meet me after all because a colleague had invited me last minute to travel with her for a publishing convention in Chicago, he'd suggested the colleague come with us for dinner, which I'd really appreciated. It saved me having to ask if Beth could tag along. Plus it was gentlemanly.

"Hello," Lief said, smiling. "If you're ready, we can go. We have reservations at an Italian restaurant in twenty minutes. My secretary says it's the best in the city."

Lief opened both of the passenger-side doors. I got in front, Beth in the back, and we were off.

"Are you from Chicago?" Beth asked Lief from the back seat after we'd been driving for a minute in silence. She knew how bad I was at small talk, and the butterflies I was still feeling were making it even harder than usual for me to come up with interesting things to say.

"No, I'm from Arizona," Lief said. "I was born in Sedona."

"Wow," Beth said. "I know that part of the country. There's not much in Sedona today. There must have been nothing there when you were born."

"There wasn't," Lief said. "My parents were living in Jerome. Alone. There was literally no one else in the town at the time. It wasn't even a town. It didn't have a hospital or a doctor. When it was time for me to be born, they drove to Sedona, to the doctor's office there."

FIRST DATE

"Do your parents still live in Sedona?" I asked, finally finding a voice.

"No. They've been divorced since I was a year old. My mother is here in the Chicago area. My father lives in Ojo Caliente, New Mexico."

"Ojo Caliente?!" Beth exclaimed. "That's another very small town."

"Yes, my father likes his freedom. He lives off the grid, in a trailer, on a few hundred acres he's bought at tax auctions over the past few decades. He accumulates old school buses and uses them to store stuff. He's got a school bus full of musical instruments from Africa and another one filled with tribal art. He's got buses packed with boxes of crystals and gemstones from South America and others with American Indian artifacts." This cowboy boot-wearing CFO was the son of a hippie living off-grid in northern New Mexico?

I could imagine the look on Beth's face. The love of Beth's life was a communist accountant named Fred. Her house in Fell's Point was like a small museum of contemporary counter-culture, so eclectically engaging that John Waters considered using it as a set for one of his movies. School buses full of treasures parked in some forgotten corner of the New Mexican high desert? That was right up Beth's alley—and mine, too.

"Do you see your father much?" Beth asked.

"Not since I was a kid."

"But your mother lives nearby?" I said.

"Yes, in a house I own in Woodstock. My ex-wife and I bought the house about a year before we split up. Now my mother lives there. During the week, I stay in a townhouse I rent in Chicago. On weekends, I go out to Woodstock. It's a nice escape from the city and a really cute little town. The movie 'Groundhog Day' was filmed on the Woodstock square."

We'd arrived at the restaurant. Lief parked around the corner then led us inside. After we'd been seated, Beth restarted the conversation.

"So you're planning to move to Ireland?" she asked, looking at Lief across the table.

"I got the idea from reading *International Living*," he said to Beth while watching me. "I've known I've wanted to live outside the States since high school. I also want my own business. Ireland seems like a good choice for an entrepreneur right now, at least if I can believe what I read in Kathleen's reports," he added with a wry smile.

"Well, I'll be able to tell you better in a few months," I said, returning the hint of challenge in his voice. "The plan is for me to make the move and open Agora's new Ireland office before the end of the year."

"That's my timing, too," Lief said. "Though I haven't given notice at work or even told anyone there anything about Ireland. I want to have things more pinned down before I let the cat out of the bag."

FIRST DATE

We continued like that, with Lief opening up and all three of us feeling more comfortable and at ease with each other as the evening went on. After a while, Lief and I were chatting like old friends and Beth was sitting silent. When he'd finished his lasagna, Lief excused himself to go to the men's room.

"This is ridiculous," Beth said as soon as Lief had gone from the table. "What am I doing here? This is a perfectly nice, normal guy, and I'm a great big third wheel!"

"Okay, okay," I said, "I'm sorry. You're right. I would like to be alone with him now."

"Of course you would," Beth said, "and you should be. No man wants the best friend along for the ride on a first date. I'm leaving. You tell him I was feeling tired and wanted to make an early night of it. Tell him thank you very much for the invitation and I hope to see him again sometime. You can also tell him that I've paid the check because I'm not letting this guy buy my dinner. Well, maybe don't tell him. Let the waiter tell him. Anyway, I'm going. And I'm paying. See you when you get back to the room."

Beth picked up her purse and walked over to the waiter to take care of the check.

"Where's your friend?" Lief asked when he returned to the table.

"She has an early morning appointment and decided she'd better call it a night," I said.

"Oh, and she paid the bill," I added, as Lief began looking

around the room for the waiter. Lief didn't respond, but he didn't look happy. The idea of not paying for our first date bothered him. I felt bad that I'd created the clumsy situation in the first place. I wasn't sorry Beth had come along, though. She'd drawn more out of Lief than I would have been able to do by myself. Plus, now she knew him, so I'd have at least one person I could talk to about the guy I hoped was going to be my new long-distance boyfriend.

I have a very poor sense of direction, but I was pretty sure that Lief took me on a long detour after we left the restaurant. I remembered having parked the car just around the corner, but now we were walking along the river. If Lief had been bothered by Beth paying the bill for dinner, he didn't seem to be any longer. He was at ease, and so was I. We turned away from the river and wandered through a park, then, finally, we were back at the lot where we'd left the car. Lief walked me to the passenger door, and, as he opened it for me, leaned down to kiss me in a way that was both sweet and confident and that took me completely off-guard. I like surprises. I felt like a schoolgirl. I almost giggled.

My first day back in the office in Baltimore, I returned from lunch to find a dozen white lilies in a vase on my desk. "When

FIRST DATE

can I come to Baltimore?" the card read. I sat down in my chair with the card in my hand to read it again. I couldn't contain my smile. And I couldn't wait to see this guy again.

Two hours later, my phone rang.

"Did you like the flowers?" Lief wanted to know. "When you didn't call to say anything about them, I was worried that maybe you don't like lilies."

"They're one of my favorites," I told him.

Increasingly, Lief's soft, vulnerable side was peeking through. On the surface, he was direct sometimes to the point of coming off like a jerk. But he wasn't a jerk. Just beneath that gruff exterior, he was a sweetheart, maybe even a romantic.

Two weeks after my trip to Chicago with Beth, Lief came to Baltimore for the weekend, then, two weeks after that, I returned to Chicago, this time with Kaitlin. It was a big step, introducing my daughter to a man I still barely knew, but it didn't feel risky. Kaitlin had met Lief in Ireland. He'd helped her to navigate the rocky landscape of the Giant's Causeway the day we crossed the border into Northern Ireland. I'd told her about our dinner date in Chicago after my trip with Beth. She laughed when I got to the part about Beth paying the check and ducking out early. When I asked if she'd like to spend a weekend visiting Lief, her big smile gave me the answer I was hoping for.

On one hand, this budding relationship with Lief was developing quickly. On the other, everything about the way things were playing out felt natural and right. Lief and Kaitlin played video games—something I never wanted to do with her—and went to see the new *Rugrats* movie. They invited me to come along, too, but I wanted them to spend time alone together and was delighted watching them interact. The three of us seemed to be fitting together almost effortlessly.

"I think I'm being swept off my feet," I told Beth. Beth didn't counsel me to take things one step at a time. She must have known as well as I did that Lief Simon wasn't just another new boyfriend.

Lief and I both needed to make a return trip to Ireland, Lief to continue his property search, me to decide where to base Agora's new office.

"Let's go back together," Lief suggested the next time he called. If he hadn't proposed the idea, I might have.

When I'd told Lief the two places I needed to choose between for my move, he said, no problem. He'd focus his property search in those two cities, too. We'd spend two weeks on the Emerald Isle together, dividing our time between Galway and Waterford. Our paths were aligning, and I was over the moon.

V

Pouldrew House

We were just ten minutes outside downtown Waterford City, but the forest was thick on both sides of the narrow road. We'd driven up and down it three times, but we couldn't find the listing.

Pouldrew House was the sixth potential corporate retreat property we would be viewing together in the week since we'd landed in Ireland. The first four had been in and around Galway, the fifth and now this sixth property, Pouldrew House, in County Waterford.

"The entrance should be right here," Lief said, referencing his notes. "How can we keep missing it?"

"There!" I shouted. "Do you see that small opening in the trees up ahead on the left?"

Lief slowed the car to a crawl, and finally our path was visible. The hidden drive ran almost parallel to the road we'd been traveling. Tall trees and high hedges blocked the sun, and we continued in near darkness. Then the growth gave way, daylight returned, and we could see an old wooden watermill turning in the river running alongside us. A minute later, we reached a black iron gate. A short stout man came out from the guardhouse and walked over to Lief's window.

"I'm Lief Simon," Lief said through his open window. "I'm here to tour the property."

"Yes, of course, just one minute." The guard turned in the direction of the gate. While we waited for him to allow us through, I read to Lief from the listing sheet.

"It says the house was built in the Palladian style by Viscount Doneraile in the early 1800s. It's on forty-five acres of mature woodland, with gardens and a lake fed by the River Dawn. It's got renovated stables with a loft overlooking a waterfall.

"It also says here that all of the windows, doors, shutters, and moldings are original. I can't wait to see this place."

Once we were through the gate, we passed the waterfall on the left, then, as we came around the bend, Pouldrew House came into view. The three-story Georgian mansion of white stone was positioned at the edge of the blue lake and seemed to float above the water.

"Wow," I said.

"Don't say that inside," Lief cautioned. My new boyfriend had learned quickly that I have zero poker face. When I liked something, I had trouble keeping my enthusiasm to myself. He, on the other hand, could spend an hour at a property and leave without saying anything more than "hello," "thank you," and "good-bye." I respected the strategy, but these big old Irish country properties were the stuff of fantasy for me. I couldn't hide the pure delight I was experiencing wandering through them, knowing that Lief might actually buy one.

This one was particularly glorious. It was situated only seven miles from Waterford City and the airport and had been recently and fully renovated.

We parked in front of the lion's head statue at the end of the drive. A tall Asian man stepped out the front door. He must have been watching for our arrival.

"Remember, please, to let me do the talking," Lief said as he got out of the car.

I followed him to the front door of the house and looked inside to see an entrance hall with rows of white columns, a double mahogany staircase, and an enormous Waterford crystal chandelier. I wanted to race inside to be part of it. This was my kind of place.

"Hello and welcome," the tall Asian man said, extending his arm to shake Lief's hand. "I'm Dr. Chen. Please come inside."

We followed Dr. Chen through the grand entrance and into the salon to the right. The house lived up to the listing sheet hype. I'd never been inside a private home as grand.

"Please have a seat," Dr. Chen said, and Lief and I sat together on the sofa. Dr. Chen sat in the armchair across the room, leaving a wide expanse between us and him that, thanks to the floor-to-ceiling windows in the very high-ceilinged room, was bathed in light. The carved wooden overmantel above the oversized fireplace was lined with antique ceramic blue and white Chinese plates and vases of red tulips.

"Before we tour the property," Dr. Chen began, "can you give me an idea of your interest? I understand you are planning to move to Waterford. Would you live at Pouldrew House?"

"No," Lief said. "I'd like to develop a center for corporate retreats."

"Ah, Pouldrew House would be ideal. The house is thirteen-thousand square feet with seven bedrooms and a dining room large enough to seat thirty guests. In addition, we have a large terrace, mature gardens, and several outbuildings that could be converted to additional accommodation or private meeting rooms. Come, let me show you."

Dr. Chen was a medical doctor from Singapore who'd bought Pouldrew House only three years before. He'd been living there with his wife, the two of them overseeing the restoration work, until his wife decided she didn't like living in Ireland and returned to Singapore. Dr. Chen had stayed behind to sell the property.

I said next-to-nothing as we toured, and Lief said exactly nothing, but he was taking more time with this viewing than he had with the others. This could be just the place he'd been hoping to find.

After our tour of the house and the grounds, we returned to the salon where Dr. Chen got down to business.

"When would you be looking to make your purchase?" he asked Lief.

"I have no timeline," Lief said. "I'm looking at many properties, and I'll have to run all the numbers before discussing anything specifically." He was keeping his cards close to his vest. I wondered how he could appear so calm. It was taking real effort for me not to let my enthusiasm show.

"Well, this is a one-of-a-kind place," Dr. Chen said. "And it's getting a lot of attention. Brad Pitt and Jennifer Aniston have inquired." I struggled harder to keep the look on my face blank.

"Well, I'll have to run the numbers," Lief said.

While the two men talked turkey, I studied the collection of Chinese snuff bottles in the glass-fronted cabinet between the two front windows. There must have been two hundred of them, lined up in neat rows.

Dr. Chen came over, opened the door to the hutch, and picked up one of the bottles.

"This is for you," he said, holding it out to me. "A small gift so you will remember your visit."

I wasn't sure I should accept and looked over at Lief on the sofa. He showed no reaction. I turned back at Dr. Chen, who was smiling as he continued to hold out his offering.

"It's too much," I said finally. "It is too nice a gift. I can't accept it."

"I insist," Dr. Chen said. "I would like you to have it."

I took the little green and white bottle from his hand.

"When you return, I'll show you the rest of my collection. I have hundreds of these bottles, in cabinets throughout the house." When he said it, I knew he was right. We'd be back.

"You seem to have made a friend," Lief said when we were back in the car. I tried not to smile. He was jealous.

"So… what do you think?" I asked, changing the subject.

"The property is perfect," Lief said, finally acknowledging his interest though with maddening calm. "Now I have to see if the math works."

"I wonder if Brad Pitt and Jennifer Aniston are really interested," I said eagerly.

"Who knows," Lief said, still nonplussed. "I'll put the figures into a spreadsheet tonight and see what I can afford."

I would have made an offer on the spot, but my new boyfriend, I was learning, took things one step at a time.

We'd allowed extra days at the end of the trip for some fun. The Pouldrew House viewing was the final item on our business agendas. Now, finally, we could be tourists. As much as I'd traveled in my years at Agora, I'd seldom been on vacation. To have no daily objectives, no schedule, and no urgent reason to be up before dawn each morning was unprecedented for me, and I'd been looking forward to these few days of freedom with Lief for weeks. Kaitlin was safe and happy with my parents in Baltimore, and I was a single young woman on a romantic adventure in a foreign country with a man I felt more attracted to every day.

Now we had a chance to get to know this county the Irish kept telling us was the country's sunniest, though, by the third day of this visit, Lief and I had agreed the idea had to be tourist board propaganda. It'd rained every day. But we didn't mind. The low skies and near constant mist made for a dreamy backdrop.

From our Waterford City base, we took off each morning of our mini holiday to explore the surrounding area. We drove for hours through rich green farmland getting lost on narrow, winding roads, not minding not knowing where we were or where we were going.

Then we headed to the coast. Ireland's oldest city, Waterford was once southeast Ireland's main seaport. The traditional sea approach was via a broad channel past the lighthouse of Hook Head and the village of Crooke. Cromwell is reputed to have said that Waterford would fall "by Hook or by Crooke"—that is, by a landing of his army at one spot or the other during his siege of the town in 1649. The beaches in these spots are considered the best in Ireland, with white sand and lapping waters. You could imagine yourself in the Caribbean if it weren't for the constant gale and the freezing water. We stood on the shore in sweaters and jackets watching the Irish swim and surf.

We walked the cliffs at Dunmore East, saw the water crash at Mahon Falls, drove along the Copper Coast, and explored thirteenth-century castles. Lief won a stuffed bear for me throwing darts at a stall in the seaside amusement park at Tramore. Then we stopped on the way back to the city so I could pick wildflowers along the side of the road to put in the little vase he'd bought for me when we'd toured the Waterford Crystal Factory.

We spent our final evenings in Waterford snuggled close together in wooden seats by the window of a pub listening to traditional Irish music. We'd make our way back, hand in hand, each night, through the mist and along the cobblestoned streets, to our hotel overlooking the River Suir. I'd confessed to Beth over a glass of wine one night before leaving for this trip that I thought I was falling in love. Now I knew I was.

Back in Dublin, the day before our return flight to the States, we stayed at a bed and breakfast called the Charleston House just outside the city. It was closer to the airport than central Dublin. Plus, a traditional Irish B&B seemed like the right place to spend our final night on the Emerald Isle.

POULDREW HOUSE

Lying in bed together the next morning, warm beneath the thick duvet, neither of us wanted to move. Getting out of bed would mean breaking the spell our two weeks in Ireland had cast over us. A trip like this one, two people alone together twenty-four hours a day, day after day, in a foreign country, accelerates the getting-to-know-each-other process. A friend once told me that, after going on her first weekend away with a new boyfriend, she'd been so disappointed by his sock and underwear choices that she'd broken things off the day they returned home.

In my two weeks alone with Lief, I'd seen no such red flags. In fact, as far as I could tell, the better I got to know him, the more Lief seemed to be the yang to my yin. While I jump quickly at anything that catches my attention and am completely open to new ideas and opportunities, perfectly comfortable leaping before doing too much looking, Lief was a man of few words who proceeded slowly, paused to deliberate before taking action, and thought hard before committing. I like words. Lief, I could see, lived by the numbers. I process the world in terms of potential. Lief seemed to value not what could be but only what he could touch and hold onto right now. In many ways, Lief and I couldn't have been more different, but we had the same ideas about what we wanted our lives to look like big picture. How many other men would be up for a move to a new country to start a new business from nothing? Besides Bill, I couldn't think of any in my circle. Lief and I were on the same path. We were navigating it differently, but I suspected that our contrasting approaches would balance the ride for both of us.

We'd stayed up until past 2:00 a.m. the night before, discussing our options. Lief's plan hinged on his ongoing negotiations with Dr. Chen. Mine were more flexible, but, the more we talked, the blurrier the lines became. As we drifted finally to sleep, we weren't talking so much about what Lief or I might do as we were agreeing what we could do together.

Though we'd been up late, we'd waked with the early-rising sun. I closed my eyes, laid my head on Lief's chest, and held him close, wishing I could keep the moment from passing. Then Lief said something that flew in the face of everything I thought I'd learned about him.

"Maybe we should move to Ireland together," he said matter-of-factly. "I mean, what if we got married?" So much for taking things slow and careful.

The thought had not crossed my mind until Lief articulated it. But I'd known from the day we'd ended up alone together in the rafters of the old barn in Sligo that Lief and I were meant to be together.

When I'd told Beth I thought I was falling in love with this man I'd known only a few months, she'd said, "After a certain age, when you're sure, you're sure. So why waste time?" Maybe she'd seen the writing on the wall. Hearing Lief's quiet, simple proposal, I knew it was the right thing. I didn't hesitate in my response, and I had no doubts. I nodded and said okay. I'd always been open to marrying again, and the idea of Lief Simon at the core of my life for the rest of my life settled my mind and lightened my heart. He was my future.

We showered and dressed, ate quickly, then loaded our bags into the rental car and started off for the airport. When I saw a public pay phone up ahead, I asked Lief if he'd mind stopping.

"I'd like to call my parents," I said.

I stood with the phone to my ear staring out the glass of the phone booth at a long row of Irish Georgian townhouses with shiny red, yellow, blue, and green front doors. My father responded to my news with a surprised "Well, congratulations!" but my mother didn't say anything at all. I understood my mother's silence. What would I say if Kaitlin were to call from thousands of miles away to tell me she was going to marry a man she'd met less than three months before? My parents were still struggling with the idea of me moving with Kaitlin to the other side of the Atlantic Ocean. Now I was asking them to accept a new son-in-law in the bargain. They needed time, and that was okay.

A double rainbow arched over the road in front of us as we drove away from the phone booth headed to Dublin airport. Neither Lief nor I had ever seen a double rainbow before. Maybe my parents had doubts, but the universe seemed happy with our union.

VI
Honeymoon

Back in Baltimore, it didn't take long for logistics to eclipse Ireland's green fields and rainbows. I put my house up for sale. Found a buyer for my car. Had a yard sale to clear out the junk from my garage and basement. In Chicago, Lief gave notice at the hotel development firm where he'd been working as CFO. Gave up the lease on his city apartment. Sold his car. Put his weekend house on the market. Gave away his furniture.

We were hurtling toward a move, but we still didn't know where we were going—Waterford or Galway? If we'd taken time to get to know the two cities better, we might have chosen Galway. As a university town, it's livelier. But, when Lief finalized his numbers from all the properties we'd toured, he decided that Pouldrew House was the right choice for his corporate retreat. Lief was moving to Waterford. Now that I was his betrothed, that meant Kaitlin and I were, too. That was just fine with me.

HONEYMOON

Ours would be a second wedding for both of us, so Lief and I agreed we didn't want a big fancy event, but we still had to decide when the ceremony would be. Lief suggested we wait and get married after we'd settled in Ireland.

"I'm not moving to another country with a man I'm not married to," I told him. I wasn't having doubts about our plan to wed, but, if we were going to be married, we should be married before we launched our new life together. For me, sooner is always better than later.

Lief didn't understand why I was reluctant to make the move with him before getting married, but, he said, "It's all the same to me. I know I want to spend the rest of my life with you. The details of when and how we get started are up to you." If I had needed reassurance, his calm certitude would have done the trick. Kaitlin and I would fly to Chicago a month before the move-to-Ireland date we'd set, and Lief and I would be married there by the justice of the peace.

First, I'd need to call Rick. When he and I finally agreed to divorce, he'd asked if his friend Storm, just graduated from law school, could file the papers. This meant no attorney fees for either of us, so I went along. Now that I was getting married again, I went in search of my divorce decree but couldn't find it.

"The paperwork was never finalized," Rick conceded when I called him to ask about it. "Storm didn't file it."

Rick and I were still married. The most surprising part of that realization was that I wasn't surprised—not that Rick's friend Storm hadn't followed through to get the divorce nor that I hadn't thought to confirm the situation until now. I don't prioritize administration and ignore anything to do with paperwork until I can't. I graduated with honors from college but almost wasn't given my diploma because I had two-year-old outstanding campus parking fines. Maybe that should have cured me of my irresponsible tendencies, but, to me, a diploma was just another piece of paperwork. They could give me one or not. I'd already gotten the education. I wasn't sure Lief would feel the same way about my divorce.

It was less than three days until our wedding date. How was I going to get divorced in forty-eight hours? Rick and I had last lived together as a married couple in Pennsylvania, meaning I needed a judge in that state to sign off on the divorce. I decided I'd drive to York, Pennsylvania, and try to find one who'd take pity on me.

And that's what I did. I took the day off work and drove the half-hour north from New Freedom to York. I parked on the main square, then walked along the four sides looking for a door plaque indicating an attorney in residence. At the first law firm I came to, the senior partner agreed to see me. As she listened to my story, her eyes opened wider and wider until she was bug-eyed and shaking her head. She picked up her phone to call the courthouse across the square where she spoke with a judge who said he'd meet with me. The lawyer filled out the required paperwork as I sat across from her then sent me off with a personal note to see her friend the judge.

"You're one lucky girl," she said as she walked me to the door smiling at me the way Beth did when I'd made a mistake I should learn from.

Across the square in the courthouse, the judge stamped my documents, and, until Saturday morning at least, I was a single woman.

Lief and I met June 20 and were married November 14 by a justice of the peace at a courthouse in Illinois with Kaitlin as our only witness and guest. Everything else about our situation was complicated. We kept this moment simple. Lief and I both wore jeans and, without planning it, Aran sweaters, an accidental nod to our Ireland plan. Lief surprised me with a pair of rings—one with a diamond for me, the other a band for him to wear. After the ceremony, Lief, Kaitlin, and I went for lunch at a diner down the road—hamburgers and a milkshake toast. The countdown to our new life in the Auld Sod had officially begun.

We decided to squeeze in a trip to Turkey before we embarked for the Emerald Isle. Our honeymoon. Lief's father had been in that part of the world for a month, shopping for gemstones, because, Lief explained when I asked, "That's what he does. He wanders around the world buying stuff he thinks is interesting or valuable to sell through his shop in Ojo Caliente. Some of it is useful for his business, but mostly my father just likes to wander around the world meeting people and collecting stuff."

When Lief got in touch to tell his father he was getting married again, Paul suggested that Lief and I come meet up with him. I'd never been to Turkey and was excited at the chance to see it. I didn't want to leave Kaitlin behind. Her whole life had been turned on its head so she was coming with us. It'd be a nice bonding opportunity for our new little family.

A few days after we'd booked tickets, Lief's mother, Syndi, invited herself along. Nothing about Lief and my experience together to this point had been conventional. Having my daughter and his divorced parents join us for our honeymoon seemed par for our course.

Lief, Kaitlin, Syndi, and I flew from Chicago to Istanbul, where Lief's father was waiting for us at the airport. With his long white hair, full white beard, and oversized belly, Paul was the picture of Santa Claus. "He works as a mall Santa in Santa Fe every Christmas," Lief said, reading my mind.

I'm an adventurous traveler, but I like to be comfortable. We'd booked into the hotel where Lief's father had been staying, and it wasn't. It was on the side of a hill that we had to drag our suitcases up. Our tub was stained, and the bathroom sink faucet leaked. When we ventured out our first afternoon to tour the Blue Mosque, every Turkish man we passed wanted to touch the top of Kaitlin's blond head for luck. She spent most of her time inside the mosque crouched behind a door, trying to avoid attracting the attention of any more Turkish admirers. Our second day, we nearly lost her in the crowd in the Grand Bazaar, and she and I both were glad when Lief suggested two days later that we rent a car and tour the countryside. Maybe we'd finally be able to relax and enjoy ourselves.

The five of us and our luggage squeezed into a midsize sedan because that was the only available rental and headed south along the coast from Istanbul to Ephesus to explore the ruins of what was once the most important trading center in the Mediterranean. Kaitlin played tour guide. She led the four of us grown-ups through the ruins and then a graveyard. She'd been studying the ancient Greeks in school, including the language, and delighted us by being able to read epitaphs on the grave markers, making me feel at once very proud and really guilty. Kaitlin had stopped attending class at Grace & St. Peter's in Baltimore when she and I flew to Chicago for my justice-of-the-peace wedding and I couldn't say when or where she'd return to school. For Kaitlin, it was like a snow day that stretched for months, but I was concerned about the lack of structure. Getting Kaitlin back in school was top of my to-do list once we arrived in Waterford.

AT HOME IN IRELAND

Meantime, I told myself not to worry about Kaitlin's time out of the classroom. She was exploring the remains of one of the world's most significant cities and, really, the most important thing right now was that she and I stay together. The circumstances couldn't have been more unsettled, but I sure was glad to be in her company. Watching her skip around the rubble of ancient temples and stadiums in her blue-jean overalls, I was satisfied to see that she was as intrigued by the history of Ephesus and the other places where we'd stopped along the Turkish coast as I was. I'd missed so much time with her when my career picked up and I'd never regretted that more than in this moment. The acknowledgement nearly brought tears to my eyes. Just look at her, I thought. She's curious, engaged, quick to smile, and completely open to the world around her. I may have kicked her father out when she was four and worked way more hours than a mother should, but I must have done something right in raising her to this point. Now I had us veering off the path we'd been on but headed where? What would this new direction mean for Kaitlin?

The week before Kaitlin and I left Baltimore, a friend had asked, "How will you know that Kaitlin will be okay with all of this?"

Before I could answer, he continued, "Well, if I know you, you just will." I hoped he was right.

While I was distracted by my concern about Kaitlin, Lief's parents bickered. They argued over the car windows—should they be open or closed—over the best place to stop for lunch—"I

HONEYMOON

don't want Turkish food again," Lief's mother would say, to which Lief's father would respond, "Well, then you shouldn't have come to Turkey"—and over where we should go each day and how long we should stick around once we got there. I did my best to block out Paul and Syndi's squabbling, but it was getting to Lief, too. He started snapping at them each time they snapped at each other. In Istanbul the final night of the trip, the stresses of the previous two weeks had us all on edge. After a tense dinner, Lief, Kaitlin, and I took a taxi back to our hotel on our own.

"4 million lire," the driver said tersely as he pulled up in front.

"That's not what it reads on the meter," Lief said sternly. It'd been another long day. We were all tired, especially Lief.

"4 million lire," the driver said again.

"You've added three zeros to the amount on the meter," Lief nearly shouted. The exchange rate between the lira and the dollar made the math almost impossible to do on the fly, and the driver figured we wouldn't know the difference. In fact, I wouldn't have. The guy was charging one thousand percent more, but it was a matter of a few dollars.

"Ignore meter," the driver said. "4 million lire."

"Why would I ignore the meter?" Lief said. "The meter is working just fine. I watched it while we were driving."

"Ignore meter. No work," the driver said. "4 million lire. "

Lief, who was in the front passenger seat, turned around to look at me and Kaitlin in back. "Kathleen, you and Kaitlin get out," he said. I opened the door to climb out and Kaitlin followed.

As soon as we two were out of the cab, Lief opened his door, slammed it behind him, spun around, threw the correct amount of lira through the open window, called the driver a name I wished Kaitlin hadn't heard, and stormed off. Kaitlin and I had to race to keep up with him as we fought our way through street touts and more Turkish men intent on touching Kaitlin's blond hair. This was a side of my new husband I hadn't seen before. For the first time since I'd agreed to marry Lief, I began to wonder what I'd gotten Kaitlin and me into.

VII
Waterford

As the train pulled into Plunkett Station a week later, I sized up my situation. I was traveling alone with three suitcases, two enormous overstuffed duffle bags, and two smaller duffle bags packed with carpets Lief and I had purchased in Istanbul. Plus I had my laptop, a backpack, and my purse.

There had been no porters in the station in Dublin where I'd boarded the train, so I wasn't counting on porters here in Waterford. Fortunately, Plunkett was the end of the line, so I didn't have to worry about getting all my bags off the train before it took off again.

Looking out the window I confirmed: No porters. No waiting queue of taxis that I could see either. I stood up and began pulling the duffle bags from the shelf where I'd stowed them for the two-and-a-half-hour trip.

"Are you on your own, luv?"

I looked up to see the Irishman who'd been sitting across the aisle from me. He wore a tweed cap and a tweed jacket whose buttons didn't meet across his healthy middle. He had a warm smile and a gentle voice that made me feel much less anxious about my circumstances.

We had no place to live so I had booked a suite at the Granville Hotel for two weeks for my family of three. I'd come on ahead to try to create as comfortable a situation as I could to receive Lief and Kaitlin, who would join me the following week. They'd gone back to Chicago together so Lief could finish closing out his life there and Kaitlin could get to know her new stepdad better.

"Yes, I am," I replied.

"Where are you headed?" he asked.

"The Granville Hotel. Would you know where that is?" I asked. "Is it far from the train station?"

"It's across there on the quay," the old Irishman told me. "Just over the bridge. We'll take you, luv," he said, gesturing over to include his wife.

"Oh, no, please, that's not necessary. Thank you, but I'll find a taxi outside."

"No, luv," the Irishman said. "You probably won't. And if you do find one, it won't be big enough to fit all your things. My wife and I have our van in the car park. Plenty of room. And we're happy to do it."

I looked up at my bags on the overhead rack and remembered how hard it'd been to load them on my own in Dublin. The friendly Irishman was already reaching up to help.

"Yes, actually I'd really appreciate it if you could give me a ride," I said, returning his smile.

We three carried my bags across the parking lot and loaded them into the van. Then we drove out of the train station, across Rice Bridge, and then left onto the quay that runs riverside along the center of Waterford City. Once upon a time, this was a bustling port town with ships lining the harbor importing and exporting to France, Spain, and beyond. When we arrived, though, in 1998, Waterford was forgotten and depressed. Which was the point. The IDA was trying to reinvigorate Ireland's economy beyond its capital city. At this stage, the Celtic Tiger's roar had yet to be heard much beyond Dublin. Waterford was sad and gray and generally in need of a fresh coat of paint.

That night, though, crossing the Rice Bridge over the River Suir for the first time as an official Waterford resident, the lights from the Georgian townhouses that line the quay twinkling in the harbor, Reginald's Tower visible in the distance, standing guard over the city as it had done for a thousand years, I could imagine the place as it once must have been, lively and prosperous. Viewed from the bridge into town, Waterford appeared magical.

My new Irish friends delivered me to the Granville and helped me drag my bags into the lobby. I checked in, and a bellman carried my things to my room. I was alone and still for the first time in a long time. I sat down in the chair by the window to regroup. I'd pulled my eight-year-old daughter away from everything she and I had known to this point—our family, our friends, her school. My new husband likewise had left his life, his professional situation. Now we were to start over as a new family in a new city in a foreign country, me looking to build a publishing business while making a home, my husband trying to buy an old house from a mysterious Singaporean to convert into a center for corporate retreats. When I boiled things down in my mind to those basic facts, even I had to admit the situation could be considered unsound.

I'd left a lot of loose ends. I have always been good at focusing sharply on a single target while blocking out everything else and ignoring objections, obstacles, and challenges. It's a trait that came in handy when making a move like I was making, but it leaves collateral damage. I feared that right now the casualties included my staff back in Baltimore who I'd left to run the *International Living* business on their own for nearly two months while I'd been distracted getting divorced so I could get remarried and then taking off for Ireland via Turkey.

I should call Lief and Kaitlin to let them know I've arrived, I thought, but, when I picked up the phone, I found myself dialing my parents' phone number. I wanted to talk to my father.

"The man who bought your car came to collect it this afternoon," my dad said after I told him I'd arrived safe and sound in Waterford, "and everything is on track for the closing of your house sale next week.

"A girl from your work called yesterday to ask if I had any idea which files you wanted her to pack and which ones she could leave behind. I told her to pack everything in your office, especially everything from your bookcase. I thought that'd be safest. It's all on its way to you now."

"Thanks, Dad," I said. In the silence that followed, I began to feel less stressed. I settled back in my chair and was glad I'd called my father before calling Lief. Talking to my dad always made me feel like everything was all right or would be soon.

"So how are you? How's Ireland? What is Waterford like?" My father had been the only one to support the idea of my move. I didn't want to admit to the growing sense of panic I was feeling and give him reason to worry about me.

"How is everything there in Baltimore?" I countered. "I know I took off in a rush and left a lot of pieces for you to pick up."

"Everything's fine, just fine," he told me, just as he'd been telling me as long as I could remember.

Kaitlin and I had spent our final night in Baltimore with my mother and father. They'd picked Kaitlin up from her last day of school, and I'd met the three of them at my parents' house for dinner and a sleepover. My parents had been Kaitlin's co-primary-care-givers. If I was honest, Kaitlin had probably spent more time with them than with me over the past few years. I didn't acknowledge that truth out loud, but I understood Kaitlin had as strong an attachment to my mother and father as she did to me. Now I couldn't tell her when she'd see them again. These were big realities, but I did what I always did when worry about my life choices began to interfere with pushing ahead with a plan. I blocked it out and focused on the objective in front of me. I believed that marrying Lief and moving to Ireland were the right thing for me and for Kaitlin, too. I wanted a new life for me and a big life for her. Nothing good comes easy. My father had taught me that. He'd also taught me not to be afraid of hard. "If you don't do the hard work," he'd say, "you never have the satisfaction of seeing it pay off."

The morning of our planned departure, Kaitlin had laid in the bed in my parents' guest room, fully clothed under the covers, crying. My mother sat at her side, holding her hand and sobbing.

"Please let her stay here, with your father and me. She can come to Ireland later, after you've gotten settled." The more my mother pleaded, the harder Kaitlin cried.

Finally, mustering the strength I needed, as I do, to push through a really hard thing, I blocked out my mother's voice and Kaitlin's sobs and focused on the practical task at hand. I pulled Kaitlin out of bed and away from her grandmother. My dad helped me carry Kaitlin and our luggage down the stairs and then loaded our suitcases and duffle bags into his trunk. As we climbed into the car, Kaitlin was still crying and now I was, too, quietly. I put on my sunglasses, hoping Kaitlin and my dad wouldn't notice. No time for second guessing now. I'd made a plan. It was a good plan. I just had to stick to the plan.

My father had fielded inquiries for the sale of my car and then delivered it to the guy who decided to buy it. He had stood with me on my front lawn all day Saturday and again all day Sunday, until the last item sold, the weekend of my yard sale. He had met the movers at my house while I was at work to oversee their packing. Now he would drive Kaitlin and me to the airport so we could take off for the first leg of the trip to launch our new life without him.

I thought about all of this as I sat in the red damask armchair by the window of my room at the Granville Hotel staring out at the empty quay and the silent harbor below. "This place is like something out of a fairy tale," I told my dad, "with ancient city walls, old churches, cobblestoned squares, and even a Viking fort." It was romantic, I reminded myself, trying hard to squelch the fear growing in my stomach.

"I met a nice Irish couple on the train down from Dublin. They drove me to my hotel. I'm in my room now, looking out over the river. You and mom will like it here. We need to talk about when you can come see Waterford for yourselves."

Yes, Dad, I thought as I continued doing my best to paint a storybook picture of my nascent life in the Old World, *please come visit. I think I'm going to need your help.*

VIII
The Granville Hotel

The waitress seated us at our usual table by the front window. From this spot, Lief, Kaitlin, and I had a view of the stone clock tower across the street. The Gothic tower was built when Waterford was Ireland's busiest industrial port, home to the biggest boat-building yards in the country. I liked imagining what the docks must have looked like back in the nineteenth century, when this was a center of global commerce, the river lined with ships coming and going, the quay crowded and chaotic with goods being loaded and unloaded and traders bustling about, calling out to draw attention to their arriving wares. The scene now was silent and lonely, no ships, no sailors, no shoppers. It made me sad to see the once-celebrated harbor so forsaken, so I looked beyond it, past the tower and across the river to the green hills at Ferrybank. That was the picture I looked forward to seeing each morning while we ate our breakfast. It was calming. So far, everything else about

THE GRANVILLE HOTEL

our experience as new residents on the Emerald Isle had been downright stressful.

"Full Irish for himself?" our waitress asked.

"Yes, please," Lief said, confirming the order of fried eggs, rashers, beans, and tomatoes he'd been enjoying every morning since he'd arrived six days before.

"Tea and toast for the three of ye'?"

"Yes, thank you. She'll have scrambled eggs with her toast," I added, nodding in Kaitlin's direction. "Nothing more for me."

I'd been in Waterford nearly two weeks, Lief and Kaitlin almost a week. Lief and I had prioritized a to-do list. First, we needed to choose a school for Kaitlin. Then we needed to find an office. We put finding a place for us to live third because we thought locating a small office to rent would be easier than shopping for the big old Irish country house I had my heart set on. So far, we'd managed to make an appointment to enroll Kaitlin in Newtown School. Not much to show for nearly two weeks' effort.

While we waited for our order, I opened *The Munster Express* to the classified ad pages. I was keen to get Kaitlin in school and we needed to find a place to live, but I was also very aware that Agora's Executive Committee back in Baltimore was standing by for a report from the scene of their new EU operations. But for the fifth day in a row, the paper included no listings for office rentals.

Waterford IDA representative Seamus wanted Agora to set up operations in the new Industrial Park just outside the city center. He couldn't understand why I was resisting the idea, but I couldn't bear the thought of spending every working day in that purpose-built, low-rise, pre-fab space. If I didn't find an alternative soon, though, I'd likely acquiesce to the pressure from Seamus, who kept reminding me politely that basing ourselves in the IDA-supported business center might be the thing to do given the IDA benefits we were enjoying as new Irish business owners. I wasn't ready to make that concession. My fairy-tale expectations about this adventure we were undertaking in Ireland had nothing to do with industrial anything.

I was used to doing things on my own—from raising my daughter and managing my household to running two publishing divisions—but I was beginning to realize that, if my vision of what I wanted our new life on this island to look like was going to play out, I'd need to find help. Quick.

For years, I'd advised our readers that when you're moving to a new country, your first important choice is whether to live among the locals or in an expat community. In Waterford we didn't have to make that decision because there was no expat community. We didn't mind being the only non-Irish souls in the city as far as we could tell, but it meant that we had no one obvious to turn to for help. We were reduced to asking for recommendations and referrals from everyone and anyone. We'd already spent days searching the local papers and walking from shop to shop, restaurant to restaurant, and pub to pub, checking message boards and asking cashiers and bar maids if they knew of offices for rent.

"After our meeting at the school, we can walk around town and stop in at the real estate agencies," Lief suggested after the waitress had brought our food. "Maybe some of them handle commercial leases. We can ask about houses for sale, too."

So, we set about our routine. We were up early each morning. After breakfast in the dining room of the Granville Hotel, we'd venture out. Waterford isn't a big city, and we'd begun to get the lay of the land, but we just couldn't seem to get anything accomplished. Nothing worked the way we thought it should. We'd expected to slot right into our new life on the Emerald Isle. The Irish speak English, after all, and this was Europe, not the developing world. Getting established in this country shouldn't be anything near as difficult as moving to Costa Rica or Honduras or any of the other Spanish-speaking Third World countries I'd been recommending to my *International Living* readers for so long. What were we doing wrong?

After we finished eating, we followed our usual route, past the townhouses with their Irish Georgian front doors each painted a different color. I smiled remembering the guide who'd led us around Dublin the first day of the *International Living* tour where Lief and I had met. She'd told us that the reason Irish doors are all painted different bright colors is so the man of the house could pick out his from among all the others when coming home late after too many pints at the local pub.

We crossed a cobblestoned square to reach the city's only taxi stand, outside the city's only shopping mall.

"Newtown School," Lief said to the driver as we got into his cab. "We have a meeting there that should last about an hour. Would you mind waiting then bringing us back to the city?"

We drove along the quay and up the hill past more Georgian townhouses with their black iron railings and doors of many colors. A few minutes later, we passed through the tall front gates of Newtown School. Nearly all the secondary schools in Waterford were boys or girls only and Catholic. Kaitlin didn't want to go to school with "just girls," so we'd made an appointment with the head mistress of Newtown School, both the only co-ed and the one non-Catholic education option in the city. The campus was behind high stone walls in Newtown. While original Waterford was built by Vikings, Newtown dated to the 1700s. To us Americans, it was all old. Trees on the Newtown campus had nearly as many years on them as the country from whence we Yanks hailed.

The school itself had been founded in 1798 by the Religious Society of Friends on the estate of the home of Sir Thomas Wyse. Originally it was intended for the education of Quakers in the south of Ireland, and until 1858 no non-Quakers were admitted. I'd attended Catholic schools for sixteen years, including an all-women Catholic university in Baltimore. Raising my brothers, sister, and me Catholic had been important to my mother, who was a converted Presbyterian. I'd grown up with a strong feeling that I wanted to believe in something but could never figure out what. I appreciated the early exposure my mother had given me to the Catholic faith and its traditions. I had been stopping in at Waterford City's Christ Church Cathedral every time we passed to light a candle and ask for guidance. I'd been lighting candles in churches for years. If someone had asked me the point I wouldn't have been able to name it—Catholicism hadn't resonated with me as the answer to my search for meaning—but I figured I could use whatever help I could get. Some of the most religious people I'd known were the least Christian. God is all about love, but religion—including Catholicism, as far as I could tell after having gotten to know it pretty well—too often wasn't.

I hadn't asked Lief about his religious inclinations until we began researching schooling choices for Kaitlin. "I'm an agnostic," he'd told me, which was fine with me and maybe described what I was, too. I wasn't sure. I'd had Kaitlin baptized Catholic, because it was taken for granted by my family that she would be, but Grace & St. Peter's, where she'd started school in Baltimore, was Episcopal. Close enough. Now she'd be going to school with Quakers. Wyse had been a famous defender of Catholicism in Ireland. I wondered if he minded his homestead having been developed by a community of Friends and, as well, if my mother might mind her granddaughter now spending her days among them. When it came to educating your child in Waterford, Newtown was definitely the non-conventional choice, which worked for us. Non-conventional seemed to be what Lief and I did best.

Our taxi parked in front of the main building, and Lief led us across the Newtown campus according to the directions we'd been given on the phone. Kaitlin and I followed him upstairs to the second floor of a stone building where Head Mistress Miriam invited us into her small, unheated office with stone walls and a wide-plank wooden floor. Kaitlin was silent and obviously nervous. Head Mistress Miriam, a short, slight woman with very good posture and a kerchief on her head, tried to make Kaitlin feel at ease. She smiled brightly in Kaitlin's direction and put her arm around Kaitlin's shoulders to settle her into one of the three straight-backed wooden chairs positioned in a row opposite Head Mistress Miriam's desk, but these efforts didn't have the intended affects. Kaitlin grew more apprehensive with every gesture. Lief and I sat on the other two wooden chairs, on either side of Kaitlin, and prepared to answer Head Mistress Miriam's questions. The woman was doing nothing but trying to make us feel welcome, but the word "interrogation" kept coming to my mind, and I wondered what was going on in Kaitlin's.

Ever since Kaitlin and I had flown to Chicago so I could marry Lief, I'd been worried about all the school time she was missing. Now that we were in Waterford, I was increasingly concerned about all the kid time she was missing, as well. She'd had no opportunity to meet other children let alone to make a friend. That would change when she started school, but, meantime, she was

Lief and my constant companion, and Lief and I were all about our getting-settled to-do lists. Our ongoing search for office space, thinking through a strategy for finding staff, and keeping up with the day-to-day operations of the business back in Baltimore were our only topics of discussion. Our conversations couldn't have been interesting to Kaitlin. I registered this truth and lamented it but couldn't see what I could do to change it, at least not in the immediate term, so we carried on, which meant dragging Kaitlin around with us for every meeting and every errand. Getting her enrolled in school would make me feel like I was at least doing one thing for her.

We had no permanent address to offer when asked for one and explained that we were staying indefinitely at the Granville Hotel while we tried to find a house or an apartment to rent. Head Mistress Miriam wasn't too put out by that fact, but, no, she was sorry, she said, she didn't know of any available rentals. I continued filling out the enrollment forms while Head Mistress Miriam tried again to help Kaitlin feel less uneasy. "What's your favorite subject?" she wondered. Kaitlin, small and pale in her purple corduroy overalls, looked over at me with such a panicked expression that I had a sudden urge to take her by the hand and lead her out of the room. "She enjoys reading," I offered instead, fighting back the impulse to flee, "and she likes to write stories." Head Mistress Miriam smiled, then, to Kaitlin's relief, turned away from Kaitlin to review the forms I'd finally completed.

"There now, dear, you're registered for third class," Head Mistress Miriam said with a big smile. "You can begin your studies with us on Monday." It was Friday. Finally, we could cross something off our list.

"Look over there, Doodlebug," I said after we'd climbed back down the wooden stairs from Head Mistress Miriam's office, pointing in the direction of the playing field across the lane. "I wonder what game that is those boys are playing. I've never seen sticks like those before."

"It's hurling," Lief said. "It's something like three-thousand years old. They learn to play as soon as they're old enough to hold the sticks. It's their baseball."

We stopped to watch for a minute. "It's kind of rough and tumble, isn't it?" I said. "I wonder if girls play, too." The boys on the field before us were whacking their axe-like wooden sticks at each other with a vengeance, whipping a small ball around the field while charging each other, barreling into each other, falling, crumbling, then jumping back up to carry on whacking and whipping and charging. Their jerseys were muddy and grass-stained, and a few were a little bloody. What kind of schoolyard game was this?

"Yes, girls play, too," Lief said, "but they call it something else. And I think body contact and tackling are prohibited in the version women play."

"Ah," I said, looking over at Kaitlin who looked smaller and paler even than she had during the inquiry with Head Mistress

Miriam. "Well, that's good to hear, isn't it, Doodlebug?" Kaitlin didn't respond. She just kept staring at the scene taking place in the field across the way.

"Let's stop inside at the main office," I said, trying to divert Kaitlin's attention. "Head Mistress Miriam gave us a list of books you'll need that we can pick up inside. And we can order your uniforms."

Unlike the navy jumper and white shirt with a Peter Pan collar that Kaitlin had worn at Grace & St. Peter's, students at Newtown, like students at all middle schools in Ireland, wore track suits. Newtown's were teal blue with a white school insignia in the upper-left-hand corner of the front of the sweatshirt. The outfit was practical and warm, I guessed, but not what I'd expected. Kaitlin still hadn't commented on any part of the whole registering-for-school experience and I didn't want to add to the misgivings she was clearly having so I kept my disappointment about her new school togs to myself.

"We'll have your track suits for you within two weeks," the lady in the office explained, as she put the receipt for the uniforms and the books on the desk in front of me.

"I don't have that much cash with me," I said, feeling again, as I'd found myself feeling often the two weeks since I'd arrived in this city, unprepared, "and we can't write a check because we haven't opened a bank account yet. Could we send the money with Kaitlin when she returns for her first day of classes on Monday?"

"Yes, of course. That'll be fine, sure it will," the lady in the office told us. "In the meantime, my dear," she said, looking over at Kaitlin, "while you're waiting for your uniforms to arrive, you can wear whatever you'd like to school each day. How's that then?" the kind lady asked. "That'll be fun, won't it now?" Kaitlin nodded slightly and tried to smile.

"You have some catch-up work to do," I said as we carried our bagsful of books in the direction of the waiting taxi. "We can get started later when we're back at the hotel, okay, Bugsy?"

Kaitlin nodded her head again but still didn't speak. Everyone we'd encountered at the school had tried hard to reassure her, but she looked now like she might break down in tears, and I didn't blame her. The morning had been overwhelming.

"Let's call Gammy and Poppy tonight," I said. "To tell them you're enrolled in your new school and that you'll begin classes on Monday. How will that be?"

"Okay, Mommy," she said, finally brightening a little.

By now we were back at the taxi. Lief got in the front passenger seat, Kaitlin and I climbed in back with our bags of books.

"We're trying to find office space to rent," I said to our driver, doing what I did every chance I got, asking another stranger for help. "Would you know of anything available?"

"It's office space you're wanting, is it, luv? No, I wouldn't know of anything. I'd say you want to speak with the estate agents."

"Yes, okay. Would you be able to take us to the biggest agency in the city?"

THE GRANVILLE HOTEL

"That'd be O'Shea O'Toole on Gladstone Street. I'll take you there now, sure."

Ten minutes later, Lief, Kaitlin, and I were sitting in the waiting room at O'Shea O'Toole, Kaitlin holding her bags of schoolbooks on her lap, while the receptionist checked to see if Des O'Shea was available to speak with us.

"Hello," Mr. O'Shea said when he emerged from behind his office door. He was tall, thin, and formal in his dark three-piece suit. "My girl tells me you're interested in office space to rent, is that it?" he said as he sat down at the round meeting table and indicated for Lief and me to do the same. Kaitlin stayed put in her chair by the window, holding her books.

"Yes. We need space for six or eight people to start, with the potential for expansion in a year, say, and we'd prefer to be in the heart of the city center," I explained.

"I don't have anything on the books that might suit at the moment," Des replied. "Have you considered the Industrial Park?"

"Yes, we've been to see it," I said, trying to hide my disdain. "We'd prefer something with more character. Something with charm. We don't want office space, per se, but an historic property, maybe something Georgian in style."

Des O'Shea stared at me like he couldn't understand the words coming out of my mouth. Then he turned to Lief, as though hoping for a translation. What was I doing wrong?

"We're also in the market for a house to buy," Lief said, ignoring the bewilderment on Mr. O'Shea's face.

"Again, we're looking for something classic Irish Georgian in style," I added. "An old stone house on a few acres in the country."

"We can have a look at our books," Des said finally. "When would suit for viewings?"

We made an appointment for Monday at 9:00 a.m. That'd give us time to drop Kaitlin off at school at 8:30. More progress, though I still couldn't figure out why the real estate agent had seemed so baffled by my property descriptions and I said as much to Lief when we were back outside on the quay.

"I don't understand his reactions either," Lief admitted. "It does seem that, while we all speak English, we and the Irish are having a really hard time getting through to each other."

Back in our room at the Granville, I spread Kaitlin's new textbooks on the bed.

"Head Mistress Miriam made a list of sections she'd like you to review by Monday," I said. "What would you like to start with, Doodlebug? Would you prefer to read or to do some math exercises?"

"I'll read," she said, and I handed her the English book open to the page Head Mistress Miriam had indicated.

"Read the text and then respond to the questions on the next page, okay? I'll review your answers with you when you're finished."

Kaitlin propped up the purple travel pillow my parents had bought her, and began reading. I powered up my laptop at the desk.

THE GRANVILLE HOTEL

Lief sat in the armchair by the window and likewise booted up.

The time zones worked in our favor. It was 4:00 p.m. in Waterford but only 9:00 a.m. in Baltimore. My staff would be just getting into their day. I replied to emails, reviewed copy for the next issue of *International Living*, and okay'd the marketing plan for the rest of the month. I owed Bill, Mark, and the Executive Committee an update, but I still didn't have anything positive to report and talked myself out of sending a note. Maybe by Monday I'd have news.

I shut down my laptop for the day at 7:00 p.m. and sat on the bed to review Kaitlin's work. She'd finished more than an hour ago and had been watching episodes of "The Simpsons" on television ever since. I told myself not to make an issue of it. She'd be back in school on Monday.

"Excellent work, Doodlebug," I said after grading her responses to the reading comprehension questions and marking a big red one hundred percent at the top of the page. "Great job. It's time for dinner, but how about if we call Gammy and Poppy first?" I wanted to hear how Kaitlin would relay the day's events on her own.

"Yes, please!" she said, more animated than I'd seen her all day.

"Poppy!" she called enthusiastically into the phone when my dad picked up. "It's me!" She was quiet a minute, listening to whatever my father was saying. "But when are you and Gammy coming to visit?" she asked. Another pause. "I know, but I want to show you my new school. I start on Monday. When you come, will you and Gammy bring ketchup? They don't have any here. Instead of ketchup they use this stuff they call 'red sauce.' It's awful. And so I have to eat my scrambled eggs without ketchup." Kaitlin had yet to complain to me about our move at all—not about the food or anything more significant either. I feared she was keeping any misgivings to herself, not wanting to worry me. I wasn't sure I could articulate how at sea I was feeling and understood Kaitlin's silent perseverance. I was happy to hear her open up to my father, even if only about her breakfast challenges. "Okay, Poppy, I miss you, too!" she said after another pause. "I love you, too! Here's Mommy."

I wanted to tell my father that the morning had been painful. That Kaitlin had been nervous in the meeting with Head Mistress Miriam then terrified watching her new male schoolmates beat each other silly with long wooden sticks. But I didn't want Kaitlin to overhear me admit that she'd been right to have felt anxious about the morning's events, and I didn't want my father to worry, so, like Kaitlin, I kept my fears to myself and just told my dad that I thought the school would be a good place for Kaitlin.

"That must be a relief," my father said, "knowing she'll be back in school starting Monday."

"Yes, I said. "I heard Kaitlin ask when you and Mom will come visit. We really do need to plan that. We're still staying at the Granville Hotel, though. As soon as we find an actual home, we'll count on you and Mom to be our first houseguests."

"We'll be there," my father said. "You just let us know when."

Like every other time I'd spoken with my father by phone since arriving in Waterford, in the instant after the conversation finished, I felt so alone and sad I almost couldn't take a breath. He was so far away.

"Come on, Mom," Kaitlin was saying. "I'm starving."

"Okay, okay! Yes, let's go eat!" I said, forcing enthusiasm. She was much less glum after speaking with her grandfather.

Kaitlin ran ahead of us, down the long hallway lined on both sides with black and white photos of Waterford City over the centuries, then down the big central staircase with the heavy mahogany banister to the ground floor. She waited for us at the bottom of the stairs, then the three of us turned to enter the pub area. Breakfast was in the dining room at the front, with the view of the quay and the river. Dinner was served in the restaurant in the back, which doubled as a bar and featured a big fireplace in the middle of the far wall. It was Friday, so the room was crowded with both locals and tourists.

The Granville Hotel, positioned at the center of the quay on the River Suir, was built by a family of Dutch merchants and bankers in the early 1700s. It's one of the oldest hotels in Ireland. With its arched entrances, ornate moldings, paned windows, and stained glass, it's a picture of the Old World. Tourists come by busloads to see the place where the world's most famous crystal is made. Waterford Crystal is the city's only real economy, and those who come to tour the factory all want to spend the night at the Granville.

On the walls in the restaurant and over the bar are more photographs of the city and its most famous sons and daughters, including Thomas and Thomas Francis Meagher. The Meaghers bought the Granville from the Dutch family that built it, and Thomas Francis Meagher of the Fighting 69th, the Irish Brigade that fought in the U.S. Civil War, was born here. Thomas Francis helped to design of the Irish flag, which was flown for the first time ever in 1848 in front of the Granville. Thomas Francis was also a seditionist who was eventually ordered to be hanged, drawn, and quartered. When he learned of his impending fate, Meagher delivered a heart-felt call for freedom from the Waterford docks that led to such an outcry among the townspeople that the death sentence was commuted. Instead, he was banished to Van Diemen's Land, eventually known as Tasmania.

Lief, Kaitlin, and I were happy to see that our regular table by the fireplace was free. We were learning that Irish buildings were never sufficiently heated, and we'd come to look forward to being able to warm ourselves in front of the open fire in the dining room come dinnertime each night.

Kaitlin opened the *Goosebumps* book she'd brought with her, and Lief and I took stock of the week. The pressure I felt to get the Agora Ireland operation off the ground and generating positive cash flow was greater every day, yet we still had no line on office space and we couldn't begin interviewing for the new staff we needed until we had somewhere to receive them other than the lobby of the Granville Hotel.

"How can it be so hard to find an office to rent?" I asked Lief.

"There's virtually no commercial space available because there's virtually no commerce," he said. "There's a reason the IDA is working so hard to attract foreign business to this town. I'm tired of beating my head against that wall. Tomorrow, let's go shopping for a car."

Buying a car sounded like a great idea to me. Walking or taking a taxi everywhere we wanted to go each day was getting old. With our own car, we'd be able to explore beyond Waterford City limits. I'd come to Ireland with visions of castles and gardens. It was time we saw some.

IX

Saturdays

We rose early, as we'd done each Saturday since arriving in Waterford, dressed, and had our usual breakfast at our usual table. We said hello to the desk staff on duty, all of whom knew us by name by now, on our way out and then nodded and smiled at the white-gloved bellman when he pulled the big brass handle to open the door so we could step out onto the quay then turn right up into the center of town in the direction of the city's only taxi stand.

"We'd like to visit some of the car dealerships just outside town," Lief explained to the driver as the three of us got into the back of his taxi. "Would you be able to take us around and wait for us while we have a look at two or three places?"

The driver stared back at Lief.

"You're wanting to go where?" he asked.

"To two or three of the car dealerships on the Cork Road," Lief

SATURDAYS

explained again. "We'd like to buy a car. Would you be able to take us from one dealer to another and wait while we shop? Perhaps for an hourly fee?"

"It's Saturday, sir," the driver replied.

Lief and I looked at each other.

"Yes…"

"Would you be wanting to do this Monday morning, is that it?" the driver asked.

"No, not Monday," Lief said. "We'll be working Monday. We'd like to go now."

"But it's Saturday."

Why did this guy keep telling us what day it was? We knew it was Saturday. Why did that matter? Why couldn't he take us to look at cars for sale on Saturday? Ah, ha, I thought. That was it, wasn't it? It was Saturday.

"Is it that the dealerships aren't open today?" I asked. "Because it's Saturday?"

"Aye, luv, of course. It's Saturday."

We'd observed from week one of our move that banks and other places, too, closed for lunch every day and that the entire city of Waterford called it quits by 5:00 each afternoon. Sundays, you saw nary a soul anywhere, other than coming and going from church or the local pub later in the afternoon. But when we were planning our day, it hadn't occurred to us that some businesses were also closed on Saturdays. So much for our plan to go car shopping.

"We'll have to try again one day next week," Lief said dejectedly and mostly to himself.

"When do they run their errands?" Lief wondered aloud as we walked away from the taxi stand. We stopped when we got to the corner, and Lief and I stared ahead blankly. I was out of ideas for next steps.

"Let's go buy today's papers," Lief said. "We can check the classified and real estate listings to see if anything new is available."

"Okay," I responded with all the enthusiasm I could muster, which wasn't much.

"You know," I said to Lief as we walked through the pedestrian center of town toward the bookstore with the only newsstand in the city where we could buy all the local papers at once, "I don't think they do."

"You don't think who doesn't do what?" Lief said wearily.

"Run their errands," I said. "You asked 'When do they run their errands?' But 'they' don't. Their wives do."

Ireland was seeing big changes, but it was still a very traditional place. Back in Baltimore, every woman I knew of my generation was working full time in a career-path position like me. For the most part, Irish women stayed home to raise their children. They could run to the dry cleaners or the bank anytime they wanted. Here in Waterford, where I'd come to run an office and build a business, I was an alien in ways that had nothing to do with my residency status.

Kaitlin started school and her life at least settled into a routine. Within a few weeks, she was talking about friends she'd made, especially Sophia, who began inviting Kaitlin over to her house after school and on Saturday afternoons. Kaitlin also joined the girls' hurling team. It was the main extracurricular activity available, and all her friends played. The girl version, she told us, was called "camogie," and she and I both were very happy to see that it wasn't nearly as rough as the form the boys played. I took her new friends and her decision to join the team as hopeful signs. She was integrating.

The mothers of the girls Kaitlin was making friends with began calling to invite me to join them for tea. I accepted a couple of times, wanting to make an effort for Kaitlin's sake, but I didn't have time for that kind of socializing and, really, it's never been my thing. I've never prioritized play. It's always seemed like a waste of time. In school, I liked homework. Now I was a career woman who craved respect and believed that hard work was the way to earn it. I was ready anytime, day or night, to jump into a planning session for the launch of a new marketing campaign or to brainstorm article ideas with a writer, but I was no good at small talk with other women. I just never knew what they'd want to talk about and had always had more male friends than female. Plus, ever since Bill had given me a taste of what it was like to build a business, I'd been bored by conversation that didn't have what I perceived as a productive agenda, preferably to do with expanding some aspect of some enterprise.

Eventually, after I'd turned them down or cancelled once too often, the mothers stopped reaching out, and I understood. I hoped I hadn't offended them by deflecting their invitations to get together and breaking our dates, but we had nothing in common. They wouldn't have been interested in my Agora Ireland growth plans, which were all I wanted to talk about, and, sooner or later, I might actually have asked one of them what she did all day and that probably wouldn't have done Kaitlin's efforts to assimilate any favors.

At the same time, I knew that my focus on career had meant that Kaitlin had sometimes been seconded and right now I was even less available for her than I'd been in Baltimore. Kaitlin's efforts to soldier on cheerfully only intensified my guilt. But the current chaos was temporary, I told myself. Lief and I would eventually figure out how to make a home for our little family among the Irish, then we'd have more time to devote to Kaitlin. The truth was, though, I'd been telling myself that most of Kaitlin's life. I was always sure that, as soon as my big project was finished, my new division was up and running, or my next business trip was over, I'd have more time for her. But there was always another important launch or meeting. The difference now was that I didn't have my parents to pick up the slack for me. Kaitlin wasn't com-

SATURDAYS

plaining, but I knew that she was struggling. She asked every day how long it would be until she'd be able to see her father and her grandparents again.

The only thing I could think to do was to work through our to-do lists, but they kept growing. We needed to open personal and corporate bank accounts, apply for a company credit card, find an Irish accountant to keep us compliant with Irish tax law, engage an Irish attorney to keep us from running afoul of local labor law, and finalize our residency visas and work permits. For years I'd been telling my *International Living* readers that the biggest challenge they'd face moving to a new country would be not knowing what they didn't know. Now in Waterford I was beginning to suspect Lief and I knew nothing about anything. We couldn't even manage to purchase a cell phone. The guy in the shop told us to come back when we had a permanent Irish address. "Care of the Granville Hotel" wouldn't cut it.

Not only were we struggling to get anything done, but whatever we did manage to do left us feeling befuddled. The attorney who drafted our fist employment contracts included a clause guaranteeing two fifteen-minute tea breaks every day because they were required by law. The residency process in Ireland is handled by the *gardai*, or local police, but Tramore station, where our cases were assigned, had only one officer. Two appointments out of three, we showed up to be told that he was out on a call, once investigating a murder, and we'd have to reschedule.

AT HOME IN IRELAND

We'd contacted the Bank of Ireland our first week in Waterford. "What documentation will we need to open a corporate account?" Lief had asked the banker over the phone. "Simply bring your passports," she'd told him. Thinking we were being very on top of things, we'd also brought the articles of incorporation for the company, which, though she hadn't mentioned them on the phone, the very young banker in the too-big navy pantsuit asked for first thing after we'd sat down across from her in her small office.

"Here you go," I said, pleased to be able to produce them.

"And I'll also need to see company proof of ownership certificates," she said with a smile.

Lief and I looked at each other and frowned. Probably we should have thought to bring the proof of ownership certificates along with the articles of incorporation, but that was why Lief had asked what we'd need on the phone.

"We were told only to bring our passports," Lief said. "We figured we'd also need the articles of incorporation so we brought those, but it would have been nice if we'd been told about the other required documents."

"No problem," the young banker said cheerfully. "You can schedule another appointment for next week."

When we showed up for that appointment, the very young banker, dressed in another oversized pantsuit, accepted our additional paperwork, and then looked up at us, and said, "Do you have your reference letter?"

SATURDAYS

"Reference letter?" I asked.

"Oh, did I not mention it?" the young banker said. "We'll need to see a bank reference letter for the company. That's no problem, though, sure it's not. We can schedule another appointment for next week."

I could feel Lief tensing up beside me.

"Could we schedule our next appointment for later this week?" I asked. "We should be able to get the reference letter in a day or two, and we've already been trying to get this account opened for three weeks."

"I'm sorry, but I'm leaving for holidays this evening. I won't be back until Thursday a week. Would that suit?" the young banker asked.

"Yes, that will be fine," I said flatly.

"Can you tell us if there's anything else at all that we'll need to open the account?" Lief added using his deepest baritone voice.

"No, no," the young banker said nervously as she seemed to shrink even smaller inside her suit. "Nothing at all."

Thursday of the following week we were back sitting across from the very young banker in her small office. Lief passed her the bank reference letter.

"I'm sorry," she said, after reviewing the document and placing it inside the folder she'd created for us during our first meeting, "but we won't be able to open this account."

"What do you mean you won't open the account?" I said quickly, before Lief could recover his power of speech. I was terrified at the thought of what might come out of his mouth when he did.

"We simply need an operating account for our new business. The Bank of Ireland opens corporate accounts, doesn't it?" I asked. My tone, I was aware, was overly direct but nothing compared with what Lief's tone was going to be when finally he spoke.

"Yes," the very young banker said feebly, so intimidated that she couldn't look at us. "However, we cannot open an account for non-residents," she explained staring down at the closed file on her desk. "We could meet again after you've gotten your residency permits. Then we should be able to consider the account."

"This is our fourth meeting with you," Lief said, trying hard to control his voice. "Why didn't you explain that you wouldn't be able to open an account for us because we're not yet residents during any of our three previous appointments?"

"Well, I imagined you understood," the young girl said in a voice so soft we could barely hear her.

"Why," Lief boomed back at her, "if we understood that we wouldn't be able to open an account no matter how much documentation we produced, would we have returned again and again with additional documentation!" Lief was now in full range boss form. He stood up and, when he did, the small young girl finally looked up at us. Her face had gone white.

"Why would you waste our time like this?" Lief said as he pushed past me and out the door of the little office without another word or a glance over his shoulder.

"Thank you," I said quietly when the young banker and I were alone. "We'll be in touch again as soon as our residency applications have been approved."

The girl couldn't respond but nodded her head. Tears slid down her cheeks. I had no idea how to smooth things over so I didn't try. I walked out of the office and out of the bank and saw that Lief was already two blocks down along the quay in the direction of the Granville Hotel. I didn't hurry to catch up. I'd give Lief time to cool down. He could return to our room. I'd go for a walk along the river. I was frustrated, too, but I felt horrible for the young banker. She hadn't communicated the situation well, but Lief had overreacted. My new husband had a short fuse. I didn't have experience with angry men. I'd never seen my father lose his temper. Or Bill either. How much should I be bothered by Lief's lack of self-control? Or that Kaitlin and I were basically on our own with him in a foreign country? *Okay, that's enough of that line of thinking…*

I continued along the quay slowly. Finally, the flowing river and the green hills of Ferrybank on the other side distracted me from my worries over my husband's temper and the embarrassing scene with the young banker. My mind began to wander. It wasn't long until it found its way to my fear that I wasn't making quick enough progress in the eyes of Agora Baltimore.

Bill had wanted to open an Agora office in Ireland for years.

His business partner Mark, also Irish and always up for an adventure, was enthusiastic about the expansion agenda, but the same could not be said for every member of Agora's Executive Committee. To most of the rest of them, Bill's globalization plan was a distraction, taking focus off the business base in Baltimore and putting start-up capital at risk that'd be better used further fueling the fast-growing operations onshore.

One Executive Committee member in particular was not a fan of Bill's interest in establishing an Agora Ireland. Buddy Hayden, Agora's CEO, didn't travel beyond U.S. shores and didn't see the point of expanding the business beyond them either. Buddy's priority was memos. He sent many every day, all typed according to a specific format on stationery he'd had specially made and required every Agora manager to adopt. Buddy also mandated the type of post-it notes we could use. If you made a note on a post-it of a different size or color than the ones Buddy allowed, you'd be on the receiving end of an admonishing memo advising you never to do it again. The office culture at Agora was casual. Bill wore khaki pants and oxford shirts open at the collar. Mark wore suits on days we had meetings with important visitors. Otherwise, he might wear jeans. Summertime, temperatures in Baltimore reach ninety-five degrees and warmer. Our Baltimore Street offices were only partially air conditioned. In July and August, editorial and marketing assistants wore shorts. Buddy wore a three-piece suit and tie every day of the year.

SATURDAYS

Shortly after my move to Waterford, Buddy began contacting me to check in on my progress. He sent emails and then began calling to ask how I was coming with staffing and whether I'd managed to open a bank account.

"Things are going to get uncomfortable for you," Buddy had told me one day, "if you aren't able to establish operations and begin bringing money in the door very soon. You let me know how I can help."

Buddy's offer of aid wasn't sincere, but that didn't matter because neither he nor anyone else in Baltimore was in a position to help even if they actually wanted to. I was fairly certain that the solutions to our doing-business-in-Ireland problems would have to be found in Ireland.

I'd written an article years earlier for *International Living*, about how it takes three tries to do anything in Panama. Say you're out to dinner with friends. You excuse yourself to go to the bathroom. The door is locked but nobody's inside. You ask the nearest waiter for the key. You unlock the door and go into the stall and see that there's no toilet paper. You find another waiter to ask for a roll. You use the bathroom then discover there's no soap in the dispenser at the sink, so you find a third waiter and ask for a refill. Fifteen minutes and three tries later, you've successfully used the facilities and return to your table to finish your meal. We'd begun to have suspicions that Ireland operated a lot like Panama. Sometimes even three tries weren't enough to get done what you were trying to get done. But how could I explain that to Buddy? He couldn't imagine how it could take so long to accomplish everyday doing-business agendas. To be fair, if it were me back in Baltimore, I wouldn't have understood what the hold-up was either. I'd sped ahead cavalierly with the move to Ireland with no idea how difficult it would be, and I knew no one back in Baltimore had any appreciation of our circumstances. Who could have imagined that two months after arriving in Waterford I would still be living and working solo in a suite at the Granville Hotel? But that was our situation.

 I needed a hug and turned around to head back toward the Granville Hotel. I hoped Lief had regained his equilibrium so I could ask him for one.

X
You Say Potatoes

"This one isn't old either," I whispered in Lief's ear so that Mr. O'Shea and his associate wouldn't overhear. This was our fourth time out looking at houses with Mr. O'Shea, and I'd had my fill of the cookie-cutter jobs he kept taking us to see in these subdivisions he referred to as housing estates.

"Shhh," Lief shushed me under his breath. "We're here. Let's just take a look."

Des O'Shea parked the car, and the four of us got out in front of another bungalow that was suspiciously similar to the four we'd just toured and also an awful lot like all the others we'd seen on our previous three days out looking. Had the Irish banished all their architects? These square structures with hollow doors, too few windows, no moldings, no trim, and no imagination certainly hadn't benefitted from the help of any. Every house we'd seen so far had been the same color—brown—and too close to all the other houses around it. Lief and I wanted views of rolling hills and patchwork green fields. The view from every one of these housing estate bungalows was of more housing estate bungalows.

Lief and I dutifully explored the house, wandering from bedroom to bedroom and throughout the rest of the house, surprised again that, yes, five bedrooms had been crammed into one-thousand-eight-hundred square feet. Before we climbed back into the car, I tried one more time:

"Mr. O'Shea, this really isn't what we're looking for."

"It's five bedrooms within easy commuting distance of the city center," Des said.

"Well, yes, right, we want a big house with four or five bedrooms. But more important than the number of bedrooms is the property overall. We're looking for something with some years on it, the more the better, situated on a few acres, maybe with a barn. We want something Georgian and stone."

Des O'Shea's response was to take us to see two more identical houses.

We couldn't say why, but we weren't getting through to Mr. O'Shea, so we agreed a new plan of attack. The next morning, after walking Kaitlin to school, we'd return to the city center and stop in at every other real estate agency in the city. We didn't seem to speak Mr. O'Shea's language, but maybe some other agent would understand what we were asking for.

Lief had mapped out a route the night before. We started with

Palmer Auctioneers on Newtown Road. Don Palmer didn't have a receptionist but greeted us himself when we entered his office and didn't seem to mind that we didn't have an appointment.

"We're looking for a house to buy," I explained. "We'd like something historic and Georgian, four or five bedrooms, on a few acres, in the country. We're wondering if you have any listings along those lines?"

Don Palmer picked up the big black binder from his desk and began going through the listing sheets. He stopped at a Victorian house with a back garden in the city center. Then he flipped to a former convent, also in the center of town. Finally he showed us the listing for a not-yet-finished four-bedroom house on a hillside in new housing estate in a place called Annestown.

"That'd be what I have to show you," he said as he closed the binder.

We thanked Don Palmer, much less surprised by the nonsensical listings he'd presented than we would have been before having spent so many days touring similarly unsuitable properties with Des O'Shea, and continued on to John Rohan's estate agency on Parnell Street. When John's secretary called him out of his office, we put our inquiry to him.

"Would you have any classic Irish country properties on your books?" we asked.

John invited us to join him at his conference table, where he pulled out his big black binder. He flipped to a series of four- and five-bedroom houses, all within the city limits.

"Do you not have any country properties for sale?" I asked.

"We've got these," John said. "They're all four and five bedrooms, as you've said you're looking for."

We thanked Mr. Rohan and took our leave. Again, we were baffled. We still weren't getting through.

From John Rohan's office we continued on to the High Street and Purcell Auctioneers, where we laid out our specs to proprietor John Purcell, who showed us listing sheets for three properties outside Waterford City, all less than twenty years old.

Back on the quay, we sat down on a bench alongside the river. Why would no agent in the whole city of Waterford show us an old stone house in the country? Surely there had to be some. Where did they keep them all?

"Come on," Lief said suddenly, pulling me out from inside my head. "I'm tired of sitting around wondering why nothing makes sense and no one understands us. I'm hungry. Let's go have lunch."

"Let's try the carvery at Reginald's Tower," I suggested.

In 914, Viking raiders and traders began settling along the banks of the River Suir. To guard their city, which they called Vadrarfjord, they built thick stone walls and, in the eleventh century, a round tower. Now the tower was a museum with a circular staircase you could climb up for the best view we'd found of the River Suir and its city. Alongside Reginald's Tower was a pub that served up what the signboard out front assured us was the best roast beef carvery in Waterford.

The lunchtime queue at Tower Pub was dozens long, as it had been every day we'd passed. We picked up trays and followed the line of lunch-goers past the chef's carving station. The big Irishman in the white chef's hat on the other side of the warming lights carved three slabs of roast for Lief, then three more slabs for me. We moved along to the next station.

"Potatoes and veg?" the big Irish woman standing behind the counter offered.

"No potatoes for me," Lief said. "Just broccoli."

The woman spooned mashed potatoes onto Lief's plate. And some broccoli.

"I said no potatoes," Lief said.

The woman added a heaping spoonful of roasted potatoes.

'Didn't you hear me?" Lief said louder. "I said I don't want any potatoes."

The woman used a pair of tongs to add a pile of French fries atop the mashed and roasted potatoes on Lief's plate. What was going on? Lief was speaking English. Why did this woman not understand what he was saying? I could feel Lief's blood pressure rising.

"I'll eat the potatoes," I said to him quietly. "It's okay."

Then, to the big Irishwoman behind the counter, "Nothing for me, thank you. The roast beef is all I want." I twisted sideways so my plate was beyond her reach and she couldn't add anything more to it.

Lief seemed paralyzed. He just kept standing there holding his plate and staring unblinkingly at the woman who'd piled it high with potatoes.

"Come on," I said. "Let's go. This way. We'll get drinks, and then we pay over there."

"But I didn't want any potatoes," Lief said, still stuck in his spot. "I kept telling her that I didn't want any potatoes," he said. Then, to the woman, "I kept telling you I didn't want any potatoes."

Lief's mind was skipping, like a needle on a vinyl record with a scratch. Meantime, the long line of carvery guests behind us was growing restless.

"Lief, please, let's just move on."

"I'm not paying for all these potatoes," he said. "I told her I didn't want any potatoes."

"I know," I said. "But I'll eat them. I did want potatoes. It's okay."

Finally, Lief turned and took a step forward. He continued on in the direction of the bar. I followed. We picked up two glasses of water, then moved along to the cashier to check out.

"I'm not paying for these potatoes," Lief said to the girl behind the cash register. "I told that woman over there that I didn't want potatoes. The more I told her I didn't want potatoes, the more potatoes she put onto my plate. But I'm not paying for them."

The girl behind the cash register looked at Lief then at me.

"It's okay," I said to Lief. "I'll eat the potatoes. Then to the girl behind the register, "Please go ahead and ring up our orders, both lunches. Thank you."

Lief paid for our carveries, and we found a table.

"What was wrong with that woman?" Lief said as we sat down, using a tone I'd never heard from him before. He sounded like he was on the verge of tears. He was no longer angry. He was desperate.

"I don't know," I said. "Maybe the Irish can't fathom someone wanting a meal without potatoes. So every time you said the word 'potatoes,' she heard it as 'more potatoes.'"

The potato debacle had pushed Lief over the edge. "They can't respond to simple requests. You ask for no potatoes, and they give you a mountain of every possible type of potato. You ask what documents you need to open a bank account and they tell you none then have you come back three more times with more documents each time only to tell you in the end that they won't open an account for you at all. You ask to be taken to see an old Georgian property in the country, and they show you newbuilt houses in the middle of the city."

"Let's just eat our lunch," was all I could think to say.

I'd been researching, scouting, and writing about property markets in Latin America and the Caribbean as editor of *International Living* for years. I knew how maddening those markets can be because the agents don't work for the buyer or the seller but for the sale. There are no multiple listing services. The listings are proprietary, and each agent has access only to the properties listed with his agency. A dozen of a certain kind of property might be available for sale at any time, but any given agent might have just one or two of those on his books. I never imagined that those emerging-market fundamentals would apply in Ireland. I'd naively assumed that Ireland was a developed market where you shopped for a house the way you shop for house in the United States, but there didn't seem to be any other explanation.

"I think," I said after we'd sat in silence for a while, "that real estate markets in Ireland operate like real estate markets in Central America. We keep expecting to be able to walk into an agency, describe the kind of house we want to buy, and be presented with every house for sale that fits those criteria. But that's not how it works here. All these agents we're meeting with don't have any listings that fit our parameters, but, just like all the Central American real estate agents I've known, rather than admit that, they're showing us the listings they do have."

How had it taken me so long to figure that out?

Lief didn't look convinced, but, for the first time since we'd arrived in Waterford, I felt hopeful. At least now I understood what we were up against. I had a lot of experience dealing with developing world real estate agents. Now that I perceived that Irish agents were the same animal, I was confident we could figure this out.

In this Celtic Tiger age, the better part of the money the boom economy was generating was being plowed into real estate—building it, buying it, selling it, one Irishman to another. Dozens of housing estates were being developed in and around every city on the Emerald Isle, including in County Waterford. It was a massive Ponzi scheme. We'd registered this fact but ignored it. The local Irish economy wasn't our problem, and, as we'd been trying hard to explain to every real estate agent we'd met with, we weren't interested in newbuilt anything. But the phenomenon explained why the listing books of every agent in Waterford City were filled with new houses.

That night, back in our room at the Granville Hotel, while Kaitlin was doing her homework at the desk, Lief and I read the local papers. At first, living at the Granville Hotel had been fun and romantic, part of the adventure. Now, two months in, our suite felt more cramped every day and the lack of privacy had put a real damper on Lief and my would-be honeymoon stage. We were desperate to find a place to live that we could make our home.

I turned to the first page of the real estate section of *The Munster Express*. There, above the fold, big and bright, was a photo of an Irish Georgian townhouse with a red front door. The caption underneath explained that the house, on The Mall in the center of Waterford, was to be sold at auction in three days' time. It was a city townhome rather than a country house, but the photo grabbed me. The two-hundred-year-old house had a classic Irish Georgian front door that had been painted berry red and sported a big polished brass Claddagh knocker. It was the kind of door that had become a symbol of Ireland for me and the first image to came to mind every time I imagined my Irish dream home.

"Look at this," I said to Lief, holding up the paper so he could see the photograph. "This house is going to go up for sale at auction on Friday."

"Let me see," Lief said. I handed him the newspaper. He sat back in the red damask chair by the window and began reading.

"Maybe it'd make more sense to be in town, rather than out in the country," I said, "We'd be within walking distance of Kaitlin's school and our office, wherever it eventually ends up being," I added smiling.

Lief studied the ad for a few more minutes. I'd learned to give him time and space to process new ideas.

"I know this isn't the country house I've been pushing for all along," I continued, layering on my argument. "But look at that door. That's the picture of old Ireland. And it could be ours in just three days!" I said with a burst of enthusiasm that was as much for my own benefit as for Lief's.

"Yes, right, okay," Lief said, finally. "If you're okay with it, I am, too. I've had enough of hotel life. Tomorrow, let's find an attorney and ask how we buy a house at auction."

XI
All Mod Cons

The newspaper ad included the time and location for the auction, but we had no idea how to place a bid, so, after we'd dropped Kaitlin off at school the next morning, we walked back to the city center and along Parnell Street, where it wasn't long before we came to a brass plaque indicating the offices of Kinsella Heffernan Solicitors. Maybe someone there could tell us how to participate in the auction for the house that Lief and I, having slept on the idea, now both were keen to buy. No, it certainly wasn't the Irish country estate I'd been stuck on, but I'm good at adjusting and adapting on the fly. In the fourteen hours since I'd seen the ad in the paper, I'd settled into this new dream. We'd be city-dwellers, at home behind that delightful red Georgian door, with the quay, the river, and, we'd confirmed by checking our Waterford maps, a section of the original city walls just a few blocks walk away. Not Irish country living but an authentic Irish experience. Bottom line, that's what I was really after.

"Bye, bye, Granville," I practically sang to Lief as we turned to enter the premises of Kinsella Heffernan, Esquires.

Inside, we explained our situation to the receptionist who was kind enough not to turn us away but to ask if we wouldn't mind waiting. Morette Kinsella would be free presently.

Seated across from the smartly dressed attorney in her office ten minutes later, we explained that we'd just arrived in town and were here to start a business and make a home for our family, meaning we were in Waterford for the long haul and wanted to buy a house. We liked the looks of the one in the newspaper ad in *The Munster Express*, which I held up for reference, and we were interested in placing a bid on it at auction on Friday. Could she help?

"Have you ever bought a house in Ireland before?" Ms. Kinsella asked.

"No," I said.

"Have you bought a house at auction before?"

"No."

"Have you been to see this house?" she said, now sounding as though she were speaking to two children.

Lief and I looked at each other. Maybe we hadn't thought this all the way through.

"No."

"If you win the bid on a property at an auction in Ireland, you must be prepared to pay ten percent of the hammer amount immediately and the remaining ninety percent within thirty days," Ms. Kinsella continued soberly. "If you are unable to make the final payment in time, you forfeit the ten percent down payment. If you'll need bank financing to fund the purchase you should have that lined up, at least pre-approved, before the date of the auction. Have you been to see a bank to find out how much of a loan you might qualify for?"

Hearing this stranger dissect our plan baldly was having the effect I figured Ms. Kinsella expected it would. The idea writ plain was preposterous.

"No, we haven't spoken with a bank," I said quietly.

"You are not my clients, but I feel I must advise against your proceeding to bid on this property," Ms. Kinsella said like a Catholic school nun reprimanding a couple of reckless third-graders. "You are not at all prepared."

After a long pause to let the weight of her admonishment sink in, she added, "I must charge you some amount for today's consultation. My secretary will send you a bill for 25 pounds. Please leave your address with her on your way out."

We'd been dismissed. We thanked the solicitor for her time, thanked her secretary, too, who we told to send the bill to us care of the Granville, then we walked the few blocks back to the hotel in silence. Deciding to buy a house we'd never seen at auction in a country where we had no experience buying property by any method and thinking we'd make that purchase based on forty-eight hours of preparation was absurd. It didn't make sense for us to buy that charming Irish Georgian townhouse with its bright red door and Claddagh knocker. But if not that house then what house? After more than two months of searching, we were back at square one, and I for one was feeling deflated and fatigued.

Back in our room, we settled into the pair of red damask armchairs at the window.

"I think we have to give up looking for a house to buy," Lief said. "We don't have to give up on the idea of an Irish country house. I know that's really what you have your heart set on, and we shouldn't let ourselves compromise on that vision just because we get frustrated.

"I think, though," my husband continued, "it's time to admit that we're not going to find the house you're hoping to find quickly. But we need to move out of this hotel room. I think we should begin looking at rentals. Maybe we can find an apartment on a month-by-month lease. Then we can take our time and keep looking until we find the house you really want. I'll go out for today's papers, okay?"

Lief was right, of course, and I nodded my head in agreement as cheerfully as I could.

After he'd returned with four local dailies, Lief opened the papers to the classified ad sections and spread them out on the bed.

ALL MOD CONS

We each picked up a red pen and began looking for listings that might suit.

"Furnished two-bed apartment. All mod cons," Lief read.

"'All mod cons'? What could that mean?" I asked.

I didn't expect a response, and Lief didn't offer one. This new world we were navigating made less sense all the time. Normally, uncertainty doesn't bother me. I find it exhilarating, but I was reaching my limit for unclearness, and Lief was long past his. He liked things to fit with his expectations, and, in this enigmatic world of the Irish, almost nothing did.

I walked over to give Lief a hug.

"Only one way to find out," he said as he picked up the phone on the desk and began dialing the number printed with the first two-bedroom apartment rental ad he'd circled in red.

XII
Your Man Mark Breen

We asked our taxi driver take us to the address for the first apartment we were to view. The listing in the paper hadn't given us much to go on. All we knew about the apartment we were to see was that it had two bedrooms, one bathroom, all mod cons—whatever they were—came furnished, and was in an area of the city we'd not yet encountered referred to as Ballybricken. I'd looked it up in my city guidebook.

Ballybricken, to the west of downtown, originally sat just outside the city walls beyond St. Patrick's Gate. This was Waterford's Irishtown, where the Vikings and the Irish were banished after the Anglo-Normans invaded. For a time, Ballybricken was the site of the biggest cattle and pig fairs in the region. It'd since been converted to an open public space, but, in the center stood the Bull Post, where livestock had once been bought and sold in great quantities. Beyond that was one sorry little park. The grass was brown and littered with candy wrappers and cigarette butts, and hobo-like characters were sprawled on the wooden benches. We seemed to have crossed a metaphorical train track.

The driver stopped in front of a two-story brown brick building. "Here you are then," he said cheerfully. I looked out the window at the building the driver had indicated and almost told him to drive on. On the ground floor was a former electronics repair store that was now, we could see through its dirty cracked window, vacant. I looked above the shop to what I figured must be the apartment for rent. Its two front windows were also dirty and broken. I try to keep an open mind and I don't think of myself as high maintenance, but the scene before me was depressing. I'd been hoping for cute and charming. This place wasn't even clean and it certainly didn't feel like a place we could look forward to coming home to at the end of the day. I stepped out of the taxi and onto the cracked sidewalk. How had we gone from shopping for an old stone house in the country to considering renting here? Lief seemed less bothered than I was. He'd already walked over to introduce himself to the real estate agent standing by the building's front door. I had no choice but to do the same.

"Hello!" the young woman said brightly, holding out her hand first for Lief to shake and then in my direction. "I'm Siobhan."

"Hello," I replied. "I'm Kathleen."

"Well, then, shall we go inside to have a look, sure we shall," Siobhan said.

The stairs were covered with stained brown carpet and smelled of mold. Still, we followed Siobhan up to the second floor and into the apartment, which was dirtier and stinkier than the stairwell. I walked in and around quickly then back down the stairs. Lief and the agent came out onto the street a few minutes later.

"Do you have any rentals that are unfurnished?" I asked Siobhan as we stood on the corner with a view of the park bums.

"Unfurnished? No, everything on our books comes furnished. Do you have your own furniture, is that it?"

"No," I said and didn't bother to try to explain further. I was ready for this experience to end. "Well, thank you very much for taking time to show us the apartment. We have several others to look at but will be in touch," I said as I started backing away.

"Why did you ask about unfurnished rentals?" Lief wanted to know as we walked down the hill in the direction of the quay where we were to meet the next rental agent. "The container of furniture that you shipped from Baltimore won't fit inside a little two-bedroom apartment," he said, and he had a point. I'd shipped the entire contents of my three-bedroom, two-bathroom, two-thousand-eight-hundred-square-foot house, including a basement full of Kaitlin's toys, a library's worth of books, china place settings for twelve, and deck furniture.

"We're going to have to arrange to put the container into storage in Dublin until we find a house," Lief added. "Which reminds me that you need to call to find out how much the long-term storage is going to cost."

"Yes, yes, okay, I'll call the storage guy," I said. "But can we stick with today's agenda, please? I asked that agent about unfurnished rentals because I'd rather live in an empty apartment than one with furniture like what we just saw. I don't think I could tell you the original color of the sofa it was so badly stained. And the carpet... what was that smell anyway? Two of the dining chairs were broken, and I think the television set in the corner was black and white.

"Furniture aside, it was so dark. There were just those two small windows in the living room. No other windows in any other room of the whole place. It felt like a cave. A dirty, smelly cave."

"Well, we'll only be renting for a short time," Lief said, "while we look for a house to buy."

"We don't know how long we'll be renting," I said. "Based on our experience so far, I'd say it could be much longer than any of us would like. I can't move Kaitlin into a place like the one we've just come from. And I don't want to live there either." The more we talked about our reality, the closer I was coming to breaking down in tears.

We viewed three more apartment rentals that morning, every one dingy, dark, and damp. By lunchtime we were both demoralized.

"I'm tired of eating out in pubs," Lief said. "Can we go to a grocery store and buy something to take back to eat in the room?"

"Sure," I said.

We walked to Dunnes and shopped for bread, cheese, ham, crisps, and a bottle of wine for later. In line at the check-out, I turned to the woman behind me, as had become my habit.

"Would you by chance know of office space for rent here in the city?" I asked, as I'd done dozens of times before in dozens of other check-out lines. Sometimes I asked first about houses for sale. Sometimes I started with apartments for rent. Today I'd seen my fill of horrible apartments and decided to try my luck with office space.

I began setting my items on the check-out counter, expecting another polite regret. Instead, the woman replied with a cheery "Yes, luv, I do, sure."

I was so surprised my brain hiccupped, and I nearly missed what the lady said next.

"A friend is looking to rent some of his space. He doesn't need all he has, you see. I could write down the address for you, if you'd like, sure I could," the woman offered.

I pulled a scrap of paper and a pen from my purse and handed them to the lady who leaned on the box of corn flakes in her shopping cart to write out the address. I picked up the items we'd been planning to buy, set them on the shelf behind us, then Lief and I stepped out of line and walked out onto the quay in the direction of the taxi stand. Lunch could wait. We got into a cab and handed the driver the slip of paper with the address. He took us to a red brick building at the eastern edge of town, across from the courthouse and the Peoples Park, with a brass plaque by the entrance indicating this was St. Catherine's Hall. It looked deserted, but the door was unlocked, so we stepped inside. There was no lobby or reception area, only a staircase. We had no suite number or business name, so we climbed the stairs and knocked on the first door we came to.

No answer.

We knocked again then pushed on the door. It opened, so we walked into the big open space with two rows of four empty desks each.

"Hello," we called out.

Around from behind the office partition separating one corner from the rest of the room came a stout Irish woman with a great abundance of curly brown hair who introduced herself as Claire. Her smile lit up the windowless room.

"We understand there might be office space available for rent here in the building somewhere," we explained. "Would you know anything about that?"

"Well, I'm not quite sure, but, yes, Ray might be wanting to rent this space. I could call him for ye'."

"That'd be great. Thank you."

Claire disappeared back behind the partition, and we heard her speaking softly into a telephone. Then she came back around into view.

"Yes, Ray is interested in renting out part of the space. We don't need it all ourselves, you see."

Yes, we could see. Claire was the only one in the room.

"When would ye' be wanting to move in?"

"As soon as possible. How much is the rent?"

We had no idea what to expect to pay to rent office space in Waterford City, as we'd yet to be able to find any other office space available for rent and had nothing to compare.

"400 quid per month," Claire said.

"We'll take it," I said before she could change her mind.

"We'll have three girls joining us within the next couple of weeks," I said. "However, at first, it will be just the two of us. Could we move in next week? And is the furniture included?"

"Yes, sure, you can move in any time. And, yes, ye' are welcome to use the desks and chairs you see here."

On the way out the door, as an afterthought, I asked Claire if she happened to know of a house or an apartment for rent, two bedrooms.

"In fact, I do. Your man Mark Breen, everyone in town would know him, he has a small cottage for rent just up the hill from here in Newtown. I could give you his number."

Maybe our luck was changing.

"We'd appreciate that very much. Could you also describe where to find the cottage so we could go by to take a look?"

Lief and I nearly sprinted back down the stairs of St. Catherine's Hall and out onto Catherine Street where, for the first time in more than two months coming and going around this city, we found a waiting taxi. The gods were with us.

Minutes later, we turned down a narrow lane between two high walls. Here, protected by the stone walls and tall hedgerows, was a brick house under construction and, farther around the bend, a small cottage. Just beyond was the River Suir. At the top of a ladder leaning against the edge of the roof of the house a dark-haired Irishman was hammering nails into black shingles.

When our taxi stopped in front of his house and Lief and I got out and began looking around, the Irishman climbed down the ladder and walked over to introduce himself as Mark Breen. Several inches shorter than Lief and wider around the middle, Mark Breen was dressed in slacks and a golf shirt. Lief and I, meanwhile, wore coats and scarves. Would we ever be comfortable in this climate?

"We're very sorry to intrude like this," I said, "but we've just rented office space in town, at St. Catherine's Hall, and the woman Claire who agreed the lease with us said that you might have a house for rent. We've just arrived in town and are looking for a place to live with our daughter."

"Yes," Mark Breen said pointing to the little red brick cottage at the end of the white stone drive, seemingly unbothered by two strangers showing up at his home and asking if they could move in. I wondered what it'd take to get an Irishman to let on he'd been taken off-guard.

"My guesthouse is indeed available for rental. It's two bedrooms. Would you like to see inside?"

"Yes, if you have time to show us around, that would be great," I said.

When Mark Breen came back with the key, we followed him across the stone drive to the arched wooden door of the cottage and inside. From the small entry area, we could either go up the stairs or down a short hall to the left.

"Here's the second bedroom here," Mark Breen said, pushing open the door at the end of the short hall to the left. I looked past him and into the room. It had a big window with a view of the back garden and the river beyond.

"Lovely," I said.

Then we followed Mark Breen up the stairs. At the top, a great room served as both the living and dining spaces, with a small kitchen off to the side. What got my attention, though, was the floor-to-ceiling arched bay window in the great room. Like the window in the bedroom below, it had a view of the back garden and the river. On this unusually clear afternoon, the sun shone brightly on the big cottage garden below. The hollyhocks and daisies danced in the afternoon breeze. *I'll make us a garden just like that when we find our house in the country*, I thought, looking down on the mass of blue, purple, yellow, red, and green that filled the window.

Between the stairs and the great room was a small hall to the bathroom and second bedroom. This bedroom was the same size as the one downstairs but had a smaller window and no view of the river. This room will be for Lief and me. Kaitlin could have the one with the view. And, with that, a weight was lifted. I could imagine us living here.

After he'd finished touring us around his cottage, Mark Breen walked us through the back garden and down to the water, where he was building a pier for the boat he told us he planned to buy. We three stood in the tall grass to watch the River Suir. It passed slowly, almost silently. Along the bank opposite ran the train track from Plunkett Station. I thought of the nice old Irish couple that had helped me with my luggage and delivered me to the Granville Hotel my first night in the city. When we turned to head back up the small hill to the cottage and Mark Breen's house, I paused. No other structure in sight in any direction, just trees, grass, and wildflowers, and no sound but the barely perceptible gurgle of the river behind us. After all our disappointing and frustrating experiences looking for a place to live, this one seemed almost too good to be true.

"What are you asking for the rent?" Lief asked.

"400 pounds," Mark Breen said. I relaxed even more. Four-hundred pounds a month was much less than we had been prepared for. We agreed our second lease of the day with a handshake, and Mark Breen told us we could move in immediately if we wanted.

"Here you go," he said, reaching into his pocket for the key to the cottage. "Take this so you can begin moving in your things whenever suits."

I felt happier than I had since that night I'd arrived in Waterford. This wasn't our forever Irish home, but it was a fine stand-in. Finally, we could begin to settle. But first, I had one more question.

"Mark," I asked, looking back after Lief and I had turned to walk back out to the street and our waiting cab, "does the house have 'all mod cons'?"

"Oh, yes," he said. "I installed central heating when I renovated the place last year."

We collected Kaitlin from school, told her our big news, then asked the taxi driver to deliver us to the Granville Hotel. "Welcome back," the white-gloved bellman greeted us as he pulled the big brass handle to open the door to the hotel lobby so we could pass through. For the last time. Inside, Kaitlin and I stood on either side of him smiling as Lief asked the front desk clerk to prepare our bill. Our little family would be checking out and moving into our new home in the morning.

XIII

Yes, I'm From America

Lief was right. Mark Breen's cottage was lovely but small. We wouldn't be able to take delivery of the container with the rest of our things until we'd found and purchased a permanent home. I needed to arrange for long-term storage on the docks in Dublin, where the container had been delivered the week before.

"Hello, my name is Kathleen Peddicord," I said to the Irishman who answered the phone. "I understand from my shipping company that my container of furniture has been delivered to you for storage?"

"Aye, luv, Kathleen Peddicord, yes, right. You're from America, are ye', luv?"

"Yes, sir, my husband and I have recently moved to Waterford. We shipped a container of household things from Baltimore that arrived last week. However, we're not ready to take delivery of the container yet, so we'll need to arrange for long-term storage.

Would this be something you could help us with?"

"Aye, yes, of course, luv. I've been to America, years ago, and I have a cousin living in New York. Do you know New York?"

Here we go again, I thought, smiling. I'm asking a simple, direct question and getting a response that has nothing whatsoever to do with it. These Irish were master deflectors.

"Yes, sir, I know New York. Our container was delivered from Baltimore. I have the reference number for you. Perhaps you could check to confirm that you have the container there as our shipping company has indicated?"

"I have another cousin living in Boston. Well, she's my wife's cousin. My wife isn't well. I've had her to the doctor three times this past week."

"I'm very sorry to hear that," I said, shaking my head and smiling. I was, indeed, sorry to hear that his wife was ill, but what did that have to do with my container?

"Could I give you the reference number for my container? So that you could confirm that you have it?"

"Aye, I've got it, luv, sure I have, no worries. I've got to run now. Got to take my wife back to the doctor. She's not doing well at all."

"Okay. Well, could I call you back? I'd like to find out the cost of storing our container with you long term. Do you charge by the month? What is the fee?"

"Aye, no worries, luv. We'll work it out, sure we will. I've got to run now…"

The line went dead. It had, indeed, happened again. Another Irishman had cheerfully ignored my agenda, leaving me more uncertain of the situation after our conversation than I'd been before it. I have no problem with ambiguity, and I was beginning to suspect that these Irish were my kind of people.

While I found the Irish penchant to ignore the practical in deference to the personal endearing, my all-business husband was really struggling in this land where efficiency was a stepchild. I braced myself as he walked over to my desk after I'd hung up.

"What did he say? Does he have the container? Can he store it for us month-to-month? How much will it cost?" Lief wanted to know.

"He says he has it, though I never was able to give him the reference number to confirm that whatever container he has that he thinks is our container is in fact our container. And he says he can keep it long term, but I don't know how much it will cost."

"You don't know how much it will cost? Isn't that why you called the guy, to find out?"

"Yes. It's hard to explain. His wife is not well, and he had to run to take her to the doctor. I'll try him back tomorrow." Lief looked slightly panicked.

"What will we do if this guy Patrick presents us with a bill for tens of thousands of pounds?" he asked, sounding as though he were in physical pain.

I was relieved when he turned, a moment later, to go back to his desk. I had no idea what to say to make him feel less worried. This guy Patrick in Dublin would charge us what he would charge us to hold on to my stuff until we were in a position to receive it. What else were we going to do? Have the container moved to another storehouse? No, we had to roll with it.

I called Patrick the next day and the next day and the day after that. He and I became well acquainted. His wife, Cara, was recovering from her illness. He'd called his cousins to tell them about his new friend from the U.S., and they wished us all the best in our new life in Ireland. Each time we spoke, Patrick asked after Kaitlin, wondered how she was getting on in her new school and whether she was continuing to make new friends. He didn't, though, ever say how much it was costing us to have our container in his shipyard.

When my father offered to help sell my car when I was preparing to leave Baltimore, he asked to see the registration. I produced it reluctantly, knowing that it was two years expired. My father shook his head and gave me a look of dismay I knew well from him. "I'll go to the Department of Motor Vehicles tomorrow to renew this," he told me. "You won't be able to sell the car otherwise."

I felt embarrassed that I'd been irresponsible and that my father had again to clean up a mess I'd made, but only because I knew it disappointed him. As far as the expired vehicle registration itself, I couldn't make myself care about it or other things like it. An invoice from Patrick for the cost of storing my container fell into the same category for me. My father had come to accept this flaw in my character. I was hoping my new husband would, too, and quickly, but I was increasingly concerned about the tension my non-accountability for anything administrative might create.

On the other hand, Lief's mastery of paperwork meant I could give up any pretense of paying attention to it, leaving me free to focus on the editorial and marketing aspects of the business. It seemed like a fine division of labor to me.

We moved from the Granville Hotel into Mark Breen's guesthouse on the river. I'd unpacked the toys and stuffed animals I'd brought from Baltimore for Kaitlin, bought a pink spread for her bed, and placed family photos on the end tables in the living room. The little cottage with the beautiful garden by the river wasn't my dream home, but the location was perfect. Kaitlin's school was a ten-minute walk away. We dropped her off each morning then carried on down the hill and past the People's Park to Catherine Street and the office space we'd rented from the guy named Ray we still hadn't met. Ray didn't seem to come to work. Claire arrived every day, though not until 10:00 or 11:00 a.m.

"Top of the morning," she'd greet us with a big smile as she came through the door. I hadn't imagined that the Irish actually use that expression, but they do.

Claire would hang her black cape and woolen scarf on the old wooden coat stand beside her desk, which she'd pulled out from behind the partition. She now shared the big open space with Lief and me. Each morning, she turned on the stereo in the corner, sat down in her chair, pulled a book out of her bag, and began reading and singing.

"Do you believe in life after love," Claire would sing along with Cher. The local station played the song, Claire's favorite, she reminded us every time it came on, at least once an hour. At first, I found Claire's lack of industry annoying. After a few weeks, though, I wasn't as resentful of Claire's laid-back approach to the workday as I was curious about it.

"What business is Ray in?" Lief finally asked Claire after our first week in our new office.

"He's created a software program to help businesses file their tax returns," Claire said, pointing to a stack of CDs behind her desk. "I process the orders and mail out the disks."

In the week we'd been sharing space with her, we hadn't noticed Claire send anything out in the post. Lief and I would arrive each morning by 7:45, in a rush, feeling like we were already behind for the day. I'd download emails from overnight, feeling more behind and out of touch as I read each one. The time difference meant that everyone back in Baltimore worked for several hours beyond when we signed off each evening about 6:00 p.m. Ireland time. I'd reply to all their post-6:00 p.m. emails, then dig into the deadlines of the day.

Between keeping up with the business, trying to carve out even a little time each day for Kaitlin, and continuing to chip away at our to-do lists, Lief and I were all out and super stressed. I was as intent as ever on earning the respect of Agora's Executive Committee, but I was also beginning question why I was so preoccupied by what a bunch of people I never saw thought of what I was managing to accomplish each day. Claire didn't seem bothered by what anyone thought of her. She was one of the most contented souls I'd ever met. I didn't want Claire's life, but I did find her lifestyle intriguing.

Okay, enough musing about Claire, I told myself one morning as I sat again staring over at her in awe of her ability to be perpetually relaxed and happy. I needed to focus. We had one remaining urgent item on our agenda.

When I'd decided to take Bill up on his offer to go to Ireland to open an EU office for Agora, I'd called my *International Living* staff together for a meeting.

"I'm moving to Ireland," I told them. "And I invite any of you interested to come along with me. We'll publish *International Living* from there."

It was a big ask, but three young female staffers, Jen, Risa, and Lindsey, came back to me to say they'd like to know more. We four went for drinks one night.

Jen, who had a serious boyfriend, said she'd like to come for a month. It was mostly a show of moral support, but I was thankful for it. Risa and Lindsey, both in their mid-twenties, were unattached and up for an adventure. I'd promised them the company would provide housing.

Now they would be arriving in two days and I still hadn't been able to find them a place to live. Lief and I had continued asking around about apartment rentals after we'd moved into Mark Breen's cottage, but we hadn't gotten a line on anything that was better than the awful places we'd toured that day in Ballybricken. Finally, it hit me: I should ask Claire. Why hadn't I thought of that sooner?

"Claire, do you remember the three girls I've told you about from Baltimore? The ones coming to work with us? They'll be arriving in a couple of days. We've made a reservation for one of them—Jen, who's coming just for a month—at the Granville. But we need somewhere for the other two girls to stay. They're planning to be here for a year. You wouldn't happen to know of anything that might work for them, would you?"

"Aye, sure, there are two new apartments available in the center of town," Claire replied brightly. "They're owned by Maura, who also owns the salon below. One of those apartments would do, sure, for a couple of young girls. Shall I set up a viewing for ye'?" As she never had anything else to do, Claire had been defaulting into a now-and-then assistant for us, making introductions and scheduling appointments. She seemed to enjoy being useful. I didn't want to offend her, but the more we came to count on her support, I wondered if we should offer to pay her.

"Yes, that would be great," I said. "Thank you."

"Maura says you could call by now, if that'd suit, to take a look at one of the apartments," Claire looked over from her desk to mine to say after she'd hung up the phone.

I jumped up, and Lief did, too. We'd learned that when these Irish opened a door, we shouldn't waste time passing through. Who knew when they'd change the topic of conversation and leave us hanging, confused, and frustrated? We pulled on our coats, scarves, and gloves and were off. We passed the souvenir shop with the leprechauns in the window where we'd never seen a customer and the Irish Tourist Information Centre with the Irish flag out front where we'd never seen a tourist. It made me wonder why this city had been so forgotten? Were we fools to be settling in this forlorn little town?

No time to ponder questions so big, I told myself, as Lief and I continued quickly along the quay. Just gotta' keep working the plan.

By now we were approaching Maura's Salon and Day Spa, where we could see two young red-headed Irish girls standing on the sidewalk out front of the brick building.

"Hello," one of the young girls said. "Are you Kathleen and Lief? I'm Roisin and this is Orla. We work for Maura. She asked us to show you one of the apartments upstairs. Just follow us, so, will ye'?"

Lief and I followed Roisin and Orla up the narrow staircase to the even narrower second-floor landing with a door directly in front, one to the left, and another to the right. Orla unlocked the door on the right, then she and Roisin flattened themselves against the door in the middle so Lief and I could squeeze past. Stepping through the open passage, we were immediately in a galley kitchen with a sink, stove, and refrigerator along the righthand side and a tiny fold-down table fixed to the wall opposite. There was no hallway or entrance space. We walked from the kitchen directly into the bedroom to the left where two twin beds were pushed against the walls to either side. Along the shared wall with the kitchen was a small dresser. Standing in the center of the room between the two beds, Lief and I took up the entire rest of the available square meters.

"Where's the bathroom?" Lief called to Roisin and Orla still standing on the landing outside.

"Out here," Roisin said. "Through this middle door here at the top of the stairs. The bathroom is shared between the two apartments. The other apartment, on the other side of the bathroom isn't rented yet, though, so you'd have the bathroom to yourselves, at least to start."

Lief waked back into the kitchen. "What's this on the wall in the kitchen?" I heard him saying.

Roisin came inside. "That's the electric heater," she said. "You buy cards for it in the shop next-door."

"Cards?" Lief asked. I peeked around the corner from the bedroom so I could see what Lief was talking about.

"Yes, you see here," Roisin explained, pointing to a slot on the meter. "You insert the card here. To pay for usage."

I hadn't realized it until Roisin brought it up, but I was cold. Lief and I were still wearing our coats, scarves, and gloves, but I was shivering. No card in the heater meant no heat.

Lief and I followed Roisin and Orla back down the narrow staircase to the sidewalk out front of Maura's salon. Through the big front window, we saw two men in overalls covered in dust plastering the back wall.

"When will Maura's salon be open?" I asked.

"In two weeks' time," Roisin said.

"We're renting the place for a couple of young American girls coming to work with us," I said. "I'm sure they'll appreciate having a hair salon just downstairs."

"So you'd like to go ahead with the rental then?" Roisin asked.

"Yes, we would," I said. "What is the rent?" I realized that asking the price after agreeing the deal wasn't super savvy, but the approach had worked out okay when renting office space from Claire and the little riverside cottage from Mark Breen. Plus, I had just forty-eight hours to find a place for Risa and Lindsey to sleep, meaning I had little time to find an alternative.

"150 pounds per month," Roisin said.

"Great," I replied. "Could we sign a lease for a year?"

Roisin told me she'd call by our office later that afternoon with the paperwork.

"You didn't think the place was kind of small?" Lief asked after we'd begun walking back along the quay in the direction we'd come and were out of earshot of the two young Irish girls.

Of course I thought the apartment was small. It was ridiculously small. There was no furniture beyond the twin beds and the dresser and no storage at all. When Risa and Lindsey wanted to sit down, their only option would be to sit on their beds. They'd have to eat on their beds, too. And eventually they'd have to share a bathroom with a stranger across the hall. But they'd be in Waterford in two days and the rentals market, we knew all too well, was thin. I'd just have to hope Risa and Lindsey brought their senses of humor with them and were able to see the awkward, uncomfortable lodgings as part of their whole new-life-in-the-Old-World experience.

"Yes, it's small," I said to Lief, "but it's also clean, bright, dry, and new. Every other place we've seen has not been any of those things. It's the best we're going to come up with within the next forty-eight hours. It will be fine," I assured Lief with a smile. "Or, well, it will have to do."

XIV
Staffing Up

I'd shown up to establish an office for a direct-marketing publishing company in a country where no such industry existed. Actually, hardly *any* industry of any kind called Waterford home. It took longer than it should have for the implications of those realities to sink in. Like rentals and many other resources, the pool of available labor was shallow. Once Risa, Lindsey, and Jen arrived to manage operations day-to-day, get the magazine out the door each month, and oversee marketing campaigns, I turned my attention to looking for the additional staff we'd need to build a long-term business. It became nearly a full-time occupation.

We'd learned that here in Waterford the best strategy for locating anything was to inquire of every person you knew and every random person you encountered. We started, of course, with Claire.

"Claire," I said one morning the week after Risa, Lindsey, and Jen had joined us, "We'd like to hire an assistant. Someone to run employment ads, schedule interviews and meetings, find vendors, and keep our calendars. We don't need experience. Just someone enthusiastic, smart, and eager to learn. Would you know anyone like that?"

"Indeed I would," Claire responded with her usual perk. "My friend's daughter Deirdre would suit for what you're describing, I'd say. I'll call her now, will I, and ask her to pop by for a chat?"

"Yes, that would be great," I said, appreciative and not at all surprised by how Claire was coming through for us again. "We could meet with her for an interview any time tomorrow afternoon if that works."

"Lovely," Claire said. "Grand. I'll ring her now, so."

Deirdre, it turned out, had been working as a groomer at a stable outside the city. She had no office experience but presented herself as a capable young woman. I've always prized a willingness to work and to learn over most everything else when it comes to staff, so we decided to take a chance on Deirdre, who became our first local hire. Deirdre's out-of-the-gate task was to run newspaper ads for the other positions we hoped to fill. We asked her to advertise in all the local dailies and in the Dublin and Cork papers, too, though Deirdre counseled that we'd have trouble attracting talent from the bigger cities.

"I shouldn't think someone from Dublin would be interested in taking a job in Waterford," she told us. "Waterford is a bit of a backwater, you might say." We told Deirdre to place the ads anyway.

STAFFING UP

A week later, we began receiving curricula vitae in the post. While in the United States, it's frowned upon or, depending on the state, illegal to ask, in Ireland, we were surprised to see, applicants offered their age and marital status right up front and a photo to boot. Most of the resumes were from unlikely candidates, career shop clerks or farm hands, but we found two to put at the top of the pile. First was a forty-eight-year-old with writing, publishing, and management experience. He seemed like someone we should meet.

Robert arrived two days later wearing an oversized three-piece grey suit with black pinstripes. He was tall, heavyset, and balding with a thick reddish beard.

"What is it ye' do here?" Robert asked abruptly after he, Lief, and I had sat down around my desk. Lief and I looked at each other. Who was conducting this interview?

"We're here to establish an Irish base for a U.S. publishing company," I said. "To start, we'll be publishing a magazine called *International Living*, primarily for North American readers interested in living and retiring overseas. Eventually, though, our plan is to grow the operations to include divisions for marketing lifestyle, investment, and health publications for the individual consumer."

Robert stared back at us blankly.

"You'll be marketing those various publications how is it?" he finally asked.

"Through mailings to Americans and Canadians," I said.

"We're a direct-marketing publishing house, as the ad explained."

"I wasn't quite clear on that," Robert said. "What is it you're meaning by 'direct marketing'?"

Lief and I looked at each other again. I nodded as if to say, I'll take this.

"We send out letters to people who we believe, based on their past purchasing history, might be interested in subscribing to our publications."

"How do you find these people?" Robert asked.

"We rent their names," I said. "We rent lists of their names."

"You rent lists of their names?" Robert asked. "Who rents lists of peoples' names?"

"Well, list brokers," I said. "List rental is a big, competitive industry in the United States."

Again, Robert stared blankly. I don't think he'd encountered list renters or direct marketers before, in person or in theory.

"Thank you for meeting with me," he said, "but I do not believe this would be a suitable position. How would my children explain my work to their schoolmates? What would my wife say when asked what her husband does for a living? Would she tell her friends that I rent peoples' names? I couldn't have that. We'd be outcasts."

While the Irish of this Celtic Tiger era shunned anything old—preferring newly built bungalows in housing estates over old country homes and multistory themed dance pubs over thatched-roofed locals—they were, at the same time, suspicious of anything new. Though it was a decades-old arena in the U.S., the Irish had never heard of direct marketing.

Robert stood up and left the room, ending the conversation as suddenly as he'd begun it.

"Maybe we should tell people we're writers rather than direct marketers," I said to Lief's back as he returned to his desk. "The Irish love their writers."

"Sure," Lief said without turning to look at me. "Whatever works."

"Onward," I said, to Lief and to myself, too. We didn't have time or energy to focus long on any particular odd experience. Exchanges like the interview with Robert were coming at us too many and too fast. We had no choice but to take unexpected interactions as a matter of course. "Onward," I said again. "Let's keep working the plan."

"Onward," Lief agreed, as he sat down at his desk to return to work.

The second resume that floated to the top of our pile was from a woman who was working as a hotel receptionist but who had had actual direct-marketing experience in New York a few years before. Praise be.

"At least this one won't get up and walk out mid-conversation because she's offended by the very idea of what we do," I said to Lief as we waited for the woman to arrive.

Indeed, Clodagh (pronounced, she explained, with emphasis

on the very long "o") wasn't embarrassed by our business or our industry. She seemed happy to have a chance to return to the work she'd done while living in the States. Clodagh's problem wasn't with us. Clodagh's problem was with Waterford.

"I won't tell my family where my new job is located," she said on the phone as she accepted the marketing manager role. "I'm delighted for the opportunity, but my family won't understand. They don't come to Waterford, and they'd tell me I shouldn't either."

What could that be all about? I walked over to Deirdre to ask.

"Yes, of course," Deirdre said after I'd relayed my exchange with our new marketing manager. "Clodagh's people are from Dungarvan. They wouldn't mix with folks in Waterford City. The way they see it, folks in Waterford City rolled over for the British."

"But that was hundreds of years ago," I said.

"Might as well have been last week," Deirdre explained. "We Irish remember."

In 1169, Anglo-Normans invaded and proceeded to conquer Ireland, which the English then claimed as part of their sovereign state. This was a watershed in Irish history, marking the beginning of more than eight-hundred years of direct English and later British involvement on the island. The Irish, understandably, didn't appreciate being serfs and launched twenty separate rebellions and revolutions against their English overlords, the first in 1534 and the final successful campaign, the Irish War of Independence, in 1919, which, three years later, resulted in the free

Republic of Ireland on the southern part of the island. The Act of 1920 carved out a chunk in the northeast that would remain part of the United Kingdom, creating a border between Northern Ireland, as it's called, and the Republic to the south that would become a flashpoint.

Waterford played a notable role in the country's history as an English fiefdom. In 1171, Henry II landed with a large fleet on Waterford's shores, becoming the first King of England to set foot on Irish soil. Henry was worried about the establishment of a rival Norman state on the island and, wanting to make the point that he was the guy in charge, proclaimed Waterford a Royal City. Some eight-hundred-and-twenty-seven years later, when we arrived on the scene, the good Irish of Waterford were still stewing over that event.

In addition to Clodagh, we hired Cathleen as designer and Martina as bookkeeper. Now we needed to find a fulfillment manager and we'd be staffed up for our launch stage. Take that, Buddy.

One day as Lief and I walked down Catherine Street to the little shop on the corner owned by the friendly Irishman named Michael who greeted us with a hearty "Hello! How are ye' keeping?" every time we stopped in, which was at least two or three days a week for lunch, I floated an idea I'd been mulling over.

"What if we offered Claire the fulfillment manager role?" I said. "She's competent, capable, and connected. We never would have gotten as far as we have without her. I'd hate to lose her, and

I wonder every day how long this Ray guy can continue to employ her. I've still never seen her mail out a single one of the accounting software CDs behind her desk."

"You have a point," Lief said, laughing. "How is that guy staying in business?"

"I don't know, but I don't want to risk Claire disappearing if and when Ray is forced to call it quits. I feel a little guilty, though," I said. "We'd be poaching Claire."

"Ray might be relieved," Lief said. "From what Therese has told us, it's nearly impossible to fire someone in this country."

Maryland was a hire-at-will, fire-at-will state. Agora's corporate attorney Matt Turner used to tell us managers that we could fire someone because we didn't like the color of the tie he'd worn to work that day. No one had ever put the theory to the test, but Matt's example made the point. In Baltimore, we didn't worry about letting someone go if they weren't cutting it. Here in Ireland, however, our attorney Therese warned us that ending someone's employment meant a big payout even if the person had worked for you only a brief time and an enormous payout if they'd worked for you longer. Plus, invariably, letting someone go meant an unpleasant encounter with the labor board. Irish labor law fiercely protects the employee and treats the employer as the enemy. We were working hard to create jobs and stimulate the local economy. How did that make us the enemy? We were hoping to avoid finding ourselves in a position where the Irish clarified for us.

"Yes, right," I said. "Maybe Ray would like to let Claire go but can't afford to!"

When we returned to the office with our sandwiches from Michael's shop, I walked over to Claire's desk.

"Claire," I said, "you've had a chance to get to know us and our business a little over these past several weeks. And you know that we're looking now to hire a fulfillment manager. This person will be responsible for having the *International Living* magazine printed and mailed to subscribers each month, as well as all the reports and books we produce and the direct-mail promotions, too, that we send out to solicit new subscribers. Lief and I are wondering if you might be interested in applying for the role?"

Claire jumped up from her chair. "I'd love to come work for ye'. That would be grand, sure it would. Thanks so much," she said nearly bursting with excitement.

"Well, would you like to speak more about the position before committing?" I said. "Also, what about Ray? We wouldn't want to leave him in the lurch."

"No, no, we don't need to speak any further. I know ye', as you say. I'd be very happy working for ye'. And don't worry about Ray. Things are a bit slow at the moment. I think he'll be fine without me." Claire ducked behind her partition to make a quick phone call to Ray that we couldn't hear, then re-emerged to say she could start the next day.

Agora Ireland was officially established, and, over the next few months, Lief and I spent our days showing our little team what they needed to know to do the jobs we'd hired them to do. Meantime, Lief continued his negotiations with Dr. Chen. The friendly Singaporean had invited us back to Pouldrew House for lunch and to Waterford's Jade Palace for dinner. Lief had run his numbers. He knew what he could afford to pay for Dr. Chen's property, and he'd stated the amount clearly. Dr. Chen not only ignored Lief's offer but referenced a higher asking price when we met for lunch and then another even higher asking price when we three got together for Chinese. Lief restated the price he could pay, and, each time, Dr. Chen acted as though Lief hadn't spoken.

For me, Dr. Chen's ability to pretend prior conversations hadn't taken place and to begin each meeting by proposing a bigger price was almost charming. I suspected he didn't really want to sell his Pouldrew House. A pretty young Irish woman arrived to the house midway through our lunch the day we were invited and behaved very at home, hanging her coat in the hall closet and heading upstairs after quick introductions. Dr. Chen's wife had returned to Singapore, but I'm not sure he was missing her terribly. His love life wasn't our concern, but the fact that he kept raising his ask was a problem for Lief. Finally, after six months of back and forth, Lief walked away from the deal.

Lief had come to Ireland to build something of his own. It was the primary reason he'd been looking to move out of the United States in the first place. The deal falling apart could have been a

STAFFING UP

dramatic development, maybe even giving Lief reason to question his whole Ireland plan. However, by the time he acknowledged that Pouldrew House wasn't happening, Lief was actively engaged with my business. He didn't have time to regret the Dr. Chen deal that wasn't because he was coming into the office with me each day and working as hard as I was.

Without being formally asked, Lief had become fully occupied with Agora Ireland. He'd helped me sift through the resumes we'd received in response to the job ads Deirdre had placed. He'd begun paying our local bills and training Martina to take over the bookkeeping role. Martina was a bright young woman studying—we learned only after we'd hired her because she'd been too modest to mention it during her interview—to sit for Ireland's charted accountant exam, making her our first actually qualified employee. Lief was training Claire, too, in how to print and fulfill the monthly *International Living* magazine. Lief had never worked in our business, but he was a quick study and showed me early on that he could figure almost anything out on the fly. With a bit of support from centralized resources back in Baltimore, Lief taught himself how to negotiate with printers and the other vendors involved with producing the magazine. He even began suggesting marketing ideas. Why not try a catalog as an insert with the magazine when we sent it out each month? He and Claire created one and sent it out with the next *International Living* issue. It was one of the most successful inserts we'd ever mailed.

AT HOME IN IRELAND

I allowed Lief to become increasingly involved in the business because I needed his help and also because I enjoyed having him in the conversation. Jen had returned to Baltimore months ago, meaning now Risa and Lindsey were our only legitimately trained staff in the country. It was easier to face building a business from nothing with Lief by my side. With his own business plan off the table, though, he was no longer pitching in to lend support to his new wife. Now he was his new wife's full-time employee. When Pouldrew house fell through, the dynamic between us changed, creating two problems.

First, Lief didn't like the idea of working for his wife, and, as quickly as I was allowing myself to come to count on him, I wasn't sure I was comfortable with the idea either. But, as with nearly everything that'd come to pass since Lief and I had met, without directly addressing the question and without allowing ourselves time to process or discuss the potential complications, we'd defaulted into a new reality. Lief could have searched for a replacement for Pouldrew House, but we both knew it could be a long while until another suitable property presented itself. Meantime, what was he going to do with himself? He'd decided to make the move to Ireland on his own, before we'd met, but now it was as though he'd tagged along to Ireland with me.

Then there was problem number two. Lief wasn't being paid. He had been working full time for Agora Ireland for more than six months without receiving a penny of compensation. I knew that wasn't right, but changing it meant a conversation with Agora's Executive Committee that I was afraid to have. We still weren't operating in the black. Now I'd created a big conflict-of-interest concern by hiring my husband without actually hiring him and without getting an okay from Baltimore in advance. On top of all that, I had no idea what to offer to pay my husband. It was a question I really needed help answering.

Finally, after discussing the idea with Lief—who responded with a sarcastic, "Oh, you mean I might actually, finally get paid? That'd be nice."—I worked up the courage to address the situation with members of the Executive Committee. I went back and forth in my head for several days, then decided to send a group email rather than scheduling a conference call. I wasn't sure how I'd hold up to a negative response on the phone. Easier to send an email, put on my Kevlar, and lick the wounds of any assault in private.

"I'd like to engage Lief as a consultant," I began. "Since arriving in Waterford, Lief has been helping with all aspects of establishing the Agora Ireland business. He has taken over the local bookkeeping role, is managing fulfillment, and is acting as liaison with our Irish bankers, attorneys, and auditors.

"As you may not know," I continued, "Lief has a master's degree in finance and international business management. He is well qualified for the role he has assumed, and I'd like him to continue in it.

"I propose we engage Lief as a consultant, to avoid the complications of trying to acquire a work permit for him. And I would appreciate feedback as to an appropriate monthly retainer amount." I crossed my fingers and pressed send.

Seconds later, I received a reply from Agora CFO Myles Norin: "We don't hire consultants."

What? Of course Agora hired consultants. Agora hired consultants all over the world all the time. What Myles was telling me was that he did not want to hire Lief as a consultant. But why not? What did Myles have against Lief?

Probably nothing, I realized after I'd had time to begin to recover from the email. Myles probably had next to no opinion about Lief. His beef wasn't with Lief; it was with Agora Ireland in general. Myles had made it clear all along that he was against the whole venture. I understood Buddy's cantankerous posturing. Buddy was an ass. But Myles wasn't generally obnoxious. His response stung. I decided not to mention it to Lief, especially as I didn't think it really had anything to do with Lief. It was a passive-aggressive attack on me.

I didn't counter right away. I thought I'd wait to hear what the others had to say. However, two days later, when no one else had offered comment, I decided to call Bill. It wasn't the professional response, but it was what I'd always done. I didn't work for the Executive Committee. I worked for Bill. He'd hired me, and he'd been my boss every day of the thirteen years since. The Executive Committee had no idea what Lief and I were going through in Ireland and didn't care. I counted on Bill the way I'd always counted on my Dad. It was a complicated relationship that went beyond employee and employer that I valued more than most any other in my life. I thought when I laid the situation out for him, Bill would understand and would want to help.

"Of course Agora hires consultants," Bill said when I spoke with him on the phone. "And if you think we need Lief's help as a consultant, well, then, we'll put him on retainer. No problem."

I don't know if Myles objected further to Bill, but he didn't argue with me anymore, and I tried not to be bothered by Bill not having spoken up in my defense without my having to prompt him. I knew he was under pressure himself related to the Agora Ireland experiment, and, more than anything, I didn't want to let him down. The drama didn't matter. What mattered was that I officially had a partner on the ground.

XV
Lahardan House

John Rohan had been taking us to see houses for six months. I wouldn't say we'd become friends or even friendly, really. The Irish were at once open, affable, hospitable, and welcoming and completely private. They'd chat your ears off for hours over pints in the pub, but, when you thought back over the conversations the next day, you'd realized that you still didn't know anything about them. So, while we'd spent days touring housing estate after housing estate and viewing property after property with him, we couldn't tell you anything about John Rohan except that he wore dark suits and was exceptional at not listening. In all the six months we'd been working with him, he'd yet to take us to see a single house that looked at all like the house I'd described for him over and over again.

Why did we stick with him? I suppose it was because he was the most proactive of all the agents in Waterford City. Now that

LAHARDAN HOUSE

we were comfortably settled in Mark Breen's cottage by the river, we'd lost our sense of urgency about finding a house of our own. But John Rohan kept following up, so we kept going out with him to look at more properties that didn't fit our description of the property we wanted to buy.

Finally, our willingness to keep wasting our time paid off. John Rohan's secretary called to say John would like to show us a two-hundred-year-old stone house on seven acres twenty minutes outside Waterford City. At last. Hallelujah.

The day we went to see the house for the first time was atypically clear and bright without a hint of Irish mist in the air. We met John Rohan at his office then took off in his car along the Cork Road, Lief up front with John Rohan, me in the back seat, enjoying the passing views.

Lief and I had come to know the Cork Road well. Technically, it's the N25 single carriageway, meaning a highway that's one lane each way, but the Irish refer to roads by their destinations and this one leads from Waterford City to Cork. For people in Cork, it's the Waterford Road. The name changes midway. Lief and I found this an odd road-naming strategy, but the Irish we said as much to didn't understand why.

The Cork Road is also the first leg of the trip from Waterford to Shannon Airport, so we'd been traveling the Cork Road at least two or three times a month since we'd moved to Waterford six months earlier. But I never tired of it. Within minutes of leaving Waterford City, the landscape opens up to a patchwork of meadows in every direction, each one a different shade of green. The N25 is a major artery, but much of the way it's little more than two narrow lanes cutting through fields of sheep and cows and, in stretches, dense forest. This time of year, the fields were sprinkled with summer wildflowers.

"His daughter wanted to marry a man he didn't approve of," John Rohan was saying, giving us the backstory to the house. "'If you'll break things off with your fellow and marry this other lad I've chosen for you instead,' he told the young lady, 'I'll build you a country home.'

"His daughter agreed, and Lord Waterford started work on Lahardan House."

John turned off the Cork Road at the Cosy Thatch pub—an actual thatched-roof local pub of the kind the Irish were replacing so eagerly with dance clubs—and traveled an even narrower lane through more heather-covered expanses. Two more right turns had us on a road barely wide enough for a single vehicle. On one side were more rolling green hills marked off into separate spaces by low stone walls and hedgerows, while the view to the right was blocked by a high wall covered with ivy.

"Here we are," John said, suggesting that the house we'd come to see was behind that high stone wall. This was promising, the kind of setting where you might actually find the kind of house we'd been searching for for so long.

LAHARDAN HOUSE

We made a final turn onto a private dirt drive. Up ahead I could see a giant cypress tree with a massive crooked limb that would be ideal for a wooden swing. Across from it, the main event came into view as we continued down the driveway. Here, indeed, was the Irish Georgian country house we'd been scouring Waterford County for months to find.

After we'd gotten out of the car, I retreated four or five steps so I could take it all in. With its stone walls, red Georgian front door, paned sash windows, and classic symmetry, it was my Irish country living dream come to life. Beyond the house was an assortment of tumble-down outbuildings of stone and wood, including old stables nearly hidden by the overgrown brush and brambles. All around, as far as I could see in every direction, were more rolling fields marked off by more low stone walls and tidy hedgerows. Not another house in sight. The only sound was the chatter of birds nesting in the enormous ash tree behind the house.

The property, John explained, had been vacant for five years. A British man had bought it for his wife who'd wanted to retire to Ireland. The couple moved to Waterford and rented a house in the city where they lived while overseeing the renovation at Lahardan House. Before the work was half-finished, though, the man's wife was diagnosed with cancer and the couple had to return to England for her medical care. When she died, the man didn't want to see the house again. He hadn't been back to

Ireland since. I felt bad for him but said a little prayer of thanks for the way events had played out. It was as though the place had been sitting here empty all this time waiting for us to find it.

Prickly vines and nettles covered the ground around the house all the way up to the stone walls, but we wanted to see all four sides so stomped through. I was glad I'd worn knee-high boots. John unlocked the front door and led us inside.

Lord Waterford had built his daughter a fine place. Its front hall led to a winding central staircase. To the right of the hall was the living room with wide plank floors, two marble-mantled fireplaces, French doors to the side terrace, and oversized double-hung sash paneled windows with their original wooden shutters. I walked to the nearest one and pulled on the shutters to see if I could close them. I nearly giggled out loud when I found that they worked. They almost never do in a house this old. Two chandeliers hung from ceiling roses, and dentil molding outlined the room at the ceiling line. I was so excited I felt almost drunk.

We'd entered the living room from the entry hall but exited through the door at the other end, then followed the back hallway past more of those beautiful paneled windows to the kitchen. The British couple had torn out the original kitchen but hadn't gotten to installing a new one, so this room was bare walls, stone floor, and empty save a giant green cast-iron oven.

"Is that an Aga?" I asked.

"No," John Rohan said more sharply than I'd heard him speak

before. "That is a Stanley, made here in Waterford and generally considered superior to the English Aga." Ah. I see.

Through the big bay window at the other end of the kitchen we could see the front drive and the fields beyond. We left the kitchen through the door to the dining room then continued back to the front hall and up the stairs. At the top was a large landing with another set of paneled shuttered windows. To either side were bedrooms with en-suite bathrooms. Turning down the hall to the right we passed three more bedrooms and the final bathroom. At the end of the hall was a door to a rooftop terrace over the utility room off the kitchen below. Through every window along the way we had more views of Lahardan's rolling green acres. I wanted to skip. I wanted to sing. And Lief—the master at keeping his feelings to himself when viewing real estate—kept catching my eye and smiling.

By the time we'd followed John Rohan back down the stairs and out the red front door, I was all in on this Lahardan House. The French refer to it as a *coup de coeur*—a blow to the heart that tells you something is meant to be. I'd known even before stepping inside that Lahardan House was our Irish home.

While he'd chatted the entire drive out from the city, on the way back to Waterford John Rohan barely spoke. He could tell that Lahardan House had gotten under my skin. Rather than taking the N25, John stuck to back roads Lief and I hadn't traveled before, which meant the return trip lasted twice as long as the drive out. Giant willow trees blocked the sun, keeping us in semi-darkness, and high stone walls on both sides of the road meant no view as we drove. I was left with only my own imagination to occupy my thoughts. The spell Lahardan House had cast over me didn't break until we were nearly back in the city. By that time, I'd already decorated and furnished Lahardan's living and dining rooms and was wondering what color to paint the walls in Kaitlin's bedroom. Hers would be the next-to-last one down the hall. It had some of the best views.

John Rohan dropped us at the end of the lane to Mark Breen's cottage. In his typically Irish estate agent way, he made no hard sell. "Give me a ring if you have any questions," he said.

"What did you think?" I asked Lief as soon as John had driven away.

"What did you think?" Lief asked back.

"I think it's exactly the property I've been looking for all these months," I said.

"I think so, too," Lief said.

Walking down the lane to our little rental, I wondered what our next step would be. Lief interrupted my thoughts, as if reading my mind. "Do you remember that lawyer we met with when we had the idea to buy that house at auction?" he asked. "I think her name was Morette something? On Parnell Street? Let's get back in touch with her. We'll need an attorney to help us make an offer."

LAHARDAN HOUSE

I took Lief's hand, stepped in front of him, and pulled myself up to kiss him on the cheek.

"I think we've found our new home, dear," I said, practically bursting with joy.

Lief smiled more brightly than I'd ever seen and kissed me, too.

XVI
Rising Damp

When I'd told him about my plan to remarry and move to Ireland, Rick had asked if I'd send Kaitlin back to Baltimore to visit him every other month. I agreed. However, as with most every other aspect of the move, I didn't think it through. Kaitlin made return trips our first several months in Waterford. She looked forward to each of these adventures, traveling solo in the care of the airline as an unaccompanied minor. But these visits took a toll, both physically and emotionally. She still hadn't embraced Ireland as her new home and was eager for every chance to visit her dad, grandparents, cousins, and old friends, but she'd return to us exhausted, disoriented, and less enchanted with Ireland than ever. Continually reconnecting with her old life was making it harder for her to open herself up to our new one. Plus, each trip meant time out of school, and she was struggling to keep up with the rest of her class.

After we'd moved into Mark Breen's cottage, we'd fallen into a routine. I'd make breakfast and Lief, Kaitlin, and I would sit down at the small round table in the kitchen to eat, then Lief and I would drop Kaitlin at school before continuing on to Catherine Street. Kaitlin would walk from Newtown to our office at the end of her day and do homework until Lief and I were ready to head home. Then we'd drive back to our little cottage on the river, have dinner, finish homework, and watch television or play a board game until bed. It was a pleasant life, but I knew that Kaitlin wasn't happy in it. At parent meetings, her teachers assured us she was adjusting, but she'd grown quiet and sullen. Some nights she'd leave the dinner table and go directly to her room, sometimes closing the door with a loud thud, the only way that she could think to express the sadness she felt.

Finally, so distressed watching Kaitlin struggle between the Baltimore life she was missing so much that it sometimes seemed to be causing her physical pain and the Waterford life I was forcing on her, I decided to stop sending her back to the U.S. for regular visits. I didn't discuss the decision with Rick. He wasn't my concern. Legally, he had no standing. Though I'd not made an issue of it, he'd never kept up with the child support payments he'd been required to make by our separation agreement. But this wasn't a tit-for-tat choice. I was worried about Kaitlin's health.

After a few months, though, I began to feel guilty about Kaitlin going so long without seeing her father and the rest of her family.

Kaitlin was trying to be a trooper and never complained. I suspected she didn't want to disappoint me, but there was no denying she'd grown despondent. She could use a dose of Baltimore, and, honestly, so could I. So, a couple of weeks after we'd been introduced to Lahardan House, I planned an extended visit for the three of us.

During our stay in Baltimore, Lief and I scheduled meetings with Bill, Mark, and the Agora Executive Committee to regroup on Agora Ireland's progress and to make plans for continued growth, while Kaitlin divided her time among her two sets of grandparents and Rick. She was thrilled to be home, as she still thought of Baltimore, so happy to be back in her element that I worried about the letdown that was likely to follow when we took her back to Waterford.

Ten days later, just before we were to return to Ireland, I began feeling nauseous. I was throwing up and overwhelmingly tired. I had a constant headache and a sore throat. I decided to make an appointment with my Baltimore doctor. Probably I had the flu but better to be sure I didn't need antibiotics before boarding the plane for the flight to Waterford.

I did need antibiotics. I had strep throat. My doctor also wanted to give me something for the nausea and vomiting.

"You shouldn't take this, though," he said, "if there's any chance you're pregnant."

"Ah, no… no chance of that!" I said laughing. Then I thought for a minute and did some quick math in my head. In fact... well... hmmm...

"You know what," I told my doctor. "Maybe we should hold off on the anti-nausea medicine."

My mother and Lief had driven me to the appointment then gone to run errands while I was seeing the doctor. When they returned, I got in the back seat of the car and explained that I had strep throat.

"Could we stop at the pharmacy on the way home to pick up the antibiotics?" I asked.

In the drug store, I gave the man behind the counter my prescription then went in search of a home pregnancy test. Back at my mother's house twenty minutes later, I took it. My math had been right. The stick turned blue. By my figuring, I was six weeks along.

I'd wanted more children with Rick, but my doctor had told me complications following Kaitlin's birth would make that difficult. After a while, it wasn't an issue, as Rick and I had more immediate concerns to contend with. Like just about every other aspect of our lives, Lief and I hadn't discussed children before getting married or since. Lief wanted to have kids. At least, I thought he did. Of course he did. He'd never said otherwise. He must. Still, I was a little nervous at the prospect of telling my still very new husband that we were going to have a baby.

I came out of the bathroom at my mother's house and called Lief upstairs. I led him into the guest room, sat him down on the bed beside me, looked him square in the face, and blurted out my news.

"I'm pregnant," I said, beaming. I couldn't hide my excitement. I was thrilled.

Lief didn't reply for a long few minutes. His face, as usual, gave away nothing. I knew the news was unexpected, but surely he'd be as happy about this development as I was… right?

"Okay," he said. My husband was a man of few words. He said only what was required to make his point and was private about his emotions. I liked these traits in him, but right now I needed a little more than "okay."

"What do you think?" I asked. "Are you happy?"

"Yes," he said finally, "I'm happy." Then he smiled and reached over to take my hand in a way that gave me all the reassurance I could hope for.

We went downstairs to the kitchen to tell my parents together. They were overjoyed, as I knew they would be.

"I wonder if you'll be as sick with this pregnancy as you were with Kaitlin," my mother said.

Lief looked over at me. That was something else we hadn't talked about.

"I had serious morning sickness with Kaitlin," I told Lief, "for the first four months. I was barely able to work, barely able even to get out of bed."

"Maybe this time will be better," my mother offered. I hoped she was right.

Back home in Waterford, I called the only woman I felt comfortable enough going to for personal advice, Gerri, the mother of Sophia, Kaitlin's best friend at school. I asked if Gerri could recommend an obstetrician. Gerri referred me to Dr. Triona Sliney, who confirmed my figuring. I was six or seven weeks pregnant. The baby would be born in late November.

That set our clock. Time to get serious about the renovation of Lahardan House. We had to be moved in early November at the latest.

The day after we'd viewed the house with John Rohan, Lief and I had stopped by the offices of the attorney we'd first contacted about the Georgian townhouse we had decided we wanted to buy at auction. As she'd done then, Morette's receptionist told us that Morette was happy to meet with us, even though we didn't have an appointment, if we didn't mind waiting just a few minutes while she finished a conference call.

"Hello again," I said as Lief and I sat down in Morette's office. "We're back because we've found another house we think we'd like to buy. And this time we've actually seen the place!" I added, trying to push through whatever awkwardness might be lingering from our meeting months before.

"Well, then, that's progress, isn't it?" Morette said smiling. Something about this calm, reasonable, obviously smart, well-put-together woman had me immediately at ease. She was a career woman, like me, the first I'd gotten to know in Waterford. We'd understand each other. Plus, she'd already seen us at our looniest, dropping into her office as though out of the sky saying we wanted to spend hundreds of thousands of pounds on something we'd never seen. I had the sense we could trust her not to be scared off by anything this couple of knucklehead Americans might get up to. And that we could count on her to do her best to keep this couple of knucklehead Americans from getting up to anything too foolish.

"Yes, we think so," I said. "It's about twenty minutes outside the city, off the Cork Road. It's called Lahardan House."

"Lahardan House," Morette said thoughtfully, pulling a legal pad from the cabinet behind her desk and beginning to make notes. "I don't know it. Well, no matter. I'll dig into the Land Registry. Shall we plan to meet again next week to review my findings?"

We returned the following week. "Everything appears in order," Morette told us. "I assume now you'd like to make an offer?"

"Yes, we would," Lief said. "And we understand that that is handled by you, our attorney? In the States, offers are relayed by the real estate agent." Not wanting to appear again like buffoons in front of this woman whose respect I instinctively wanted to earn, we'd looked up the steps to buying a home in Ireland before coming in for the meeting.

"Yes, that's correct," Morette said. "Here it's I who handles the conveyancing on your behalf." She meant the property purchase.

While Morette was drawing up the paperwork to put our offer out to the seller, Lief and I decided we'd like to have the property inspected. No one had mentioned a home inspection, and, when we'd asked Morette about the idea, she'd told us it wasn't obligatory in Ireland. The bank would require us to test for termites and a couple of other specific risks, but they wouldn't call for an overall inspection of the kind we take for granted when buying a house in the United States.

No home inspection industry meant no home inspectors, but Morette's husband David was an architect. "He'll know someone who could visit the property and give you an opinion on the state of things, if you'd like," Morette offered.

Morette's husband put us in touch with a man whose profession no one could name but who spent the better part of the next Saturday on site at Lahardan House. A week later, we received a twelve-page report. "The living and dining rooms would benefit from re-decoration," it noted and then went on to point out that, "The gardens might be cut back."

Lief and I read the report together over dinner one night. When we'd finished, we shook our heads in bewilderment. What about the wiring, the plumbing, and the heating? What kind of home inspection didn't address those items?

"I guess buying a house in Ireland is a caveat emptor experience," Lief said finally.

"Indeed," I said. "These Irish like to keep things loose, don't they?"

We didn't understand this so-called home inspection report, but that didn't seem like a reason not to proceed with the purchase of our dream house. The seller had accepted our offer, the Bank of Ireland had agreed to give us a mortgage, and Morette was finalizing the contract. No one else seemed concerned that we'd received no assurances as to the condition of the house, so we decided we wouldn't worry either. Instead, we'd focus on mapping out a plan for making the place habitable by the time the new addition to the family arrived.

We asked Claire and Deirdre if they knew a general contractor who could come to the house and review our to-do list with us then give us a quote for the various work to be done. Deirdre said she knew a "decorator."

"A decorator?" I asked. "Well, we're not at the decorating stage yet. First some repair work is needed. Some woodwork, I think, and some re-plastering. We'd also like to review the electrical and plumbing systems."

"Yes, right," Deirdre said. "Decorating."

"Okay, great," I said, undaunted at this stage by feeling like I never understood the Irish and that they never followed me. "Yes, would you please put us in touch with your decorator friend?"

"I'll ring him now," she said. "His name is Noel."

I arranged to meet him the following day. When I pulled down the muddy drive, I saw a tall, lanky, smiling red-headed Irishman standing in the drizzle studying the exterior of the house. Noel.

"I'm Kathleen. Thanks very much for agreeing to meet me so quickly. We have a fair amount of work to accomplish and a short window." I added, deciding not to explain further. I was never sure how forthcoming to be with these Irish. Though they chatted constantly, they didn't give much away. I was trying to follow suit.

"Shall we go inside out of the rain?" I said.

Noel followed me through the big red door, then I let him take the lead. I walked a few steps behind as he went from room to room, upstairs, down the hall, back down to the living room, then again across to the kitchen, where he turned, finally, and declared, "I'd say there's a bit of damp."

"Yes, it's very damp in here, isn't it?" I said.

"No. You have damp."

"Ah..."

"Look, here," Noel said walking over to one of the kitchen walls. "Do you see? Damp." He pointed and I focused and finally registered hundreds of tiny paint blisters that I hadn't noticed until this moment. It was like the wall had a bad case of chicken pox.

"I know a damp guy. I can call him for you if you'd like."

"Yes, okay, that would be great, thank you," I said wondering what in the world it meant to "have damp." And what was a "damp guy"?

A few days later, on another chilly, misty Irish morning, I was back at Lahardan House for the meeting with Noel's damp guy. While I waited, I wandered from room to room, imagining where I'd place our furniture when we finally got it out of storage in Dublin—which reminded me that I needed to call Patrick. I wanted to let him know that we'd decided to schedule delivery of our household goods to Lahardan House mid-October. Noel promised the renovation work could be mostly finished by then, giving us a four- to six-week window to unpack and settle in before the baby's arrival.

When I heard the car pull up on the gravel out front, I went to the front door to look out and saw a small, bent-over Irishman get out of a dented and mud-splattered Toyota and begin walking toward me. When he reached the portico, he paused to scrape his mud-caked boots on the slate tiles, then leaned back so he could look up, tipped his cap, and said, "Is himself inside?"

"Himself?"

The little bent Irishman mumbled something in the direction of the slate porch tiles that I couldn't understand and then continued on through the big red Georgian door into the entryway of the house and from there, without pausing, on into the living room. I followed.

"Himself isn't at home?"

"You mean my husband? No, he's at work..." I guess little old Irishmen weren't accustomed to discussing business with the woman of the house. He'd have to get over that.

He pulled a screwdriver from the back pocket of his woolen

trousers and began poking it into things. I stood off to the side as he pushed his screwdriver into every piece of wood he passed, starting with the window casings, then the shutters, the skirting boards at the bases of the walls, the French door frames, and the floor boards.

After he'd finished in the living room, the bent Irishman continued into the dining room, poking as he went. Then the breakfast room and the kitchen, the entry hall and the stairs. He poked his screwdriver into every step as he climbed. On the second floor, he started over again, poking his way through each of the five bedrooms, all three bathrooms, and up and down the hallways.

I wasn't sure what I was watching but noted that the little Irishman's screwdriver penetrated every surface he stuck it into, sometimes down to the handle. That couldn't be good.

Finally, he turned and looked up at me and said, "Rising damp. All throughout."

"What... um... what does that mean?" I stammered as I tried to keep up with the little man who was already halfway back down the stairs.

"Means you've got to treat it," the bent Irishman said as he walked out the front door without another word or even a glance back in my direction. I watched him drive away, then picked up my phone to call Noel. Maybe he could help me understand what the screwdriver-wielding Irishman was talking about.

Noel explained that on this island where it rains more than it doesn't, the earth is constantly wet. Water seeps into the foundation of a house and rises as much as six feet before gravity takes over. Stone walls weep. Plaster walls bubble. Wood rots. Rising damp is big business. Ireland may not have home inspectors, but it has rising damp guys.

We engaged Noel's rising damp guy, the little bent Irishman, to rising damp-proof the place. This involved tearing the plaster from every wall on the ground floor to expose the stone beneath and then injecting a chemical into the mortar to create a damp-proof membrane. It also meant pulling up every floor board and pulling out every shutter, every piece of wood paneling, and every window and door frame. I'd spent months looking for a traditional Irish Georgian country house, and I wanted to make sure it remained a traditional Irish Georgian country house. It was important to me to preserve the architectural integrity. This meant replacement shutters, frames, and moldings had to be custom ordered, which would add months to the renovation timeline and thousands to the budget, on top of the three months and thousands of pounds the rising damp treatments would require. Our quick remodel had turned into a total gut-job renovation, and my euphoria over having found the Irish country house of my dreams was now replaced by worry over whether we'd be able to manage this project in addition to everything else we were doing. Could we possibly get this house in shape in time for the birth of the baby? Once again, it felt like we'd taken two steps forward then one big step back.

XVII
Dinner With Morette

My main means of communication was email. It was how I kept in touch with staff and the Executive Committee back in Baltimore and how I corresponded with freelance writers and editors we worked with around the world. I even used it to handle most issues with our team in Waterford. Our office was unusually quiet, with little conversation person to person.

So I was taken aback when Morette, the attorney we'd been using to help us purchase our home, informed us matter-of-factly during our first meeting that she didn't do email. She couldn't type. Instead, she'd call. In the beginning, she got in touch when she had an update regarding the property purchase, but, eventually, she began calling just to check in. "How are you getting on then?" she'd ask.

Ordinarily, random phone calls without a business agenda annoyed me. They were a waste of time. But whenever I'd answer the phone and hear Morette's voice on the other end, I'd smile and feel my body relax. I'd sit back, wherever I was and no matter what else was going on at the time, and indulge in what became a kind of therapy. What did Morette have on her mind today, I'd wonder and then settle in to find out.

Morette would ask after Lief, then Kaitlin, then Kaitlin's school. She'd wonder when my parents would be visiting next. She'd inquire about work, but, before I could give much response, she'd move on to other topics. From the very start of our friendship, Morette was constantly trying to distract me from business. Completely out of character for me, I didn't mind. She always had something else to talk about that I found interesting enough to set aside whatever work agenda was on my mind, at least for a few moments. Some days Morette would call eager to pass along a new data point to do with Irish real estate markets. Her practice was focused on property law, and she was involved with some of the biggest transactions taking place both in Waterford and in Dublin, where she was from and where much of her family still lived. Other times she'd get in touch to share details on the opening of a new exhibit at her favorite gallery in Paris, where she and her husband David had an apartment and visited for long weekends. Whatever was on Morette's mind I found also caught the attention of mine.

After several just-checking-in phone calls, Morette invited Lief and me to join her and David for dinner at their home. They lived in Tramore, a seaside town a half-hour south of Waterford City that had started its life in the 1600s as a fishing hamlet. Tramore was positioned on the northwestern corner of Tramore Bay on a hill sloping down to the strand and overlooked by the famously asymmetrical tower and spire of the Gothic Revival Holy Cross Church. Morette, David, and their two sons lived in a Georgian-style townhouse at the end of a terrace of similar homes on a cliff overlooking the Celtic Sea. It'd been built about 1850, during the time when Tramore became recognized by the residents of nearby Waterford as a pleasant retreat to the sea, leading to a tourism boom and a spate of development.

We followed the directions Morette had given me over the phone, and, twenty minutes later, Lief pulled down to the end of Morette and David's small lane and parked the car across from the final house in the row, as Morette had instructed. We sat for a moment taking in the scene. It was everything I loved about Ireland all in one view. To our right was the row of Georgian townhouses, each with a brightly colored door and a big brass knocker. To our left, an open field allowed a long view of the waves crashing against the coast. Behind us, the Holy Cross spire loomed, in front the open sea. Getting out of the car, we were hit with the smell of ocean salt and the wind in our face, the same gust creating the surf we could hear raging below us. It was early spring, meaning, at 7:00 p.m., the sun was still well above the horizon, but it was cold, and I shivered even though we'd known to wear coats and scarves. We lingered enjoying the natural spectacle so long that Morette came to her front door to wave to us.

"Here we are," she called out. "You've arrived!"

Morette welcomed us into her home like family returning after a long time away. She took our coats and scarves and ushered us down the high-ceilinged hall with its deep dentil molding and ornate ceiling roses that ran from the vestibule to the kitchen where the Aga had been cooking our dinner and warming the room. David stood at the counter peeling potatoes.

"Hello, David," Lief and I said together. David turned away from his kitchen duty long enough to reach out to shake our hands in turn. "Welcome, welcome," he told us with a smile that made us feel it.

"Your home is lovely," I said, looking into the living room where a fire burned slowly and the windows on either side of the fireplace opened to the sea. I made a mental note of the molding in the living room, wondering where I might incorporate the style at Lahardan House. I couldn't wait for Noel and the little bent damp guy and their crews to finish their dirty work so I could get to my version of decorating our new home.

"Sit down now, will you," our gracious hostess said, gesturing toward the semi-circular built-in bench beneath the kitchen window. "Now what will we have to drink? What do you think, David? We're having a roast, nice I'd say on this chilly evening, so I'd propose a bottle of red wine. What does everyone think?"

DINNER WITH MORETTE

"That sounds perfect," I said.

Lief and I sat on the window bench and Morette poured wine all around then joined David at the counter. David finished the potatoes while Morette spooned apple filling into the crust she'd unfolded into a baking tin.

"Now, where is young Kaitlin this evening?" Morette wanted to know. "She should have joined us. Why didn't you bring her with you?"

"She's having dinner with her friend Sophia tonight," I explained.

"Ah, well, she'll join us next time. Is this your first time in Tramore?" Morette continued without a pause, looking over her shoulder as she finished transferring the apple filling into the pastry.

"We were here briefly during a visit to Ireland we made together before we were married," I said. "Lief won a stuffed bear for me throwing darts in one of the staffs in the amusement park."

"But did you go swimming?" Morette asked. "You haven't been to Tramore until you've swum here."

"No," I said. "It was August, but Lief and I wore sweaters. No way I was going in the water!"

"This beach," Morette explained, "is one of the most popular for the annual Christmas Day swim."

"The what?" I asked.

"The Christmas Day swim!" Morette repeated. "Well, sure

you've heard of it? No? David and I do it every year, just over there," she pointed down the coast, "at the Guillamene. Until the early 1980s, the Guillamene was a men-only swimming cove. Women and children were restricted to swimming at Newtown. The 'Men-Only' sign is still there, but today we all swim at the Guilliamene together, and a dip there is one of the greatest delights you'll ever know."

"But on Christmas Day?" I said.

"Yes, of course!" Morette said. "It wouldn't be Christmas without a jump in the sea to start the day. You two and young Kaitlin, too, you'll have to join us this year, will you?"

"I don't think so, Morette," I said. "But maybe we'll come watch."

"Our coast here," she said, moving on to her next topic, "was also the site, in 1816, of a famous shipwreck. The transport ship *Sea Horse* foundered in Tramore Bay with the second battalion of the 59th Regiment of Foot on board. Nearly four-hundred men, women, and children died. We have a monument to the event on Doneraile Walk and an obelisk marks the burial plot at Christ Church on Church Road. Perhaps after we've eaten we'll walk over to have a look. It was the connection to this tragedy that led to the image of a seahorse being adopted as a symbol of the town of Tramore and later as the logo for Waterford Crystal."

Lief and I agreed, driving home after the evening had ended, that it was one of the best we'd ever enjoyed. I was certain that Morette was someone I wanted to know better. Fortunately, she

DINNER WITH MORETTE

seemed to feel the same way and invited us for dinner again two weeks later. Then she and I went for lunch together, just us two girls, and I told her I was pregnant. I'd told no one else yet, other than my family, Bill, and Beth. Sharing my big news with Morette gave me tremendous satisfaction. I'd made my first Irish friend.

When Noel had told us that the rising damp afflicting our Lahardan House would add ten to twelve weeks to the renovation timeline and thousands to the budget, turning our quick remodel into a major renovation, we'd had no choice but to agree to the work, telling ourselves and each other that the added hassle and expense would be worth it in the long run. Now, a few weeks later, as Noel and the little bent damp guy were getting going in earnest, tearing out every piece of wood in the house and jack hammering the plaster from the stone walls so they could inject the damp-proofing chemicals, I could no longer deny that my mother's wish, unfortunately, was not to be. This pregnancy was not going to be better than my pregnancy with Kaitlin. This pregnancy was going to be much, much worse.

XVIII
Waterford Regional Hospital

I opened my eyes and stared up at the ceiling. What time was it, I wondered. How long had I been asleep? I looked over at the big clock above the entrance to the ward. 4:45 a.m.

The curtains were drawn around my bed, but I could see through a crack in them to the window at the end of the room. Outside was pitch black. The room was bright, though, as it always was. They kept lights on twenty-four hours a day so the nurses and doctors could see coming and going. It was quiet, but I could hear carts in the hallway outside. Breakfast was on its way. Mine would be tea and toast. I wouldn't be able to eat it, but they'd want me to try.

This was my fifth admission since the start of my pregnancy. Previous stays had been for as many as ten days. When I'd been admitted the afternoon before, the nurse had suggested this visit might last that long again. I'd lost four more pounds, making for a total of twelve pounds lost in the four months I'd been pregnant, and my blood pressure was so low they'd told me not to try to stand up without a nurse's help. That was fine with me. I had no interest in trying to stand up.

The official diagnosis was hyperemesis. It's morning sickness gone rogue. The primary symptom is excessive vomiting. In extreme cases like mine, it leads to dehydration requiring IV fluids to make sure the baby isn't put at any risk and to keep the mother's blood pressure from falling so low that she's not able to function.

I heard the rattle of metal wheels turning the corner then smelled the eggs and toast being brought into the room on a cart. My stomach lurched. I reached over to grab the green plastic bedpan from the bedside table just in time. After I'd finished throwing up, I put the bedpan back on the table and hoped a nurse would come by to swap it for a clean one before I needed to use it again.

"Good morning, luv," the nurse said with a bright smile as she put the tray of tea and toast on the meal table at the foot of my bed. The smell of the toast had the effect it always had, and I reached again for the bedpan.

"Ah, my, luv," the nurse said after I'd finished. "Let me take that."

She took the full bedpan from me and returned a minute later with a stack of three fresh ones. "Here you go. This should hold you for a while now," she said, still smiling. "I'll be back in just a bit to see how you do with your breakfast. Try to take a few bites, will you?" Then she checked my IV fluids and carried on to deliver breakfast to the woman in the next bed.

Forty minutes later the nurse was back. I hadn't touched my food tray, but thankfully she didn't make an issue of it. She checked my IV again and asked if I needed anything. I shook my head no as she walked away, then closed my eyes and fell asleep. When I woke up, I felt well enough to sit up in bed and wished I had my laptop. Lief had refused to bring it. I'd insisted on having the laptop on every previous admission, but each time the doctors had objected and ordered me to shut it down when they caught me using it. The doctors telling me I couldn't work was stressful but so was not being able to download emails.

At the same time, reading my emails was hugely upsetting. Each one reminded me of something else I wasn't doing. I'd become increasingly detached from the day-to-day operations of the business. I was just too sick and couldn't keep up, not with emails, not with conference calls, not with deadlines, not with anything. I hadn't been in the office or able to work in a focused way for two months. If I let myself think about it, I panicked. I couldn't imagine what Buddy Hayden, Myles Norin, and the other members of Agora's Executive Committee were thinking. As far as they were concerned, I'd gone dark overnight. When I'd called to explain the situation to Bill he had told me not to worry. "Rest and relax and put your feet up," he'd said. "We'll be here waiting for you when you're ready to return." I appreciated Bill's support, but I knew the others didn't share his understanding position. Nothing I could do about that now, so I tried to push all thoughts of Agora Baltimore out of my head.

Beds in the ward were lined up ten along each wall and mostly full. All women, all here for gynecological procedures, conditions related to pregnancy—like me—or because they were about to give birth, and they all had lots of visitors. Formal visiting hours were 5:00 to 8:00 each evening, but if a woman was going into surgery or about to have a baby, her family was allowed in at any hour. The room was generally lively and noisy. Except by my bed. Lief would stop in each evening on his way home from work, and, sometimes, if she didn't have an after-school activity or too much homework, Kaitlin would come with him. Otherwise, I'd had no company. My family and friends were in a different country, but, honestly, I wasn't bothered by it. I felt too bad to want to chat with visitors.

I opened the bag Lief had packed and saw that it contained two books—*A Moveable Feast* and *The Garden Of Eden*. Lief knew that Ernest Hemingway was one of my favorite writers, and I smiled thinking that he'd taken time, in our rush out the door the day before, to pack things he thought would make me happy. I read the first ten pages of *The Garden Of Eden* then felt so sick that I had to lay back and close my eyes. I was alone and adrift, my entire life beyond my control. It took all the energy I had in me not to let that reality freak me out.

I must have fallen asleep again. When I opened my eyes, a young nurse I hadn't seen before was sitting in the chair by my bed. She was blond and plump, bent over with her chin in her hand, reading a magazine in her lap. She must have been on break. How many nurses in the States would use their break time to sit alongside a sleeping patient?

"Hello, luv," she said quietly when she noticed I'd opened my eyes. "I thought you might want some company when you woke up."

I appreciated the young nurse sitting by my side now but couldn't manage a response to her.

"I know you're struggling, luv," she was saying. "Don't let it get you down. Some days you might only manage a shower and nothing more, and that's okay. Some days maybe you can't even manage a shower, and that's okay, too," she said smiling. I looked over at her and tried to smile back.

"Okay, I'll leave you to it now," she said. "I'll stop back tomorrow around the same time, okay?" I nodded and tried again to smile. I'd never felt sicker nor, oddly, better cared for. I fell back asleep.

When I woke, I looked again up at clock. It was 6:15 p.m. I'd slept away another day. Lief would be by soon. I laid back and closed my eyes. The girl in the bed across from mine was on the phone telling a girlfriend about her new boyfriend. "He wants to come to visit me," she was saying, "but I've told him no. I couldn't bear for him to see me looking like this!" When she hung up, she pulled a bottle of nail polish from her purse and began painting her nails. The smell of the polish made my head ache and my stomach turn, and I reached for the bedpan on the table.

The woman next to the girl polishing her nails pulled out a packet of cigarettes. I closed my eyes and braced myself. Cigarette smoke was my worst trigger. What were these women doing smoking in the maternity ward anyway? My head began to throb fiercely, and I felt tears coming down my cheeks. I wasn't crying exactly, but my body was reaching its limit for pain. I grabbed for the bedpan but couldn't sit up and had to lean over the side of the bed to throw up. When I'd finished, I laid back and closed my eyes.

"Hey."

It was Lief. I opened my eyes and his face was in front of mine smiling. He kissed me on my wet cheek then handed me a tissue.

"How are you doing?"

I didn't respond but tried to smile.

"I brought you the usual," he said, holding out a white china plate with two pieces of roast beef and a small scoop of mashed potatoes.

During my first hospital admission, Lief had asked if there was anything I thought I could eat… anything at all. The roast beef from the carvery at the pub at Reginald's Tower came to mind and for whatever reason didn't make me feel like I was going to throw up.

"Okay," Lief had said when I told him. "I'll bring some for you tomorrow."

The next day he'd walked to Reginald's Tower after work and asked the man at the carving station if it'd be possible to buy a plate of roast beef and mashed potatoes for takeaway. The pub at Reginald's Tower doesn't do takeaway, but the man didn't question Lief's request. He'd pulled a white china plate from the stack, carved the meat, added the potatoes, then wrapped it all with aluminum foil.

"Bring back the plate when you can," he'd told Lief. Where else in the world would the chef give a man a china plate to take home with him?

Lief had been going back every day since, returning the plate from the day before and taking away my dinner on a fresh one. I couldn't finish the food but was able to eat a few bites, enough to keep my stomach from gnawing at itself overnight.

"So, how was your day?" Lief asked.

"Very funny. You know how my day was. Let's talk about your day… and Kaitlin. How's Kaitlin?"

"She's good. I dropped her off at Sophia's. She's going to have dinner there, then Gerri will bring her to our place later. That means I can stay a little longer tonight. Look. I brought a plate of carvery for myself so we could have dinner together," he said holding out a second white china plate.

"Did I tell you that Kaitlin asked if Sophia could sleep over Friday night? She said they want to have a spa day on Saturday. When I asked her what that meant, she told me that she and Sophia want to go down to the riverbank and cover themselves with mud. They read in some magazine about the healing properties of river mud. I told her Sophia could spend the night but that I didn't think the mud bath sounded like a good idea. She wanted me to check with you, though. She thinks I don't understand but you might, skin treatments being a woman thing and all."

Lief had started laughing halfway through his story. By the time he'd finished, I was laughing too, for the first time in days.

"Morette called, to ask how you're doing," Lief continued with his daily update. "I told her you're back in the hospital. She said she'd like to come see you, but I told her you're really not up for visitors."

"No, I'm not fit for company," I said. "But please tell Morette I appreciate her concern and that I look forward to the day I'll be able to eat again so we can plan another dinner. Tell her I'm missing spending time with her in her kitchen."

"Have you thought of a girl's name yet?" Lief asked, returning to one of our most common topics of conversation. We'd agreed on a boy's name, but I didn't like any of the girl's names Lief suggested and he hated all of my ideas.

"No," I said. "Nothing new."

"If it's a girl," we might have to wait until she's old enough to name herself," Lief said.

"Ha, ha."

"Work at the house is going well," he continued. "Noel's crew has nearly finished stripping all the rotten wood out of the place. That should make you happy, I hope," he added, looking up at me from his plate of carvery.

"Yes, it does," I said. "It's progress. If only I could get up and go see it for myself."

XIX
Jackson

Over the next three months I was admitted to Waterford Regional Hospital five more times. In between those visits, I spent hours lying in my bed or, on my better days, on the couch in the living room of Mark Breen's guest house. At least when I was in the cottage, I got to see Kaitlin every morning and afternoon. For the first time in her life, I was there waiting for her when she came home from school. I couldn't get up to greet her, but I could keep her quiet company while she did her homework and she me—at the kitchen table if I was on the sofa or on the floor of my room if I was in bed—while I laid still with my eyes closed. Just being in the same room with her was comforting for me and I hoped for her, too. Some days Sophia would walk home with her and the two would sit at our little round kitchen table doing their homework. I delighted in their gossip. They'd whisper and giggle, reliving moments of their day. Sophia, I overheard, liked a certain boy named Ciaran. "Shh!" Kaitlin screeched when Sophia began to respond to name the boy Kaitlin had her eye on. "My mother's right there!"

Finally, in my seventh month of pregnancy, I was well enough to go back to work. I'd done my best to keep up with the business over the five months I'd been sick, but the load really had fallen to Lief. He'd held things together, both at home with Kaitlin and in the office, where our transplanted operation now employed a staff of twelve. For the first time in my life, I'd had no choice but to give up control, and it was hard for me to see that the world had carried on without me while I'd been in forced hibernation. Kaitlin was still alive and more settled all the time, our little rental cottage was in good order, and Lief had kept the business afloat. Agora Ireland was chugging along nicely. It should all have come as a relief, but mostly I felt guilty for having had to drop the ball at home and panicked for how out of the loop I was in the office.

As soon as I was able to return to the world, my primary focus was the renovation of Lahardan House. It was early September, meaning there were just two-and-a-half months until my due date, and the damp-proofing work still wasn't finished. Meantime, Noel and his crew had indeed stripped the house of its doors, windows, paneling, moldings, and floor boards and shipped off all the wood to be made right. Sections with dry or wet rot had had to be cut out so they could be replaced to match the original.

Two days after my return to the office I was feeling well enough to make the drive out to meet Noel and check on progress. As the house came into view, my heart sank. I was aware that every door and window had been removed, but seeing Lahardan House full of holes was alarming. I pulled up alongside the front entrance, where our red Georgian door used to be, stepped out into the mud and hurried toward the house to get out of the rain. I had to pull myself up mentally before taking my first step inside. The floor was missing. Being told that our house had no floors and now actually seeing that our house had no floors were two different things. The living room and the dining room were rubble. Someone had placed planks to create pathways so you could walk around the place without descending into the open, dusty pit.

As I stepped carefully onto the plank in the entry, I heard jack hammers start up in the kitchen. The little bent Irishman was doing his thing. I walked across the plank to the stairs then up them to the second floor, where, I was relieved to see, the floors were still intact. I heard Noel's voice. He was in the room that would be the baby's nursery.

"Hello," I called out as I walked into the room, trying to appear cheerful but again catching myself as I looked down and saw that, while the floors were intact on the landing and in the hall, they were missing here. More planks had been placed, and Noel and another fellow I didn't know were in the corner of the room bent over a plan of the second floor. Then I saw the hole where the window used to be and the pits in the wall on either side where the big wooden shutters used to be and whatever small bit of cheerfullness I'd mustered leaked right out of me.

"Hello!" Noel replied genuinely enthusiastic. "It's great to see you up and around. How are ye'? Better, I'd say?"

"Yes, I'm much better, thank you," I said. "I'm a little concerned, though, Noel," I said. "It looks like there's still an awful lot of work to be done here. What's the status of the doors and windows, for example?"

"I'll ring the lads," Noel said brightly, "to see how they're getting on."

He'd ring the lads to see how they're getting on? Wasn't he in touch with the lads every day? If I were managing this project, I know I would be. You shouldn't have to ring the lads. You should know the status of every aspect of this job without having to ring anyone.

I thought those things but didn't say them. The Irish didn't respond well to that kind of forthright feedback. I'd learned that, if you spoke overly directly to them, they backed off. Sometimes they even walked away entirely. I couldn't afford for Noel to walk away. I needed Noel fully engaged. I fought back tears as I stood in the middle of the room with my expanding belly and looked around at the place where my new baby, due to arrive in a matter of weeks, was meant to sleep.

"When will the destruction phase be over?" I asked Noel. "When will you be able to begin putting it all back together?"

When would it be a house again?

"Let me ring the lads and get back to you with an update," was all Noel could offer.

We'd known we were taking on a half-finished renovation project and we'd understood that no home inspection meant we were buying as-is, but we'd had no idea what we were getting ourselves into with the purchase of Lahardan House. The damp, the rot, and the mold were only the start of it. In addition, the furnace didn't work. No, we hadn't thought to turn it on ourselves or to ask about it specifically. The Stanley cooker in the kitchen was meant to provide supplemental support, but it would have to do all the heavy lifting of heating the drafty old stone house until we could afford a new furnace. More than the cost was the mess. Replacing the furnace would require another phase of destruction, and I just wasn't up for it. I needed things to get better, not worse. I couldn't take much more worse.

We'd organized for Patrick to deliver our container-load of furniture and boxes the second week of October, and we'd given Mark Breen notice that we'd be moving out of his rental cottage November 1. My due date was November 30. Noel had assured me that everyone understood that these important deadlines loomed, but I wasn't convinced. Watching the crews as they worked reminded me of a story told by one of the speakers who'd addressed our group during the tour of Ireland where Lief and I had met. "In Latin cultures," he'd said, "*mañana* doesn't mean *tomorrow*. It means sometime… just not now. We Irish," he'd explained, "don't have a word to express that level of urgency." Now I got the joke.

Patrick had our container trucked down from Dublin October 12, as we'd agreed. I'd been hoping finally to meet him, but he wasn't able to come along for the delivery. His men unloaded everything and packed it all carefully into Lahardan House's living room, where Noel had put down more wooden planks because the floor was still missing. Now the floor couldn't be re-laid until we were able to place the furniture in other rooms of the house and unpack the boxes. The good news was that the bill for the storage in Dublin the past eleven months, now finally presented, was less than 1,000 pounds. Patrick had sent it with his driver along with a handwritten note congratulating us on moving into our new home. Cara sent her regards.

I wanted to dive in to begin unpacking boxes and placing furniture in rooms, but the house was still a construction site top to bottom. Slowly, though, over the month to follow, Lief and I were able to drag dressers and bed frames from the mountain of stuff in our living room. We organized Kaitlin's room and ours as best we could, and Lief assembled the crib we'd bought in the nursery. At night, the moon shone directly on it.

November 1, we packed up our things from Mark Breen's cottage and moved into Lahardan House. The master bedroom's ensuite bathroom was unfinished but usable, but the other three bathrooms were shells. All the windows and doors were again in place, but we had no kitchen. We had the Stanley for cooking, a mini-fridge, and a faucet coming out of the wall but no cabinets, counters, or sink. Noel had put us in touch with a cabinetmaker named John Kerr who I'd worked with to design a kitchen and who was custom-building the cabinetry and countertops in his workshop. He'd promised it'd all be fully fitted by the time the baby arrived. I wanted to believe him.

Each morning, we'd leave the house as Noel, the little bent Irishman, and their crews were arriving, then we'd return each evening as they were packing up to call it a day. They stored their tools—including the jack hammer and a rented cement mixer—in the entry hall. I tried to look beyond it all and see not what was in front of us but what we were working to build. Normally, that's no problem. Normally, seeing beyond the reality of my surroundings and enjoying only the vision in my imagination comes naturally. But my romantic nature was being put to the test.

We ate dinner together, Lief, Kaitlin, and me, on the bed in the master bedroom, then I'd wash the dishes in a bucket positioned beneath the faucet coming out of the kitchen wall then, when I'd finished, dump the dirty dishwater behind the barn. I swept and dusted each evening, but everything was constantly dirty. I told myself not to be bothered by the mess, and I finally stopped asking Noel for status updates. The work would be done when the work was done.

One afternoon, a week before my due date, I felt compelled to organize my desk in the office, to make sure everything was in its proper place and nothing was left unaddressed. Then I asked my marketing manager Clodagh to sit with me for a few minutes at the end of the day to review current projects and schedules and so I could show her where to find priority files and papers in my cabinets.

"Just so you'll know where to find everything you might need… in case I'm not in tomorrow," I told her.

We picked Kaitlin up from ballet practice then drove home. I followed Kaitlin through the front door, and, as I stepped onto the wooden plank in the entry hall, being careful not to bump my belly into the cement mixer to my right, I turned around to face Lief, coming in through the door behind me.

"We need to go to the hospital," I said. "It's time."

My water had broken.

Gerri had offered to have Kaitlin stay with her and Sophia for a few days when the time came for the baby. We got back in the car for the drive, one more time, to Waterford Regional Hospital. Lief drove in silence. The narrow, unlit roads weren't easy to navigate in a rush in the dark. Kaitlin sat in the middle of the back seat leaning forward so her head was nearly up front with Lief and me, as though she were trying to help propel the car forward. "Are you okay, Mom?" she checked every few minutes.

This wasn't my first baby, so I had an idea what to expect. Lief, though, was at a loss but remained his usual calm, cool self. I wasn't having contractions or any other labor symptoms, so we didn't feel panicked.

"I'll take Kaitlin to Gerri's," Lief said, after we'd arrived at the hospital and the nurse had checked me into a room, "and come straight back."

I gave Kaitlin a hug and a kiss. "Next time I see you, Doodlebug," I said, "you'll have a baby brother or sister." She smiled and followed Lief out the door.

A few minutes later, a nurse came in to attach a fetal monitor to my belly. A few minutes after that, she returned to read the printout. She tore the paper from the machine and walked quickly out of the room. A minute later she was back with the doctor on duty. In Ireland, over the course of your pregnancy, at your regular check-ups, you meet every doctor in the obstetrics department of the hospital where you're planning to go when you're in labor. Whoever is working when you present is the one to deliver the baby. Somehow, though, I'd never seen this doctor before.

"We're going to deliver your baby now," he said as he came into the room holding the printout from the fetal monitor.

"What do you mean?" I said, feeling caught off guard to the point of panic. I'd been preparing myself for hours of contractions and a natural delivery. Now, suddenly, this man I'd never met was telling me I needed an immediate C-section. I thought of stories I'd heard of doctors in the States who deliver babies by

JACKSON

cesarean if the timing is inconvenient for them. How did I know this guy didn't have a dinner date he didn't want to miss?

"Deliver my baby now? You mean by cesarean? Why? No. No, you can't do that," I told him.

"Your baby can't wait," the doctor said calmly but firmly. "Your baby is in distress. We must deliver now."

"But my husband isn't here," I said. "He'll be back soon. Couldn't we wait so that I can talk this over with him?"

"There's nothing to talk over," the doctor said. "Your baby must come out now." The tone of his voice made his point. I stopped arguing.

The nurse removed the fetal monitor from my belly and helped me to stand up. Then she led me across the hall into the operating room. I laid down on the table. The nurses draped me and washed my belly. The doctor came in in his scrubs and, just three minutes later, he had my baby in his hands. The doctor laid the tiny, wriggling boy on my chest.

"He is one lucky little lad," the doctor said. "He'd wrapped the umbilical cord around his neck not once but twice. But he's fine. Fine and healthy." As if to confirm, the little bundle screamed out for the first time.

A nurse wheeled us into the recovery room, where Lief was waiting.

"What happened?" Lief said jumping up from the chair where he'd been sitting. "When I got back, they said you'd been taken in for a cesarean section." He was more agitated than I'd ever seen him and pale.

"Yes, he'd gotten himself wrapped up in the umbilical cord, it seems," I said. "But he's okay. It's all okay."

"He?" Lief said.

"Yes, it's a boy."

"Good thing," Lief said. We'd still never been able to agree on a girl's name. But we had a boy's name, one that we both loved and that, seeing the little guy now, seemed to suit him.

"Hello, boy," Lief said as the nurse handed him the baby wrapped in a blue and white striped blanket. "Hello, Jackson."

An hour later, the nurse wheeled me and Jackson, now washed and swaddled, into the private room where we'd spend the next three days together. I reached for the phone by the bed to call my parents. Back in the States, it was Thanksgiving Day. I wanted to let Mom and Dad know they had one more thing to be thankful for.

XX
Dad

We brought Jackson home to Lahardan House seventy-two hours later. After we'd settled in bed Kaitlin came in with a present, a book she'd made called "Jackson's Story." It showed the advent of her baby brother through a series of cartoon sketches. First was me with a big smile the day I found out I was pregnant. Next was me bent over and throwing up. Then Kaitlin had drawn me with a big tummy. On the next page was a drawing of Lief, me, and her in the car, rushing to the hospital, the night Jackson had been born. Finally, she'd sketched me walking through the big red front door of our Irish country house carrying Jackson in a blanket of blue.

"Thank you, Doodlebug," I said, reaching out to give her a hug and a kiss. "I love it."

I had prioritized Kaitlin's room, so she had a semi-comfortable place to sleep, and the master bedroom. Jackson would sleep in a

Moses basket alongside our bed. Otherwise, the house was still a construction site with just one usable bathroom and no kitchen. John Kerr now promised cabinets and counters by Christmas. He told me he was working fourteen-hour days to meet that deadline. I told him I really appreciated the effort but didn't suggest he let up. The damp-proofing work continued, but at least we were finally past the jack-hammering stage.

My mother and father came to stay the following week. It wasn't only their first chance to meet their new grandson and see Lahardan House but also their first time in Ireland. In the year since Lief, Kaitlin, and I had made the move, we'd traveled to Baltimore several times, but we hadn't been able to coordinate dates for my parents to come visit us. I had been looking forward to this opportunity to show off our new life, and I knew that this chance to spend extended time with her Gammy and Poppy in her new home would do Kaitlin a world of good.

My parents must have been exhausted when they walked through our front door, but they didn't slow a beat. After we'd introduced them to their new grandson, who they agreed was perfect, Lief helped them carry their suitcases up to the guest room, such as it was. They dropped their bags and came straight back downstairs. My father, seeing that we had no kitchen table, looked around the house until he found the box containing the to-be-installed dishwasher. He dragged it around from the boiler room and placed it in the middle of the kitchen. Then he pulled chairs

DAD

from the piles of furniture in the living room and positioned them around the dishwasher box to create a gathering place in front of the Stanley. My mother began digging through boxes in search of a tablecloth and napkins.

"It's cold in here, isn't it?" my father asked, looking down at newborn Jackson and me sitting now on one of the chairs around the dishwasher box.

"Yes, it's always cold in here," I said.

"I'll go check the boiler," my father said.

"Don't bother," Lief said. "It doesn't work. We're using the Stanley to heat the house and to provide hot water until we can figure out what to do about the boiler."

"Ah, okay, no problem," my father said, upbeat and undaunted as always. Then he set to inspecting the big green stove, turning dials and adjusting settings. "There," he said a few minutes later. "The place should get warmer now."

My father was an engineer, with his own firm in Baltimore, who'd built the house where I'd grown up himself, according plans drawn up on a card table over months of late nights. He and my mother worked months more of late nights and long weekends, with me and my three siblings helping as best we could, which mostly meant trying to stay out of the way, to finish the country house on ten acres that we moved into when I was nine. My father's father had likewise built with his own two hands the house where my father had grown up. That was during the Great

Depression. When my grandfather lost his job in the city, he dismantled the house he owned there and used the lumber and the nails from the city house to build a new one on land the family owned north of town. My father knew how to make or fix anything. It was in his DNA. He would have set to work building a kitchen on the spot except I explained we'd already engaged a cabinetmaker who promised we'd have a fitted kitchen by Christmas.

I could imagine what my father must have been thinking about this old stone house with no proper heating, no kitchen, and one working bathroom that we'd just brought our new baby home to. I *had* to imagine because he made no negative comment. He never did. He just kept looking around to see what else he could do to improve the situation.

"Okay," he said after he'd turned up the heat, "now let's take a look at the bathrooms."

"That would be great," I said. "We're close to finishing the master bathroom. We bought a claw foot tub that I'd like to position in the center of the room, but that requires running a pipe beneath the floor. A girl in the office put us in touch with a plumber who came two weeks ago to take a look, but he wanted 5,000 Irish punts to do the work. That's more than $7,500."

When we'd told Deirdre about the Irish plumber who'd quoted 5,000 punts for our small bathroom job, she'd responded with a knowing smile. "Ah, he's a chancer," she'd said. "He's chancing his arm, suggesting a ridiculous price thinking the silly Americans might be daft enough to agree to it."

"Chancing his arm?" I'd said. Deirdre had gone on to tell us the story of the Butlers of Ormonde and the FitzGeralds of Kildare.

In 1492, the two families were feuding over who would be Lord Deputy.

The Butlers holed up in Saint Patrick's Cathedral. The FitzGeralds followed them to the church and asked them out to make peace. But the Butlers weren't convinced. They thought it could be a trick and that they'd be ambushed if they came out. After a while, Gerald FitzGerald cut a hole in the cathedral door and thrust his arm through, as if to say, "If I can trust you, you can trust me." The Butlers were persuaded that the FitzGeralds were serious about a truce and came out of hiding. The Irish have used the expression "to chance your arm" ever since to mean to take a flyer, or a risk.

"Show me the tub," my father said after I'd told him the story.

"I can install this bathtub for you, Kath," he said, "no problem. I'll just need a few things from a hardware store."

Lief gave him directions to three we knew in Waterford City, and my dad set out early the next morning with his shopping list. He didn't return until hours later.

"I went to the three hardware stores that Lief told me about," he explained to my mother and me as we three and sleeping Jackson sat huddled around our dishwasher box in front of the Stanley, "and to two others that I found, asking for solder. I found everything else I needed in the first place I stopped, but everyone I spoke with everywhere I went told me they didn't have solder. How could a hardware store not carry solder?

"Finally, in the fifth place I tried, I could see rolls of solder on the shelf behind the counter. But, when I asked for it, the man insisted he didn't carry any. I pointed to the rolls behind him. 'Ah, you mean *sodur*!' he said with his brogue. The way he said it, it rhymed with *older*. Honestly, it didn't sound that different to me from the way I'd been pronouncing it all along, but, oh, well. We had a good laugh over it, and the man told me to come back to him if I need anything else for the job. He said he'd take care of us. Awfully nice folk, these Irish, once you can understand what they're saying."

My father installed the tub, and the master bathroom was finished. In Kaitlin's room, he hung wooden shelves that my mother had painted "every color of the rainbow," as Kaitlin has requested, then helped her to unpack her toys and dolls onto them. My mother made drapes for the dining room windows using red and gold brocade she'd brought for me from Baltimore, and my father found a way to install the dryer temporarily while we waited for Noel's crew to finish configuring the laundry room for its permanent installation. They'd been struggling with the set-up, which was foreign to them since the Irish hung their wet laundry on lines outdoors. "So we can complain about the clothes never dry-

DAD

ing," Deirdre in the office said with a sly smile when I asked her why more Irish woman didn't insist on having dryers, especially considering it rained nearly every day on this island.

My parents couldn't stay for Christmas, but, before they left, they went with us to the tree farm in Williamstown to help us choose and chop down our first Irish Christmas tree. We set up in the master bedroom. My mother and I dug through boxes in the living room to find tree trims and strands of white lights. We came across Kaitlin's stuffed Rudolph, whose nose lit up red when you pressed it, and stood him beneath the tree after we'd decorated it. Christmas morning, Lief sat on the bed holding Jackson while I helped Kaitlin open her presents then we all went downstairs for pancakes in our new kitchen. John Kerr had kept his word. He'd finished installing the counters and cabinets December 23.

At long last, the dirty work of the renovation of Lahardan House was complete. Noel and the little bent Irishman with the screwdriver had moved on to their next jobs. I was almost sorry to see them go. They'd become regular fixtures around the place, like part of the family.

The day after Christmas, I sat down at the desk in our bedroom, which I'd positioned in front of one of our windows so it had a long view of green fields, stone walls, and wandering sheep, to write my parents a letter. "Thank you," I told them, "for doing so much to move us along the road to making our dream of Irish country life come true…"

When I allowed myself moments like this one, sitting quietly and alone looking out at the Irish landscape, I couldn't imagine any better life, but that contentment came and went in a flash. The American in me felt guilty indulging in it. Sitting here idle was wasting precious time. I should finish the letter to my parents and go check emails before starting dinner. December 26 was a holiday in Ireland but not in the States. Everyone in Baltimore would have been at work. What had I missed by taking the day off?

I told myself to get up and get back to business, but I kept staring out at the green fields and my mind turned, as it'd been doing often lately, to the Irish women I was getting to know. Claire, Deirdre, Martina, and the other young women in the office were different than the young women I'd worked with in Baltimore. They worked hard, but they didn't live to work. Morette, our attorney, fascinated me. She was a partner in her own law firm, ambitious and successful, but, unlike every attorney I'd known in the States, she never seemed stressed. She was straightforward but relaxed, business-minded but not all business, as likely to want to talk about the best place in the city to buy fresh salmon as the legal issue on the table. From the first time we'd met with her during the process of purchasing Lahardan House, I'd walked out of our meetings feeling calm and reassured as if I'd spent time with a supportive friend.

I looked down at what I had written to my parents about our advancements and realized I was posturing, projecting confidence

DAD

that I didn't really feel. We'd made progress, sure, but I wondered if we weren't still at the just-getting-started stage of this journey.

At first, Ireland had been my escape hatch. I'd run away to this island when I'd felt I had no choice but to remove myself from Baltimore. But now that I was getting to know her, I suspected Ireland was meant to play a much bigger role for me. All my life I'd wanted to believe in something. My Catholic school education had left me cold, and, eventually, I'd defaulted into career as doctrine. I found great satisfaction in building a business and convinced myself that Agora provided all the guiding principle I needed. Now, as I opened myself to her, I was realizing that Ireland, especially her women, seemed to have new truths to show me that might just land me in the place I'd been racing toward my whole life but couldn't name. Finding something worth believing in would require letting go of what'd I'd substituted for faith to this point. Maybe I was ready to do that.

My whole life I'd wanted to be in charge, and, after separating from Rick, I'd had no choice but to do everything for myself. Maybe now, at last, I'd be able to let Ireland take the lead and see where she'd take me. Maybe that was the real reason I'd walked away from my life in Baltimore and crossed an ocean to start a new one.

XXI
Thom

After Jackson was born, we were a fully fledged family, but we spent precious little time together. When I'd become pregnant and then sick, Lief cut back on his travel completely, but, once Jackson arrived on the scene, he returned to his usual schedule. He was on the road two weeks out of four at least, scouting markets we were developing for the business and hosting conferences, meaning for half the month I was a single working mom again, without my parents for support. I was too ashamed to admit it, but loneliness and fatigue were leading to resentment.

When Jackson was eighteen months old, Lief planned an especially extended trip. We wanted to open up Europe for the *International Living* readership. Historically, we'd focused on Central America and the Caribbean, regions offering what we knew our readers prized—affordable, accessible living in the sun. Part of the agenda behind bringing *International Living* to Ireland was the chance it would create for us to expand our editorial and advertising programs to include opportunities in the Old World.

Lief took off, with Mike Palmer, one of our editors from Baltimore, for a three-week-long excursion to explore stretches of the Mediterranean coast in Spain, France, and Italy, hoping to identify property developers interested in becoming advertising partners.

Without Lief, I was on my own to take care not only of Kaitlin and Jackson, but of the house and the office, too. My days began at 5:00 a.m. We'd gotten a puppy, a border collie Kaitlin named Daisy, who was resisting our attempts at potty training. Step one each morning was cleaning up Daisy's messes from overnight in front of the Stanley, where she slept. Step two was planning what we'd have for dinner and making a list of what I'd need to stop for at the market on the way home. Then I'd pack Jackson's lunch and diaper bag, throw in a load of laundry, shower and dress myself, wake and dress Jackson, then call Kaitlin down for breakfast. My goal was to leave the house by 7:00 a.m. so I could drop Jackson at daycare then Kaitlin at Newtown in time for me to make it to my desk by 8:00 a.m. Even on mornings when I was able to keep to that schedule, I felt behind by the time I sat down to download emails and went into overdrive mode trying to catch up. I'd fly through the day, then, at 5:30 p.m., rush out the door to run my circuit in reverse, collecting Kaitlin, then Jackson, before racing home to make dinner, give Jackson a bath and put him down for the night, review Kaitlin's homework, finish the laundry I'd started in the morning, clean a bathroom or vacuum the living room, then collapse into bed to fall asleep alone. Weekends were about trips to the grocery store, household chores, and errands I hadn't had time for during the week. I loved my children and the home we'd made at Lahardan House, but this didn't feel like quality time with either. By the end of week two of Lief's Mediterranean adventure, I was exhausted.

Lief and I had been able to speak only twice since he'd left Waterford. By the time Lief was somewhere he could call me, I was ready for bed, and when I had a few free minutes Lief was nowhere to be reached. Finally, the evening of the second Friday he'd been away, I heard the phone downstairs in the kitchen as I was settling Jackson in his crib. I rushed out of the room and down the stairs trying to make it to the kitchen before the ringing stopped.

"Hello!" I nearly yelled, out of breath, as I grabbed the phone and held it up to my ear.

"Hey," Lief said on the other end. "The call rang so long I was beginning to wonder where you were."

He was wondering where I was? Where else would I be? During the day I was at work. At night I was home with the kids. Did he think I'd gone out dancing?

"I was putting Jackson down for the night," I said, realizing the words were coming out with a sharper tone than I'd intended. "Where are you?" I asked, even more sharply.

"Mike and I are in Estepona on the Costa del Sol. I can't talk long. We have to leave in a few minutes to meet a developer for dinner."

"Well, thanks for finding time to call," I said, now intentionally sharp.

"What is that supposed to mean?" Lief asked. Could he really not realize how badly I needed some support? An on-my-way-out-the-door phone call wasn't enough. I wanted to tell him that Jackson had gotten into a fight at daycare. Roisin had bitten him on the cheek! And that Kaitlin and Sophia had a ballet recital on Sunday. I'd been waiting for days to tell him that results from the big new-subscriber campaign we'd launched earlier in the month were coming in, and it was looking to be a home run. And I really needed to tell someone that I was feeling lonelier than I could ever remember feeling, including after separating from Rick. I was desperate for a few caring words, but when I started talking what came out wasn't a sweet, "Could we just chat for a few minutes" but a cross, "It means you could have called earlier, before you were already late for your meeting." I was picking a fight, and I didn't care.

"I don't have time for this," Lief said. While we'd been talking, I'd walked with the phone up to the landing at the top of the stairs. We'd had bookcases built on either side, with the big shuttered window in the center, creating a small library. I sat down in one of the two red armchairs I'd positioned on either side of the window and looked out at the night sky. No lights for miles meant a sky full of stars. I stared at the white twinkles in the sea of black. I thought of Morette, who'd become my closest friend in Waterford. I'll call her in the morning, I told myself. Maybe we can meet for lunch one day next week. But what I really craved was a session on the couch in Beth's office. I missed Beth and everyone else from Baltimore, horribly. Beth had come to visit once, the year before. Besides my parents we'd had no other visitors.

"Are you there?" Lief asked.

"Yes, I'm here," I said flatly.

"Well, I have to go. I'll try to call again over the weekend. Give Kaitlin and Jackson a hug and a kiss from me."

"Yes, okay," I said. "I will."

"All right," Lief said, "well, I'm late. I love you."

"I know," I said. "I love you, too."

The line went dead. I held the phone to my ear a while longer, looking out at the Irish night sky, feeling smaller and lonelier all the time.

"Mom, will you come watch me do this pose? I think I'm getting better, but what do you think?" It was Kaitlin calling from her bedroom, where she'd been rehearsing for her big recital.

Kaitlin was adapting to our new world. In addition to the ballet classes with Sophia, which had become the highlight of her week, she'd decided to continue on the girls' hurling team. Playing was an important part of fitting in with her classmates, which she was trying her best to do. She was getting good grades, going to parties, and hosting sleepovers, but she still went out of her way to make it clear that as far as she was concerned Baltimore was her home. Ireland was a detour. I ignored the point when she made it, but it hurt every time because I couldn't think of how to make her feel better. I couldn't command her to open herself up to Ireland. I could only try to show her the potential rewards if she did. As she gets older, Kaitlin would see the beauty of the new life we were trying so hard to build here on this Emerald Isle. Wouldn't she?

I returned the phone to its cradle on the kitchen counter and started quickly back upstairs to Kaitlin's room. Yes, she was adjusting. She just needed more time. Right now, I'd do what I could to support her ongoing efforts to assimilate and go watch her practice her arabesque.

Two weeks later, Lief had returned from his travels on the Med and I was feeling less exhausted and abandoned but still missing everyone from Baltimore. As I was downloading emails first thing after arriving at the office one morning, a message landed in my in-box that brought an instant smile. Thom had written. I clicked to read, and my smile broadened. Thom was coming to Waterford, arriving in two weeks and staying for three. I couldn't wait to tell Kaitlin. A visit from Thom was just the balm we both needed. Thom was my lead copywriter but, more than that, he was my greatest confidant after Beth and had been one of the most constant and trusted presences in Kaitlin's life since her father and I separated.

In the years before leaving Baltimore, when I'd been working well past 5:00 p.m. each day and Kaitlin was attending school at Grace & St. Peter's a block from my office, some days my parents would collect her, take her to dinner, and then have her ready for bed by the time I got home. Other days, I'd walk across the street to collect Kaitlin at 3:00 p.m. and bring her back to my office with me, where she'd sit either in my visitor chair or on the floor in front of my desk in her blue uniform jumper to do her homework. It wasn't an ideal arrangement for a second-grader, but Kaitlin and I both were glad just to be together. My staff enjoyed Kaitlin's visits, too, and welcomed her into the Agora tribe. Bill and Mark had installed a gym on the top floor of the building after they'd purchased it, as part of the conversion to office space. Some afternoons after their workdays were through, Thom and others would go up to play basketball. They'd stop by my office on the way to see if Kaitlin had finished her school work, and, if she had, they'd take her with them. She and Thom became especially close. After their games, they'd walk to the shop on the corner for a snack, then Thom would return Kaitlin to my office as I was ready to shut down my laptop. Thom had four children who he saw just twice a month after his divorce. Kaitlin enjoyed the chance for male bonding, and spending time with her seemed to take some of the sting out of not being able to see his own family more often for Thom.

The son of a Baptist preacher, Thom had been a television evangelist, host of a show called "His Place," and owner of a Christian newspaper. When his business failed and his marriage fell apart, Thom called Bill, whom he'd known from years before in D.C. "Sounds like you need a change of scenery," Bill had said. "Why don't you come to Baltimore? You could write for us." That's what Thom did, initially for one of Agora's financial divisions, then for me at *International Living*.

I'd first met Thom at a birthday celebration we were having for Bill in an Agora conference room. We were milling around, eating cake, when in walked this tall guy wearing faded jeans and a torn T-shirt, his hair in a ponytail, a guitar slung over his back. The clothes and the guitar got our attention, but what struck me more was the fellow's demeanor. One glance and you knew this was one of the easiest-going guys you'd ever meet. His posture was relaxed, his face calm, Zen even, but his eyes twinkled. This fellow didn't take life too seriously.

"Thom!" Bill had called out. "You're just in time. It's my birthday. Play something."

Thom pulled his guitar from its case and led the room in a jazzy round of "Happy Birthday." I was instantly charmed. When he went straight into a rasta rendition of "No Woman, No Cry," I knew he was one of the rarest and dearest encounters of all—a kindred spirit. Most people didn't get to know me well enough to realize it, but beneath my all-business exterior, I had free-wheeling, fun-loving instincts, a wild side I'd rarely indulged since my Bratwursthaus days with Rick. My professional ambitions had long ago trumped my appetite for daring but they hadn't buried it, and maybe the thing I appreciated most about Agora was that my role allowed me to work hard and chase adventure at the same time.

Thom moved into the Agora intern dorms the night of Bill's birthday party and started work as a copywriter the next morning. I had little time for friends and rarely made an effort to seek out new company, but the week after Thom arrived in Baltimore, I walked over to his office to ask if he'd like to have lunch with me. When we did, it was like two lifelong friends reuniting after an extended absence. I opened up to Thom the way I did only with Beth and Bill, admitting to feeling lonely since leaving Rick and like a bad mother for working such long hours. He took it all in stride and never judged.

Two days later, I was reviewing copy for the next issue of *International Living*. It wasn't nearly as ready for production as I'd hoped it would be. It looked like I would have to work through lunch. Thom appeared in the doorway to my office. "Are we having any fun yet?" he said playfully. I looked up, more than a little annoyed by the interruption, until I saw that Thom had his guitar in his hands and his pick at the ready. He smiled big, and I smiled back in spite of myself. When he started strumming "Brown Eyed Girl," I surprised myself even further by settling back to listen. For the next few minutes, I forgot the deadline complications and every other crisis of the day. Then, as quickly as he'd shown up, song over, Thom took his leave, leaving me humming to myself as I returned to my work and feeling a little lighter.

That was the first of dozens of private office serenades. Sometimes, on Fridays when Thom knew that Kaitlin was spending the weekend with her father, he'd come by at 5:00 with a bottle of wine, and we'd share a glass while he played and I finished up for the day. By the time I left Baltimore, Thom was more than my chief copywriter. He was one of my closest friends, an important part of my personal support infrastructure, and the third Agora person I'd told about Lief, after Beth and Bill. Some probably suspected otherwise, but there'd never been any romantic tension between Thom and me. We simply recognized each other instantly as the kind of friend you're lucky if you get even a handful of in your lifetime—someone who sees you for who you really are and likes you unconditionally anyway.

At dinner that night, I was excited to share the news. "Guess who's coming to visit?" I said to Kaitlin as I spooned shepherd's pie onto her plate. The classic Irish dish, on the menu of every pub we'd frequented anywhere in the country, had become one of our favorites. I'd experimented with recipes, much easier since Claire had told me about pre-mixed shepherd's pie seasoning packets, and we'd agreed that we preferred it made with ground beef, which is technically the English version, rather than minced lamb, the Irish adaptation. I didn't admit this to Claire.

"Who?" eleven-year-old Kaitlin asked, showing no real interest in the answer.

"Thom," I told her.

"Thom?" she said. Now she was paying attention. "Thom from Baltimore?"

"Yes," I said. "He'll arrive two weeks from today and stay with us for three weeks."

"He's going to stay here? With us the whole time?" She was beaming. In the three years since we'd left Baltimore, Kaitlin had seen Thom only a few times during our visits, when I'd brought her with me to Executive Committee meetings at Agora, but I knew her attachment to him remained strong. Thom represented everything she was missing about "back home," as she still referred to it. She seemed as pleased as I'd hoped she'd be at the thought of being able to spend time with him in her actual home.

"Yes," I said, "he'll stay with us the whole time."

I said a little prayer of thanks for Thom's visit. I wasn't trying to deny Kaitlin anything from her old life. I only wanted her to give the new one a chance. Maybe Thom could help us build that bridge.

THOM

Thom walked through the door of our office a little after 4:00 in the afternoon, with his suitcase, his laptop, and his guitar. In the years since I'd met him, Thom had cut his hair and upgraded his wardrobe. Over his jeans and t-shirt he wore a plaid sport coat. It was a good look. Setting eyes on him made me even happier than I'd expected, and I gave him a big hug.

Lief hadn't had much chance to get to know Thom, seeing him only occasionally at staff meetings, but he liked Thom. Everyone liked Thom. "We'll finish up quickly," I told him, after Lief had come over to say hello and shake his hand, "then we can go. You must be exhausted. We'll need to stop to pick up Kaitlin from ballet practice and Jackson from daycare, then we'll head home for dinner."

An hour later, Lief loaded Thom's suitcase and guitar into our car, and the three of us headed up the hill to Newtown and the Waterford Dance Academy. Kaitlin came running out in a pink leotard, tights, and ballet slippers and rushed over to the car. *She's so excited to see Thom that she didn't take time to change out of her ballet costume*, I thought. When Thom got out of the car, Kaitlin barreled into him, throwing her arms around his waist.

"Hello!" Thom boomed, matching Kaitlin's enthusiasm and hugging her back. "So, are we having any fun yet?" Thom asked with a big smile.

"I'm so glad you're here," Kaitlin said.

We picked up Jackson then set off down the Cork Road for Lahardan House.

"Now, when you see the house," I said, trying to set Thom's expectations, "don't be shocked. It's still very rough around the edges outside, and inside it's definitely a work in progress. You should have seen it when we bought it, though. I wish we'd taken more before photographs. It's hard now to explain the extent of the work we've done." I'd been boasting for more than a year to everyone back in Baltimore about the historic stone country house we'd bought and restored. Other than my parents and Beth, Thom was the first of them to see it for himself, and I worried that he might be disappointed. Maybe Thom would think I'd been posturing in the reports I'd been sending back. I knew he'd be relaying the details of his visit to everyone at Agora Baltimore, and what they thought of the life we were building for ourselves on this Emerald Isle still mattered to me more than I knew it should.

I was relieved when, a few minutes later, as we'd turned down our drive and Lahardan House came into view, "Wow!" was the first word out of Thom's mouth.

"What are you talking about, Kath?" he said. "This place is amazing. How did you ever find this?"

"Ah, well, that's a story better told over a bottle of wine. It's a gripping tale of a couple of hard-headed Yanks who refused to give up on their dream."

Lief showed Thom to the guest room, then the two came into the kitchen, where I'd started dinner. The one concern I'd had about Thom's visit—that he might not find Lahardan House as exceptional as I did—had been alleviated. Now I could relax and just enjoy Thom's company. "We're having Irish stew," I said as he and Lief passed by.

"Sounds great," Thom said as he followed Lief into the family room, where Kaitlin and Jackson were opening a bucket of Legos. Thom sat on the floor with them, making himself comfortable as usual, and picked up the booklet to look for ideas for what to build. "How about this dinosaur?" he said to Kaitlin, pointing to the T-Rex in the picture. Kaitlin smiled then began choosing out the green bricks they'd need to get started. She handed one to Jackson, then attached the one in her hand to it. Jackson smiled brightly for his sister and reached out for another Lego.

We'd put down thick wall-to-wall carpeting in the family to allow for precisely the kind of scene I was watching right now. I paused a moment as I was setting the table to appreciate it. I'd found an old wooden farmhouse table and six Windsor chairs that I'd painted the blue Monet used for his dining room. I'd recovered the two sofas in the family room in red and white plaid and painted the walls of both rooms daffodil yellow. It was a bright, cheery space and, glancing around it now while I finished warming the stew, I felt pleased with how it'd all come together.

"I was thinking that we should spend some time on staff training while you're in the office," I called over to Thom. He, Kaitlin, and Jackson had nearly finished T-Rex's body. "Every member of our team here is completely green. Only one of them, Clodagh, had ever even heard of direct marketing before coming to work for us, and her experience is limited and dated. I thought maybe you and I could host a couple of Direct Marketing 101 bootcamps. What do you think?"

"Sounds great," Thom said without looking up.

"Also, for the second day, I'd like to ask each member of the team to prepare a short list of their goals for their piece of the business. I want to see what they come up with."

"Sounds like a plan," Thom said, finally looking over as he held up the finished Lego dinosaur for everyone to admire.

After we'd eaten, Thom pulled out his guitar. He was on the sofa in the family room tuning up. "What shall I start with?" he asked as Jackson and I sat down together opposite him.

"Can't Buy Me Love," Kaitlin said quickly. Thom accommodated, and Kaitlin and I sang along while Jackson bopped on my lap. Lief sat back in his armchair. He wasn't much for singing, but he looked as contented as I'd ever seen him. Thom was doing what I'd hoped he'd do, injecting a little of the best of Kaitlin and my former life into the heart of our new one.

What more could anyone want? The trouble was that, while I told myself the response to that question should be nothing, my honest answer was a long list that started with a bigger, more profitable business and the respect of Agora's Executive Committee. I recognized the incalculable blessings our time in Ireland had brought us, but I still felt unsettled, like I was on my way but not moving forward fast enough. I was distracted constantly, including now. Left to its own devices, my mind invariably came back around to work, and now I had my number-one ally Thom in residence.

Bill's business partner Mark, a second mentor to me, had for years encouraged me to embrace my business instincts. "You seem afraid to admit them," he'd told me more than once. "But you shouldn't be. If you were a man, you'd be applauded, not only for your acumen, but also for your drive. You have a true entrepreneur's spirit. Don't hide it. You have it in you to be a shark. So let yourself be a shark." Easy for him to say. He wasn't a woman. I genuinely wanted to be a good wife, mother, and homemaker and I valued the life Lief and I were building together, but I couldn't not think about work. I didn't *want* not to think about work. I liked work. And whenever I wasn't thinking about work, I felt like I was cheating—on myself, on Agora, and on Bill and Mark. Then, when I thought about work constantly, I worried that I was being disloyal to Lief.

Okay, I'm not going down that rabbit hole again right now, I thought.

"Time to call it a night, Doodlebug," I said. Kaitlin had lain down on the sofa opposite Thom and was struggling to keep her eyes open. "Thom will play for us again tomorrow, I'm sure," I said.

"Okay, Mom," Kaitlin replied grudgingly. Too many nights,

Kaitlin refused Lief and me when we asked her to hang out with us in the family room after dinner and went off to be alone in her room. How nice to have to tell her it was time to go up to bed.

"Feel like watching a movie?" Lief asked after Kaitlin was in bed. Because of our remote location, we had neither network nor cable TV. When we mentioned this to family and friends back in the States, they were aghast. How were we surviving without television? We didn't have a radio in the house either. I'd come to appreciate how disconnected we were at Lahardan House. Weekdays were a mad dash, but weekends we set the rest of the world aside. I liked movies, though, so we'd built a library of DVDs.

"Actually, I was thinking of heading into town," Thom said. "I'd like to see if I can find a place where I could play, just for fun, while I'm here. Would you mind if I borrowed the car?"

"Keys are in the bowl on the table by the front door," I said.

I walked Thom to the front door and waved to him as he pulled away in our car. It's like having a third child in the house, I thought, smiling and shaking my head as I turned to head back to the family room. "Did you find a movie?" I called out to Lief.

"How about a 'Thin Man'?"

"Ah, perfect," I said. Myrna Loy was my favorite actress, and I loved the character she played in the "Thin Man" series. "Choose whichever one you want and go ahead and start it. I'm going to run upstairs to grab a pad of paper and a pen so I can make notes for next week's training bootcamps while we watch."

XXII

Agora Ireland

"Two things matter most to a direct-marketing publishing house," I began. "Copy and list."

Thom and I stood together at the front of the room, with a white board on an easel behind us on which I'd written the words "Copy" and "List" in big red letters. Before us was the Agora Ireland team—Lief, Claire, Deirdre, Clodagh, Martina, Cathleen, and Conor, who we'd hired just two weeks earlier to take over fulfillment manager duties from Claire after she'd been promoted. Thom and I had given this standard "Copy and List" training session many times but never before for a crowd so green. I wondered if anything we said would resonate. Our employees had already been doing their jobs for months, but they'd been working according to checklists, following instructions. They didn't see how what they did fit into the bigger picture. They understood small pieces of the practice of our business but none of the theory. It was time to change that.

"The idea is to identify people who might be interested in reading whatever it is you're publishing, in our case *International Living*," I continued. "Then we send them an invitation to take a look. The people you mail the invitation to are the list. At the start of the conversation, they are someone else's list. You pay the list owner a fee, and he allows you one-time access. Then you mail your letter to those names you've rented. A letter that you hope inspires the person receiving it, first, to open it rather than throwing it in the trash, and, second, to take you up on your offer—again, in our case, *International Living*. Make sense?"

I was giving the equivalent of a basic anatomy lesson to a group of people I'd hired to perform surgery. I paused to study my audience. Everyone appeared engaged, but what could they be thinking? I tried to read their faces but couldn't. The Irish must make good poker players. They never give any indication of what's really going on inside their heads.

It took months for the dots of our business to connect for new staff in Baltimore, where everyone had grown up with junk mail, which, boiled down, was the business we were in. Direct mail didn't exist in Ireland. What could Thom and I say to help this eager but raw crew understand what was going on here?

"That invitation you send out to the names on the list you rent is the marketing copy," Thom chimed in. "Those who respond by filling out the order form and sending you a check or their credit card information become your subscribers, meaning they're added to your list. Then you begin sending them the subscription service they've paid for. That's the editorial copy. "

I felt at once proud of the little team we'd assembled, sitting up at attention and listening so earnestly, and worried for them. What chance did they have of learning what they needed to know to be good at their jobs?

"Really," I said, "we're in the business of helping our readers explore the benefits and upsides of a life lived, at least in part, across borders… of a life like, well, like the one Lief and I are enjoying here in Waterford."

Thom and I spent the next few hours drilling down to help our young team understand those upsides. "People sign up to begin reading *International Living*," I explained, 'because they're looking for options for retiring sooner and cheaper. They're worried they won't be able to afford retirement in the States, so we show them where and how they could retire better overseas, even on a really limited budget."

At 1:00 p.m., it was time to wrap up our bootcamp and return to the work of the day. "Everyone was listening intently," I said to Thom, as he, Lief, and I headed out of St. Catherine's Hall and across the street for a walk in People's Park so we could regroup on the morning's meeting in private.

"Yes, they were," Thom said, "but nobody asked any questions. Not a single one. That's not a good sign."

"That worried me, too. Well, let's see what they come up with for tomorrow's Goals exercise."

When we reconvened the next morning, I launched into a discussion of the ways we looked to make the business profitable. Thom passed around copies of the most successful advertising inserts *International Living* had run in the past that I'd selected to use as examples. Most presented real estate offers in key markets overseas, from beachfront lots in Costa Rica to oceanside villas in Belize.

"To grow our insert advertising program, we need a long list of new product ideas," I explained. "So what new products and services can you imagine that our readers might perceive as valuable?"

Over the next two hours we made a list of new property offers to test through advertising inserts. That was exactly what I'd hoped would come of the meeting. Unfortunately, not once during that conversation did a member of our Irish team join in. Like the day before, they'd sat looking alert and appearing engaged but silent as Lief, Thom, and I brainstormed. I told myself not to be discouraged. These were big new concepts.

But were we getting through to them at all?

"I asked each of you to prepare goals to share with the team," I began. "Clodagh, can we start with you?"

"Yes, alright," Clodagh said. "Well, you asked me to set circulation growth targets for the magazine for this year and next. But I looked at our current subscriber count, and it has grown. We already have more readers than we did this time last year. How many readers is it you want? I didn't really understand how to set a goal for readership growth when, really, the readership is already growing enough."

Growing enough? What did that mean—to grow "enough"? How many subscribers did I want? How long is a piece of string? I wanted as many subscribers as I could get. I wanted more next month and more the month after that and many more next year and many more the year after that and on and on. I wanted constant growth. How could my marketing manager not understand that? That was marketing's raison d'etre. Growth… and then more growth.

"Well, yes, we have had some increase in subscribership over the past year," I agreed, trying not to let the disappointment I was feeling come out in my voice, "and that's great. But it's still only a starting point. Our objective, no matter how much growth we've had, is more growth. No matter how many readers we have, we want more readers. Do you see what I mean?"

Clodagh looked confused and mildly annoyed. We weren't off to a good start. I tried to keep mindful of the big cultural divide Thom and I were vaulting across. No matter how much we have, we Americans are programmed to go after more. The Irish, on the other hand, seemed very able to be happy with whatever they already had. Philosophically, that perspective might make them more evolved, but this wasn't a study of metaphysics. This was business.

I decided to take up the conversation with Clodagh privately after our meetings.

"Okay, let's stick with marketing," I continued, trying to get the conversation back on track. "Claire, what objectives do you have in mind for your new role as marketing assistant?"

Claire told us her main goal was to cut marketing expenses by fifteen percent, an objective my accountant husband and I both applauded. Next, Office Manager Deirdre had ideas for reducing local expenses, again, making both Lief and me happy. Martina told us she aimed to have financial reports ready for our review by the fifteenth of each month. Super. Then Cathleen proposed we invest in new software that she said would make the process of producing the magazine much more efficient and that would also allow for more creativity when designing ads and inserts. Great idea.

I was heartened. Those were specific and worthwhile goals. Nothing earth-shattering but at least all relevant and showing signs of life. All that was left was to hear from our newest hire, Conor, who'd been working as a clerk at a filling station before he'd joined our team earlier that month. He had been the sole respondent to the ad we'd run in the local papers for a Fulfillment Manager. He had zero relevant experience, but, as Lief had put it after we'd interviewed him, "he's young, seems capable, and he showed up on time." We decided to take a flyer, as the Irish put it, and give the kid a chance. When speaking with him about today's Goals session, I'd told him that we understood he was only beginning to get his feet under him and didn't expect much but maybe he could meet with Claire and the others to come up with preliminary thoughts for his new role.

"Conor," I said, "were you able to speak with Claire about the responsibilities of fulfillment manager? What are your thoughts at this just-getting-started stage?"

In response, Conor, who'd gone pale and looked terrified, stood up, turned, and, without a word, walked quickly across the room and out the door.

Thom and Lief wore *what-in-the-world-just-happened?* expressions that must have matched my own. The rest of the team was staring straight ahead blankly. They didn't seem nearly as shocked as Lief, Thom, and I were. What did they know that we didn't?

"Aye, poor lad," Claire spoke up finally. "I wasn't sure he was going to work out. He was intimidated by ye', sure he was," she said. "Frightened."

"Of me?" I said. They didn't all feel that way, did they? I felt suddenly a little sick to my stomach.

"Aye, of ye' and of Lief, both," Claire said. "And, if I'm honest, he wasn't comfortable working for a woman, either. He never should have taken the job, sure he shouldn't."

At Agora in Baltimore, I'd been in charge of a staff of thirty by the time I was thirty-two, including as many men as women, some ten and more years my senior. It didn't matter to me if you were a man or a woman if you could do the job I needed done and I didn't think my gender should matter either, but these Irish seemed to get stuck on the point. Sometimes, I'd found, when it was a man on the other end of the conversation—from the little bent rising damp guy with the screwdriver who only wanted to speak with "himself" to Seamus from the IDA and the government tax guys who came to audit our books every year—I had trouble getting their attention. They looked through me to Lief, unable to process the idea that Lief worked for me, not the other way around. I found it annoying mostly because it hindered progress. If these guys didn't want to do business with me, they should get out of my way.

"I'll repost the ad for Fulfillment Manager," Deirdre offered. In other words, we shouldn't expect Conor to return.

"We'll find someone else quick enough, sure we will," Claire offered. "And don't worry about Conor. He'll go on the dole, no worries. He'll be grand, sure he will."

Go on the dole? *Angela's Ashes* flashed in my mind. Lots of Irish on the dole in that story, but was it really still a thing? Sure, in famine days, folks needed help, but who, in this Celtic Tiger era, would walk away from a good-paying job promising training and upside and choose to go on unemployment? And why did Claire seem to think that was a reasonable life choice or that we'd be worried about Conor anyway? I had no sympathy for Conor. He'd walked away from opportunity and that was on him.

"Yes, that would be great, if you'd repost the ad, Deirdre, thank you," I said and bit my tongue before saying anything more. Sometimes I felt like we were closing the divide between us and the Irish, then I'd witness a new element of their world view that left me wondering if we'd ever come to understand each other.

As we got in the car at the end of the day to pick up the children, Lief, Thom and I looked at each other and, at once, started to laugh. It was a release. We had yet to speak about the morning's meetings or the Goals exercise that had resulted in our first staff departure. It was difficult to talk about anything delicate in the office. Everyone could hear everyone else's conversations.

"I'm so frightening that the poor guy chose to flee the room rather than respond to my question?" I said.

"Well, I find you terrifying sometimes," Lief said, laughing. I reached over from the passenger seat to punch him in the arm.

"Has anything like that happened before?" Thom asked from the back seat.

"Well, we had one guy get up from an interview and walk out," I said, remembering marketing manager candidate Robert. "But, no, no other staff has run out on us. Today was another unprecedented experience. They come quick on the heels of each other, we're finding."

AT HOME IN IRELAND

It was an early summer Friday evening, unusually sunny and warm, the sky high and blue, and we were headed to the coast for dinner with Morette. Maybe this straight-talking American boss woman sent some Irish hightailing it in the direction of the nearest exit, but I wasn't going to let that bother me. In twenty minutes time, I'd be relaxing on the window bench in Morette's kitchen table and that was one place where work worries couldn't find me.

XXIII
The Most Legendary Mystery In Irish History

"You eat salmon, of course, don't you, Thom?" Morette said as she took the whole fish from its brown paper wrapping. "I got it just now, on my way home, from Billy Burke in Ballybricken," she continued, before Thom could respond to her question. Since we'd arrived ten minutes earlier, Thom hadn't had a chance to say much of anything except thank you for the invitation to dinner. I'd prepared him, explaining that Morette was one of the most gracious hostesses I'd ever known for many reasons including her ability to keep the conversation interesting and unfaltering.

"I only buy salmon from Billy Burke," Morette was saying. "I call ahead to make sure it's fresh. This was caught this morning off our coast. I'll roast it with a bit of honey. We'll love it, sure we will," she said taking a roasting pan from the cabinet and turning on the oven.

After welcoming him to her home, Morette had installed Thom by my side on the bench beneath her kitchen window. Kaitlin sat next to him, Jackson on my lap, then Morette sent Lief off in search of extra chairs from the dining room and returned to preparing our meal.

"We'll have a tart for dessert. I hope you like pear," Morette said to the room, pulling a bowl of chopped pear from the refrigerator. "I have the filling already made. Just need to roll out the pastry. Won't take a minute. What will we have while we're waiting for the dinner? I know," she began, answering her own question, "a glass of prosecco. I have some chilled. It will be lovely on this warm summer evening." She walked over to the hutch against the far wall and pulled out eight crystal flutes.

It was a scene I knew well but savored every time, and now I was able to share it with Thom.

"A fine day, wasn't it?" Morette continued. "A grand summer's day. David will be home soon. He and the boys have been swimming. They'll have good appetites.

"Now, Thom," she said, "you must tell us about yourself. We want to hear all about you. Is this your first time in Ireland?"

"Yes, it is," Thom said, then, before he could expand on his answer, Morette broke in again.

"Ah, well, you need to see something beyond Waterford, then,

THE MOST LEGENDARY MYSTERY IN IRISH HISTORY

don't you? We should plan a day out. I know! We'll take a drive along the Copper Coast. Kathleen and Lief have seen a bit of it, but we should plan a proper tour. It's glorious, and this is the time of year for it. Long days and clear skies. We'll go this weekend." Before Thom could agree or demur, Morette wiped her hand on her apron and turned from him to look in the direction of the hallway. "Ah, I hear the door. That must be David and the boys."

"Straight upstairs to change from your wet things," she called out in the general direction of the front of the house. "The salmon will be ready in fifteen minutes," she said as she laid the table with china and silver for nine. "Now I'd better get the tart in the oven," she said opening the door of her Stanley. "Yes, the salmon is perfect. I'll just swap it out for the tart, and we'll be grand, won't we."

A few minutes later, David, Edmund, and Jamie arrived to the kitchen in dry clothes, introduced themselves to Thom and wished him a hearty welcome, then we all settled in for Morette's salmon with potatoes and parsnips.

"David, we want to show Thom here something of this green island before he goes. This is his first time here! We don't have any plans for Sunday, do we?" Morette asked as she refilled our flutes with prosecco. "We can stop for lunch in Stradbally. Have we told you the story of the Stradbally postman?"

"The Stradbally postman?" I said. "No, I don't think so."

"In all this time we've never told you about the Stradbally postman," she said dramatically as she began serving the salmon.

"David, we've been remiss. How can we not have told Kathleen and Lief the story of the Stradbally postman? It's perhaps the greatest mystery in the history of Ireland. Certainly in the history of County Waterford. Thom, you'll appreciate this, as well. Christmas Day, 1929, the postman of Stradbally disappeared. He'd delivered the mail, all the packages for Christmas... then was never seen again."

"Delivered the mail?" I said. "On Christmas?" I knew Morette would explain the guy's disappearance, but I wanted to know why he was out on his bicycle delivering the mail on Christmas Day in the first place.

"Aye, yes, of course. At that time here in Ireland, Christmas presents were sent through the mail to family and friends in other parts of the country. The postmen were like Santa Clauses. They would work Christmas Eve and Christmas Day, to make sure everyone got their gifts. That Christmas morning in 1929, the postman of Stradbally set out to make his rounds. When he hadn't returned by the following morning, his wife sent out the alarm. The gardai were called and, when they searched, they found the postman's bicycle and empty post sack on the side of the Kilmacthomas road. That's where the postman lived. In Kilmachthomas.

"Now, don't speak of this when we stop in Stradbally on Sunday. No one in Stradbally ever speaks of the missing postman. And for decades no one but those who were there on the day knew what had happened to the poor man."

THE MOST LEGENDARY MYSTERY IN IRISH HISTORY

"So what did happen to him?" I asked from the edge of my seat.

"Well, the man drank too much in the local pub, fell down, hit his head on the bar, and died, right there on the floor of the pub, with a roomful of fellow drinkers looking on," Morette said.

"So it was an accident?" I said, thinking the climax of the story didn't quite live up to the build-up of the story.

"Well, there was also a fight, between the postman and another of the patrons in the pub. But, yes, the cause of death is believed to have been the fall. The trouble was that no one could admit to the accident because no one could admit to having been in the pub. It's illegal to sell or to buy alcohol on Christmas Day. It was in 1929 and it is still today. If the postman's accidental death in the pub got out, the owner of the pub would be in great trouble. More than that, the pub was full of gardai! They were there drinking alongside the rest of them. So they covered it up. The gardai and the village folk who'd been witness. Covered up the whole incident. Still, to this day, the postman's body has never been found. We'll take you to the pub where it happened when we visit."

How could an entire town keep a thing like where and how a poor postman's body had been disposed of a secret for decades? What drama.

We agreed to meet Sunday morning for our guided tour of the Copper Coast and villages along the way. I'd wanted to see more of the Copper Coast since we'd made the move to Waterford. We rarely allowed time for these kinds of outings, and an entire day doing nothing but being part of the Irish landscape was overdue.

Alas, the trip was not to be. When we returned home that evening, after I'd put Jackson to bed, I booted up my laptop to check emails one more time for the day. Bill had written to say that he, Mark, and members of Agora's Executive Committee were in the UK, meeting with managers of Agora's London office. They hadn't planned to come to Ireland as part of this trip but had decided that it'd be a shame to miss a chance to get together. They'd be arriving Monday, staying three days. "We can review your financial statements, marketing reports, and anything else you'd like to talk about," Bill said in his email.

I switched gears without a thought. Gone were the logistics of caravanning to the shimmering Copper Coast, shoved aside to make room for a review of current marketing reports and financial statements. It'd take every hour between Friday night and the Executive Committee's arrival in Waterford on Monday for me to prepare for the last-minute meetings, and that was okay. We could tour the coast another time. Plus we *had* had some successes in our efforts to get Agora Ireland off the ground, and I wanted to take this chance to shine a light on them. My Agora muscle memory took over.

I called Morette, who wasn't surprised to hear I was canceling our trip because I'd decided I needed to work through the weekend. I'd backed out of plans with her because of work conflicts at least as often as I'd kept our dates. Then I set about preparing my presentation. I knew what I was in for. We weren't where we wanted to be, and I was sure the Executive Committee members coming to town with Bill and Mark wouldn't miss any chance to remind me of that. I dreaded that part, but that apprehension was secondary to the excitement I felt at the chance to spend a few days with Bill and Mark. They understood me like no one else. They weren't intimidated by my shark side. They appreciated it. And they were familiar with the internal conflicts that ruled my every day. I was hard-core and insecure at the same time, worried always that I wasn't working hard enough or moving fast enough, sure of what I wanted but always open to a better option if one presented itself, both hard-boiled and sentimental, pragmatic and romantic, a wife and a mother with a consuming job. I was a mixed-up mess that they found charming company and a capable business partner.

I couldn't wait for Agora Baltimore to get to town.

XXIV
Rody Keighery's Auction Rooms

Bill, Mark, and the Executive Committee came to Waterford and gave me a quick Agora fix. I wouldn't say I enjoyed the meetings, with Myles taking every chance to point out that Agora Ireland wasn't meeting minimum profitability expectations, but I made the best of the time with Bill and Mark. I was able to have lunch with them privately one afternoon, where we discussed plans for Agora Ireland's growth big picture. We three had wanted for years to diversify the *International Living* publishing group to include a real estate marketing division and maybe we were getting close to the point where that'd be a realistic possibility. We also talked about my personal experiences in Ireland. Lief and I were so busy building this new life that we rarely took time to pause and reflect on it. I appreciated Bill and Mark giving me a chance for that.

At the same time, I felt guilty about the time I spent alone with them. I knew that it bothered Lief, who'd been jealous of my at-

RODY KEIGHERY'S AUCTION ROOMS

tachment to Bill and Mark since early on when he'd recognized the strength of it. I didn't think I should have to apologize for relationships I'd had since long before I'd met him, but neither did I want to knowingly be causing Lief distress. It was another ongoing conflict that I dealt with by actively forcing it from my thoughts whenever it snuck its way into them.

After the Agora traveling show pulled out of town, Lief and I returned to the routines we'd built, and I took up the next phase of our creating-a-home plan.

All the wood planks of the floors had been re-laid and the windows and doors made right and replaced. Lahardan House had been transformed into the Irish home of my dreams—with one problem. After we'd placed the furniture that I'd shipped from the States, we saw that the contents of my little two-bedroom home in Baltimore didn't go far filling the five-thousand square feet we were now occupying.

In the two houses I'd owned in the U.S.—the home in New Freedom with Rick and the one I bought in Baltimore City after we separated—I'd found that I liked decorating and had a flair for it. If I hadn't found my way to Agora, where I'd learned I could support myself as a writer, I might have tried to make a living buying old houses to renovate, decorate, and flip. Now, with all this delightful Old World space to fill, my imagination was on overdrive. I'd been importing wallpaper from Baltimore, filling a suitcase with as many rolls as I could stuff in every visit, because I couldn't find the damasks and toiles I wanted in Waterford. My mother had been making drapes for me, likewise bringing fabric with her over successive visits because the one shop in Waterford carried only dressmaking options. She'd hand-stitched a gold edging onto a red brocade for the window in the back hallway and blue damask valances for the French doors in the living room. I'd lay awake at night wondering how to fill the beautifully appointed rooms.

Finally, one Saturday morning as Lief stood over a skillet of sizzling rashers while I scrambled eggs in the rich Irish butter we'd all come to love, I decided it was time to address the topic that'd so long been on my mind. "I was thinking," I said to Lief without turning my head to look in his direction.

"That's always trouble," Lief said before I could continue.

"Ha, ha. No, listen. I've made a list of the pieces of furniture we still need," I told him, "and I was thinking that, after breakfast, we could drive into the city to stop in at Rody's shop. Just to see what he has in stock."

"Again, you thinking is always trouble," Lief said, smiling and leaning over to kiss me on the forehead. "I don't think we're ready to go furniture shopping yet, dear. We've just finished paying off Noel and that little guy with the screwdriver, as you like to refer to him."

"I know, I know," I said. "But we could just take a look. Only window shopping, I promise. We haven't been into town on a Saturday since Jackson was born. It'll be a fun outing."

I like furniture with a history. Back in Baltimore, I'd spent one or

RODY KEIGHERY'S AUCTION ROOMS

two Saturdays a month poking around antique shops on York Road. My mother would meet Kaitlin and me at the Ashland Diner for breakfast, then we'd walk from shop to shop until we found something I convinced myself I couldn't live without. It was how I'd come to accumulate the furniture that'd been loaded into the container I'd shipped to Dublin.

I'd noticed Rody Keighery's Antiques on William Street shortly after our arrival in Waterford but hadn't had time to stop in until one day, while we were looking for a place to have lunch, Lief and I saw a big red and white banner on the sidewalk out front indicating "Auction Monday. Viewing On."

"Look," I'd said to Lief, "Let's stop."

Lief seemed as intrigued by the idea of an antiques furniture auction as I was. "I used to go to live auctions with my father in Santa Fe," he'd said. "They're lots of fun. Yes, sure, let's take a look."

"Hello to ye'," came a deep Irish voice from the other side of the room after we'd pushed open the front door and the bell overhead had jingled to announce our arrival. "Come on in, will ye' now, come right on in. What is it I can help ye' with today? What is it ye' are in the market to buy?"

"We're just looking," I said.

"Well, of course, of course," the big, jolly man said. "Come straight on in, so, and look around, no bother. We're having an auction Monday, you may have seen," the man continued. "Here in this room and upstairs are items for sale as you like. Items being offered at auction are in the back there, through that passageway. I can give you a catalog. No charge, as you're new to town. It's the least I can do to welcome ye'.

"I'm Rody Keighery, so you know," the man said as he handed Lief an auction catalog.

"Thank you," I said. "We'll just have a look around."

"Yes, of course, of course, no bother, no bother at all."

After we'd walked through the shop downstairs and up, Lief and I moved on to the area beyond the passageway to see what would be for sale at Monday's auction. Stepping into the auction hall, we stopped short. The massive space was packed with more antique furniture than I'd ever seen in one place at one time, large and small pieces, lined up and stacked on the floor, hung on the walls, and dangling from the twenty-foot ceiling. I could have spent all afternoon nosing around and I was on track to do so until Lief finally persuaded me it was time to leave by promising that we'd come back Monday after work.

When we returned on auction day, we heard Rody's booming voice before we'd even entered the premises.

"Peter Scott print," he was saying. "I have an opening bid of 20 punts… 20 bid… 20 bid… 25!... at 25… 30 bid… at 30… 35 bid… at 35… selling at 35… going at 35… sold at 35…

Then, with barely a pause to take a breath, Rody was on to the next lot.

"Oval mahogany dining table with extra leaf… who'll give me

RODY KEIGHERY'S AUCTION ROOMS

150 pounds for it… 120?… 100?… who'll give me 100 for it… lovely table… any interest… 100 bid by the lady in blue… at 100… at 100… any advance on 100… anyone else… very cheap… you're a robber, there, aren't ye', my dear lady in blue… selling at 100… last time at 100… sold at 100!"

Kaitlin had met us at the office after school so she, Lief, and I could walk over to Rody's together. Now we sat in three straight-backed wooden dining chairs near the back of the cold crowded hall—lot seven hundred and eleven, the stickers on them indicated—because they were the only three seats together we could find. The ballroom-sized space was filled to capacity. Hundreds of our fellow Waterfordians were sitting quietly all eyes forward.

In the center of the room at the far end stood Rody Keighery behind a heavy wooden podium, calling lot after lot, marking the sale of each with a swift crack of his hammer. It was 6:00 p.m. We should have been getting home for dinner to give Kaitlin time for homework, but I was entranced by the show Rody was putting on. He'd been at it since 10:00 that morning, and he had seven-hundred-and-fifty-eight lots to auction. The oval mahogany dining table with the extra leaf was lot five hundred and twenty-two. By my calculations, Rody would be entertaining bids from his big wooden podium until well past 10:00 p.m.

"Carved oak hall chair… 25 pounds for it… 25 bid… any advance on 25… 30?… anyone at 30?… oh, now, come on, no interest… who'll give me 30 for this lovely hall chair?"

I picked up the white card printed with number six hundred and forty-nine that we'd been given with our catalog and held it up in the air.

"Ah, the young lady in the back… 30 to you, miss…

"Any advance on 30? No… selling at 30… standing at 30… fair warning at 30… sold at 30… thank you, miss."

I'd bought a chair. I didn't need that chair and had no idea where I'd put it. At the time, we were still living in Mark Breen's furnished cottage with barely room for our luggage much less additional furniture. Plus, I hadn't discussed buying a chair or anything else with Lief.

"Framed antique map of Waterford… a tenner… who'll give me a tenner for it?"

I put up my bid number.

"I have 10 pounds… at 10… anyone else… any advance on 10… 10 bid… 10 bid… at 10 last time… fair warning… I'm taking no prisoners… I'm here to sell… sold for 10 quid!"

Lief took the bid card out of my hand and put it in his lap.

"Antique grandfather wall clock… 40 quid… surely, 40 quid… that's very cheap for this beautiful grandfather clock… keeps perfect time… you'd understand what a bargain this is at 40 quid if I told you in whose house this clock hung for a century… 40 quid… ah, come on, for a grandfather clock like this one… 40 quid… 40 pounds…"

I grabbed the bid card from Lief's lap and held it up high.

"I have 40 quid in the back now… 40 quid… any advance… 45 quid in the front here… at 45…"

RODY KEIGHERY'S AUCTION ROOMS

I held up my card.

"50 in the back… at 50 in the back… 55 down front… at 55…"

I held up my card.

"60 to the young lady in the back… at 60… at 60… at 60… you're out, are ye', here in the front… it's your bid, miss, in the back… at 60… at 60… at 60 on the hammer… come see me after and I'll tell you whose house this clock came out of…"

I didn't dare look over at Lief as Rody moved on to his next lot.

"It's getting late, and I think you've bought enough," Lief finally said, breaking the spell I'd fallen under. "But now we need to wait until the end to pay for everything."

Lief seemed a bit bothered, but I was thrilled. Taking part in the auction had been great fun. "I'll walk Kaitlin home," I said, "if you don't mind staying to settle things."

A few hours later after I'd put Kaitlin to bed, Lief came to the door carrying the hall chair and the map.

"They agreed to keep the grandfather clock overnight," he said, "when I explained that I was walking home. We'll need to stop by tomorrow to pick it up. But what are we going to do with it? What are we going to do with any of it? Where do you want this chair?"

I put the chair at the foot of the stairs.

"I can't fit by there," Lief said. "I'm going to bump into that chair every time I turn that corner." Not if you're careful, I thought.

Practicalities like access were far down on my list of decorating priorities. As far as I was concerned, the foot of the staircase in Mark

Breen's cottage was an ideal place for the high-backed oak hall chair. Still, I didn't want to make an issue of something so silly as where to place a chair.

I had an idea. Maybe Rody would sell the chair for me at his next auction.

"Of course," Rody said, when I put the question to him the next day. "No bother at all."

I set a reserve price for the oak hall chair of 40 pounds, and Rody sold it for that at his next auction six weeks later. I'd gotten my investment back including the costs of buying and selling, and the chair was permanently out of Lief's way. Plus I'd learned something. Rody was up for acting as my personal broker.

When I decided to make the move to Ireland, I resolved to take all the antique furniture I'd bought during my shopping outings with Kaitlin and my mother with me. I thought having those familiar things around would give Kaitlin and me some continuity. Plus, I didn't know what awaited us in Waterford. Would I be able to replace the household's worth of furnishings I'd spent years accumulating? It had seemed safer to bring it with us.

My experiences with Rody showed me I needn't have worried. His shop was stuffed every time I visited and his catalogues overflowing for every auction with dining tables and chairs, settees, divans, sofas, beds, tallboys, armoires, credenzas, dressers, desks, sideboards, davenports, carpets, paintings, prints, chandeliers, crystal, china, silver, candelabras, and on and on. The inventory was constantly turning

RODY KEIGHERY'S AUCTION ROOMS

over, and the prices were half or less what I'd paid for pieces in Baltimore that weren't as old or as nice. Shortly before I'd committed to the move to Waterford, I'd spent $150 for a pair of iron garden urns at one of the shops on York Road. Out back of his shop on my first visit, I saw that Rody had a store of dozens of urns. A pair similar to but bigger than the ones I'd bought in Baltimore was priced at 40 pounds.

Ireland is Europe's attic. Big volumes of old stuff finds its way onto the island and then cycles around. The country is awash in pieces that the shopkeepers I'd frequented in Baltimore would have fought over. Rody'd told me once that nearly all his auctions were attended by East Coast dealers who'd make the trip to Waterford to buy container-loads of inventory to ship back to their U.S. outlets. To the Irish, the pieces these dealers were willing to travel thousands of miles to have a chance to bid on were commonplace. Why get all hot and bothered over this eighteenth-century inlaid desk or that Victorian overmantle when another was sure to come along presently?

The Saturday morning that Lief agreed to make the trip to the city to visit Rody's shop for the first time after Jackson was born, I kept my promise. I didn't buy anything, just strolled Jackson up and down the aisles. I did, though, note the date of the next auction, two

Mondays away. From Rody's shop we went to Reginald's Pub for a carvery lunch, and I started working on Lief.

"Did you notice the date for the next auction?" I asked, as I picked up Jackson from his stroller so I could give him a bottle while we waited for the waitress to bring our order. We'd dropped Kaitlin at Sophia's for the afternoon. Gerri would bring her home after dinner.

"I did," Lief said.

"I was thinking maybe we could plan to stop by after work that day."

"What did I say about you and thinking?" Lief said, smiling. *I'll take that*, I thought. *That wasn't a no.*

After lunch, we went the long way home, traveling the back roads John Rohan had introduced us to the day he'd taken us to see Lahardan House for the first time. It was as fine a summer day as we'd seen, and I savored the view out the car windows of giant willow trees and high stone walls on both sides.

A half-hour later, we made our way down our drive and Lief pulled around behind the house to park. I got out, opened the back door, and picked Jackson up from his car seat. "Will you get the stroller out of the trunk?" I asked Lief. When he did, a silver dollar fell from it onto the white gravel we'd laid.

"What is that?" Lief asked.

"Ha!" I said. "I'd say that's from Rody. He must have slipped it into Jackson's stroller when I wasn't looking. We can thank him when we stop by for the auction in a couple of weeks."

XXV
An Irish Cottage Garden

Over the coming months, I was in Rody's Auction Rooms at least three times a week. I'd walk over from the office at lunchtime or stop by before starting my work day. There was always someone in the shop by 7:30, and I got to know Rody's staff well. I was a regular fixture at every auction, seated as near to the front as possible. Rody and I developed a shorthand. If he saw that I was going to bid on something that he didn't think was good value—because the guide price was too high or the piece was damaged—he'd ignore my raised bid card and shake his head slightly. I'd put my card back down in my lap until the next item I had a mind to buy came up for bid. I'd wager that I was Rody's number-one customer as I was outfitting Lahardan House. In time we formed a real friendship.

I bought enough tables, chairs, sofas, paintings, mirrors, carpets, and prints through Rody to furnish Lahardan House several times over. Literally. Every time I found something in Rody's shop or at auction that I thought was a better fit than something I already had, Rody would send one of his lads to deliver the new piece and carry away the one it was replacing, which he'd add to the catalog for his next auction, just as he'd done with the oak chair. Detail by detail, I was making Lahardan House the Irish Georgian country home I'd carried in my imagination since the day I'd decided to make the move to Waterford.

The grounds and the outbuildings of Lahardan House's seven acres were another story. When we'd moved in, we'd laid white gravel in a perimeter surrounding the house, so we could come and go without getting muddy. Otherwise, our rolling acres remained an overgrown, tumbledown mess.

I'd been buying books on traditional Irish gardening and had it in my head that I wanted to create a cottage garden on the side of the house in a spot where we'd be able to see it from the windows of the kitchen and the family room. Irish cottage gardens are informal and dense. In a fully-fledged cottage garden, no soil peeks through the mass of ornamental and edible plants. Originally, the cottage garden was a practical attachment to every cottage, providing vegetables and herbs for the kitchen and including fruit trees, sometimes a beehive, and even livestock. It was one vestige of English rule the Irish didn't seem to object to. They'd made it their own, prioritizing heather, bog rosemary, sheep's bit, and other flowers common on their island. In my cottage garden, the flowers would dominate. I'd have primroses and violets, old-fashioned roses and lavender for their scents, and daisies of many colors.

One Saturday during our second June in the house, when it was finally warm enough to venture outdoors, I put eighteen-month-old Jackson in his red wagon and pulled him over to my garden spot with me. Kaitlin was playing in the clubhouse my Dad had created for her in one of the outbuilding ruins behind the barn, and Lief was busy with his own projects, doing what he could to repair and make useful the various farm structures he continued to uncover from beneath decades of brambles and brush. The more he dug his way into the growth all around the house, the more wood and stone sheds and storerooms he unearthed.

I left Lief to carry on with his archeological efforts and positioned little Jackson so he could watch from his wagon perch, put on my gardening gloves, picked up my hoe, and began hacking at the mass of weeds all around. I whacked and walloped at the ground, dragging away bunches of thorny vines into a pile for burning, then, thud. What was that? I'd struck something inorganic. Hacking a few more times, I revealed a rusted bit of some piece of farm equipment I couldn't name. Lief and I had been discussing renting a dumpster, which the Irish called a skip. He was finding mounds of old tools and tractor parts, plus rotted wood and burlap bags of refuse inside the outbuildings he was working his way through. Meantime, until we'd had a skip delivered, Lief had created a kind of landfill area behind the barn. I'd carry this thing, whatever it was, over there.

After I'd dragged it to our make-do garbage dump, I returned to my work spot. A few more hacks and, again, thud. This time I'd hit rubber. An old tractor tire. I knelt down to try to uncover it enough so I could drag it away, but I was getting tired and Jackson was growing fidgety. I'd been at it for more than an hour, and, though I'd made no discernable progress, my shoulders and back were aching. As a kid, my brothers, sister, and I were enlisted regularly to help my father with the yard work—raking leaves or clearing underbrush from around the house. Sooner or later, we'd each grow tired. When we did, we'd ask our father if we could take a break. His response was always the same. "You really don't think you can do anymore?" he'd ask. To which whichever one of us had made the request would nod solemnly. "Okay," he'd say, "then fifteen more minutes. When you've done all you can do, do fifteen more minutes. Then you can be done."

"So, little guy," I said to Jackson in his wagon, "Mommy's pretty tired. How about we work fifteen more minutes then call that enough for our first day and go see what Daddy's up to?" Fifteen minutes of hacking later, I stood up to brush the dirt and brambles from my knees then picked up the handle to Jackson's wagon and pulled him toward the barn and his father.

The next Saturday and the Saturday after that followed suit. By now it was July, and I'd still made no progress anybody could notice

AN IRISH COTTAGE GARDEN

in my efforts to prepare the bed for my cottage garden. I finally had to admit I was no match for the great Irish outdoors. I needed help. Gerri was a professional landscaper. Kaitlin and Sophia had become inseparable, so Gerri and I were having lots of chances to get to know each other better. Gerri was slight but strong, a single mother living in an old cottage she was renovating herself. Every time I stopped by to drop off Kaitlin or pick her up Gerri would invite me inside to show me her latest project. She'd just finished re-plastering and painting Sophia's room and had hung netting with gold stars from the ceiling over Sophia's wood-framed bed creating a fairy princess setting. Gerri had a great sense of style. Plus, she knew everything about plants. I gave her a call, and she agreed to come size up the situation.

The Saturday morning I was to meet Gerri to discuss a plan for our yard, I pulled Jackson and his wagon over to where I'd hoped to put the bed and stood alongside him with one of my gardening books open to a double spread of a mature Irish cottage garden. Behind me, at the end of the driveway, were plastic pots of the flowers I'd bought—roses, violets, lavender, and daisies, plus delphiniums, phlox, lupins, lavender, hollyhocks, peonies, and foxglove. I imagined the flowers mocking me. They knew I couldn't put them in the ground until I'd prepared the earth. *Okay, okay*, I said under my breath. *Just hold on. Help is coming. You'll be planted soon.*

In my hacking, I'd discovered an old stone wall that I figured had once bordered someone else's garden effort. That became my goal—to clear a twelve-foot stretch along the length of the wall. From the garden spot, I had a full view of the back of now renovated Lahardan House. The front and sides of the house were exposed stone, but, at the back, the stone had been plastered over. We'd painted that back wall yellow and the back door, which opened to the mud room off the kitchen, red. On either side of the door I'd hung baskets of geraniums from iron hooks. Just outside the door was the hand pump for the property's original well. I'd planted more geraniums in a big clay pot and positioned the pot alongside the pump. I enjoyed the red of the clay pot, of the geraniums, and of the mud room door against the backdrop of the white stones we'd had brought in by truckloads and raked around the house. We'd put up a three-rail wooden fence to separate the house grounds and the stables. Now our border collie, Daisy, was running back and forth between the house and the fence, and Kaitlin was carrying a tray of snacks out the mud room door. She was headed to her clubhouse to wait for Sophia.

The sound of Gerri's tires on the white gravel pulled me out of my dream state.

"Well, now," Gerri said, as she sent Sophia off to play and turned toward me "let's see what we've got to work with."

I held up my open book so Gerri could see. "This is what I'd like to create," I said.

"Yes, well, that's lovely, isn't it? You want to build that here, where we're standing?" Gerri asked.

"Yes, well, I'd like to plant a garden all along this stone wall here," I said, pointing. "I like the idea of framing the garden with the wall. Plus, we can see this spot from every window in the kitchen and family room, so we'll be able to enjoy a view of the garden every morning and evening."

I liked Gerri for the same reasons I liked so many women I was getting to know here in Waterford. She didn't waste words, and she didn't blow smoke. She told me what I needed to hear whether this hard-charging, Type A, "I can do anything and I can do it all by myself" American woman wanted to hear it or not.

"Kathleen, this is no small undertaking, what you're suggesting here," Gerri said, as she kicked in the brambles with her boot to expose another stray tractor tire. You need more help than I can give you. You and I can design the garden and place the plants, but we can't clear out this area." Looking at Gerri, all five feet six inches and maybe one-hundred-and-twenty pounds of her, I knew she was right.

"What you're proposing will require a pair of big strong arms. I know the man for the job. You remember Ian?"

Gerri had told me about Ian one Sunday evening when she'd come over to collect Sophia after a sleepover and I'd asked her to hang around for a while and have a glass of wine with me. Ian was Sophia's father, but Sophia had never met him. Gerri hadn't given me many details, but she had explained that Ian was British and living in the UK.

I nodded. "Yes," I said. "I remember you telling me about Ian."

"Well, he's moved to Waterford. Last week," Gerri said. "He wants to meet Sophia."

"Ah, wow," I said. "What does Sophia think of the idea?"

"I wouldn't say she's excited," Gerri admitted. "And neither am I, frankly. Ian has never been a part of our lives. I'm not sure how this is going to work out. But Sophia has agreed to meet her father, and I've agreed to allow him to spend time with her at the house but I've made it clear he's not living with us. He needs to find his own place. We'll take this one step at a time. Meantime, Ian needs work. He's capable. He could be able to clear all this out for you in a couple of weeks. Then you could have a load of good black soil delivered and Ian could spread it around for you. Then you and I could plant."

Maybe it was a risk to engage the estranged father of Kaitlin's best friend to do field work for us, but that seemed to be the way here. Any time I'd asked anyone in the office for a suggestion for how to get something done, the response invariably involved kinfolk. "Oh, my cousin can lay tile"… or "I believe my niece could help cater your party." I didn't mind. Usually, I didn't have any alternative.

I engaged Ian on a week-by-week basis. The tall, lanky, pale Brit with a red beard and a full head of scraggly hair to match was friendly and chatty. He arrived each morning by 8:00 and carried on with his labors until after we'd returned from the office each evening. As Gerri had predicted, in two weeks, Ian had cleared away all the remaining garbage in the area where I imagined my cottage garden and had leveled the earth along the stone wall. We ordered a truckload of dirt, which Ian spread to create a beautiful garden bed.

The following Saturday, Ian, Gerri, and Sophia returned together. Sophia ran off to join Kaitlin in the clubhouse, and I put Jackson in his wagon and parked him alongside the fresh garden bed. Gerri and I pulled out the map we'd drawn and began positioning pots to match the plan we'd devised. Ian came along behind us and dug the holes. Then Gerri and I placed the flowers, strategically, taking into account what she had taught me about distancing, height, color, and balance. When we'd finished, our starter plants didn't make quite the same impression as the mature garden in the double-page in my book.

"Everything grows quickly this time of year," Gerri said. "Don't worry. These plants will fill out. Next year this time this will be a showplace."

She needn't have been concerned. I couldn't have felt more satisfied. Once again, Ireland had rewarded my persistence by allowing me to realize one more piece of the dream I'd chased to her shores. Time to push ahead to the next item on our to-do list…

XXVI
Stone Walls

I was as busy in the office as ever but distracted myself on weekends with Lahardan House projects. Slowly, we were assembling the pieces of an Irish country life. We had the old stone house, the rolling green fields, the stone walls, the outbuildings, and the gardens. We'd set the scene. Now we needed to populate it.

Kaitlin wanted a pony. We had told her that as soon as we were in a position to be able to take care of a horse, she could have one. That promise had been the single thing about the move Kaitlin had embraced. All those nights our first year in Waterford when she had sulked away from the dinner table and gone off to her room to be alone and sometimes cry herself to sleep, I'd tried to comfort her by painting a picture of the life I was trying to create for us. I'd describe the old country house we were going to buy. "It'll have stables and pastures," I'd tell her, "and you'll be able to ride every day if you want." Finally the time had come when we could make good.

STONE WALLS

Over the months that he'd worked to build the cabinets and countertops for our kitchen, we'd gotten to know John Kerr well. Evenings and weekends he'd spent in our house, he'd chatted with us about his other greatest interest besides carpentry. John Kerr bred horses. After he'd finished our kitchen, we'd kept in touch. He'd invited us over one Saturday to see his house and his stables. I couldn't say which made John prouder—the big beautiful home he'd built for his family just over the hill from Cahir Castle or the dozens of prize horses and ponies he was raising in the fields all around it.

When we were ready to take ownership of one, we got in touch with John to ask what kind of horse he'd recommend.

"I have a gentle mare that would be an ideal first pony for Kaitlin," he said. "Why don't you bring her to my place next weekend so she can see for herself?"

Early the next Saturday morning, Lief, Kaitlin, Jackson, and I made the forty-five-minute trip to John Kerr's home in County Tipperary. Lief negotiated a price that seemed a bargain to me. John delivered the horse to our rebuilt stalls the next day. Kaitlin named her Chesapeake.

The trouble was that none of us had experience with horses. John gave us basic instructions for Chesapeake's care and feeding and we enrolled Kaitlin in riding lessons at an equestrian center nearby. Then, fortunately, before the consequences of our having no idea what we were doing became too apparent, a week after we'd taken possession of Kaitlin's new pony, another tall, sinewy Irishman came down our driveway. He walked up to our back door, knocked, and, when we answered, asked if we'd be interested in renting our front field to him. He lived in Portlaw, about ten minutes away, and he had noticed in passing that we'd put up fencing.

"I have two horses," he said, "and not enough grass for them to graze in. I thought, now that ye' have a fence, ye' might be interested in coming to an arrangement."

Terry didn't want to rent for cash but to trade for services. He'd help around the place if we'd let his horses live in our field. Seemed like a great deal to me. Plus, I was excited for the chance to get to know another Irishman. As I'd come to expect, Lief was less quick to agree but eventually came around. We told Terry he could keep his horses in our field if he'd do odd jobs around the property and, more important, help Kaitlin with Chesapeake. Terry brought his two horses to our field the next morning and then returned every day to tend them and spend time with Kaitlin and her pony. We were relieved to have an experienced horseman on sight every day. He showed Kaitlin how to feed, exercise, and brush the horse. After she'd grown more confident as a rider, he suggested that she begin participating in regional horse shows. He even let us use his trailer to transport Chesapeake to and from. It wasn't long until Kaitlin was winning blue ribbons at the competitions and finally seeming to enjoy Irish country life. Plus, with the three horses in

STONE WALLS

the field, Lief never had to mow. It was a win-win-win.

The week his horses took up residence in our field, we'd assigned Terry his first project. The stone wall bordering my cottage garden was at risk of toppling over. We asked Terry to rebuild that wall. He'd assured us the work would be no problem, but, over the weeks that followed, we checked for progress day by day and couldn't notice any. When we asked Terry about it, he assured us he was working away, but, a month later, we hadn't seen him lift a stone and the wall looked no different. Terry didn't seem to be in any hurry about our wall, but, as with everything, we sure were.

I didn't want to create a fuss with Terry and was happy as long as he was helping with Chesapeake, but I didn't want to lose my wall either. I called Ian. "Would you be up for rebuilding that stone wall bordering the cottage garden?" I asked. Ian said he could start the next day, and he did. A couple of days after that, I returned home from the office to find Terry waiting for me by the back door.

"Why would you pay that Englishman to work on that wall?" he asked as I got out of my car. "I was rebuilding that wall."

Ah, ha, I thought. Terry has discovered that Ian is doing the work he was supposed to be doing himself. And, to add insult to injury, he knows that Ian is British. I'd wondered if that would be an issue. I knew the British ruled the Irish for hundreds of years, but wasn't it time they put that phase of their history behind them? I remembered Deirdre's response when I'd suggested as much to her. "Maybe English rule was generations ago," she'd said, "but we Irish remember."

"But you seemed to have your hands full helping Kaitlin with Chesapeake," I said to Terry, "which we really appreciate. Ian has done work for us in the past, and we thought maybe he could help out again now. We understand that you just haven't had time to focus on it, but we didn't want the wall to collapse. It's really not a problem."

"It's a problem for me," Terry said. "No need for that Englishman to be here." Then, without another word, he walked over to his car, got in, and drove away.

A few days later, we came home to find our fields empty. Chesapeake was in her stall, but Terry's horses were gone. Bewildered, the next morning in the office, I shared the tale of Terry, Ian, and the stone wall with Claire.

"Aye, well, sure, Terry couldn't carry on working with ye' as long as the Brit is there on the property, working for ye', as well. If you want Terry to come back, you'll have to apologize to him."

"Apologize? For what?"

"Ye' have insulted him," Claire explained. "You shouldn't have hired an Englishman to do his work."

When I twisted my mind around to try to think like the Irish, I could see Claire's point, kind of, but I couldn't buy into it. All that mattered to me was saving the wall. I'd waited a month for Terry to fix it, and there'd been no progress. Ian, on the other hand, had

STONE WALLS

rebuilt half the length of the wall in a matter of days. Why would I apologize to Terry? Terry should apologize to me. But Terry had taken his stand, and I'd learned that the Irish don't compromise.

By now, Kaitlin was able to take care of Chesapeake on her own, so we relegated the Great Stone Wall Debacle to memory among the many other Irish experiences we knew we'd never understand. Ian worked two more weeks rebuilding our wall. Then, after he'd finished, without warning, he, too, took his leave. Gerri told me that Sophia wasn't that impressed with what she'd seen of her father. "I've never had a father before," Sophia had told her, "and I don't need this one now." Ian had kept stopping by to visit Sophia, but she'd begun refusing to see him. The situation was crushing for Ian, who'd come to Ireland to build a new life with a new family. When Sophia finally made it clear she was no longer interested in spending time with him, he decided to return to the UK. I thought Ian gave up too quickly. In my experience, this place rewarded patience and persistence. If Ian could have stuck it out a bit, maybe Ireland would have had a chance to work her magic for him, too.

XXVII
Dead Bats And A Friendly Ghost

Our third summer in Lahardan House passed too quickly. Kaitlin was becoming expert riding Chesapeake. My cottage garden was flourishing and kept me company while I cooked or cleaned in the kitchen. I had a full view of it from the window over the sink. My parents came to visit, and my father built us a chicken coop. It was Kaitlin's job to collect the eggs each day. She helped, too, weeding the vegetable garden we planted at the top of the hill behind the house. We'd discovered the remains of Lahardan's original kitchen garden in that spot and tried to recreate it, putting in raised beds, erecting a picket fence around that we painted yellow, and adding an arched trellis at the entrance.

Then, the days grew short again, colder, and wetter. It was dark by the time we got home from the office each evening, and we returned our attention to inside projects. The initial renovation work we'd carried out with Noel's help had restored the place

DEAD BATS AND A FRIENDLY GHOST

to a habitable baseline, but I had endless ideas for further improvements and had begun speaking with Morette's husband, David, about adding a back staircase and converting the storage room above the boiler and utility area behind the kitchen into a proper library.

Meantime, we were discovering quirks about our Lahardan House, starting with the plumbing. The realization that it wasn't what might be considered up to code back in the States came as a shock one chilly fall evening as I was preparing Jackson for his bath. I started filling the tub then took Jackson into the next room to undress him and lay out his sleeping clothes. When he and I returned to the bathroom, black feathers and tiny animal parts floated on the surface of the water. I let out a scream then ran out of the room and down the stairs carrying Jackson and calling for Lief.

"There's something in the bathtub," I told him when I found him in the family room reading the paper. "Would you please come take a look?"

"Something in the bathtub?" Lief said. "What do you mean?"

"Please just come see for yourself. I don't know what it is, but it's kind of gory."

He followed us upstairs and had a look. "It's a bat," Lief said. "A dead bat."

"How in the world did this happen?" I wondered aloud after we'd cleaned up the bat pieces and I was scrubbing the tub with Clorox.

"I have no idea," Lief said.

Two days later, whatever had happened happened again. More dead bat bits in our tub. We got more serious about trying to understand what was going on. We knew that the water tank for the house was in the attic, but we'd never gone up to inspect it. The night the second dead bat came out in furry bits from the faucet, Lief pulled down the attic stairs from the ceiling of the back hallway then climbed up them. I stood beneath the attic opening awaiting Lief's report.

"You're glad you're not up here seeing this for yourself," he said after he'd shone his flashlight into the black space. "The water tank isn't covered, and floating in it are several more dead bats and at least one dead mouse plus lots of dirt and dust."

"Yikes," I said. "Yuck."

"Get me a bucket and a shovel," Lief said.

I ran down the stairs to the boiler room, where we kept the tools, grabbed a bucket and a shovel, then returned upstairs to the foot of Lief's ladder. I handed Lief the shovel then held the bucket up over my head, as high as I could. Lief scooped a dead bat off the top of the water tank and dropped it into my bucket. Plop. Then he scooped a second dead bat and a third. Then the dead mouse. Plop, plop, plop. Then Lief ran the shovel along the top of the water in the tank like a blade, to skim off the floating animal body bits. Splash, they went into the bucket. Splash, splash, splash.

I carried the full, heavy bucket of body bits down the stairs,

DEAD BATS AND A FRIENDLY GHOST

out the mud room door, and across the yard to behind the barn, where I emptied it as carefully as I could, trying not to get any of its contents on my white sneakers.

"That's one of the most disgusting things I've ever had to do," I said to Lief after I'd rinsed out the bucket, washed off the shovel, and returned them to the boiler room.

"Tell me about it," Lief said.

"Do you think we should we put a cover on the tank?" I asked.

"Yes, I'd say that might be a good idea," Lief said, sarcastically. "We can stop by the DIY if we have time on the way home tomorrow to see what we can find that might work."

We didn't have time to stop by the DIY the next day or the day after that, then, that night, we found mouse bits in Jackson's bath, fortunately before I'd put him in it.

"Okay, Okay," Lief said. "I'll make time tomorrow to stop at the hardware store on the way home. I promise."

When he did, Lief found that the DIY didn't sell tops for home water tanks nor, they told Lief, did anyone else. The Irish didn't seem to think it was important to protect the home water supply. Lief bought a piece of thick corrugated plastic and cut it to fit atop our tank.

"How do people live like this?" I said, "I mean, I wonder if the water tank is installed in the same way in other houses or if whoever put the water tank in this house was daft or just asleep on the job."

"I don't know," Lief said, "but it does make you wonder."

I didn't want to offend anyone, but I couldn't help but raise the question the next day in the office.

"We've just realized," I said to Clodagh, "that the water in our house isn't drinkable. Is that the case in houses in general?"

"What do you mean?" Clodagh said defensively. "Of course you can drink the water in your house."

"Well, we've been having crazy things come out of the spigots. Last week, bat bits and then the other night tiny pieces of a decaying mouse came through the faucet into the bathtub. Lief went up into the attic to check the water tank and found that it had no cover and inside were more dead things—mice, bats, bugs, etc. It was awful. We can't drink that water, though we have been all this time. I'm just wondering if it's the same in all houses here or if Lahardan House is an anomaly."

"You can drink the water out of the tap at the kitchen sink," Clodagh said. "The pipe from the well connects directly to the kitchen faucet," she continued, as though speaking to a child. The Irish spoke to us like we were children often. We'd stopped letting it bother us.

"Then the water is diverted to fill the water tank," Clodagh explained. "Other taps in the house are fed by the tank, so you wouldn't drink from those, but, yes, of course, you can drink the water from the kitchen sink."

I wanted to say "What kind of a way is that to plumb a house?

DEAD BATS AND A FRIENDLY GHOST

It means you're bathing in water polluted by rotting animals!" Instead, I nodded politely, said, "Ah, okay, I see," and walked away. I knew that pushing the point could cause an incident that Clodagh might never recover from. The Irish, I reminded myself, have long memories.

We had dead bats in Lahardan House and live ones, too. When my parents came to visit, they stayed in the guest room across the landing from Lief and my bedroom. One night during their visit our second fall in the house, Lief and I were awakened by sounds of a struggle across the hall. We jumped up, ran across the landing, and pushed open the door to find my mother at the open window and my father on the other side of the room waving a broom in the direction of a bat that had settled atop one of the armoires. My mother was nearly screeching, her arms flailing. Dead bats weren't enough. Now we had live ones attacking my parents in their sleep.

Lief had sized up the situation quickly and taken off down the stairs. He was back in a flash holding a long wooden stick with a heavy wooden ball on one end. It was one of the African tribal pieces that we kept in the brass stand by the front door. Lief collected them. I'd bought this one for him at Rody's most recent auction, as part of a lot of African spears and weapons. I stepped out of Lief's way and he walked slowly and quietly into the guest room then, with one swift strike, walloped the bat on the armoire on the head and volleyed its corpse out the open window into the black night.

"Well, thank you, Lief," my father said. "Handy of you to have that thing there within easy reach. What do you call that bat whacker anyway?" my father wanted to know.

"I guess we'll call it a Bat Whacker," I said smiling in Lief's direction. My mother closed the window, and we all went back to sleep.

The next day in the office, I shared the tale of Lief and his bat-whacking adventures with Deirdre.

"You should be careful about retelling that story," she said. "Bats are protected in Ireland. All the construction on the island these past couple of decades has eliminated many of their roosting areas, so a law was passed to protect them. You aren't supposed to kill them or even disturb them. You could be fined."

"Well," I said with a grin, "that's the first bat we've killed, but two others have turned up dead in our bathtub. Please don't turn us in."

Settled into Lahardan House, we were haunted by the dead in other ways, too.

One night, as I was serving dinner, two-year-old Jackson turned his head suddenly to look past me to the back hallway.

"Oh, hello," he said cheerfully, as though he were speaking to any of us.

I lifted my head to look around to confirm. Yes, Lief and Kaitlin were still seated at the table and, yes, the back hallway was empty, but Jackson definitely thought he saw someone there. Who was he

DEAD BATS AND A FRIENDLY GHOST

talking to so clearly and directly?

This wasn't the first time young Jackson had engaged with personalities in the house the rest of us couldn't see. Maybe he had imaginary friends or maybe, as I was increasingly inclined to agree, we had a ghost living with us at Lahardan House. I'd never been one to believe in these kinds of things, but, as I'd told Beth on the phone, while I didn't believe in ghosts generally, I didn't *not* believe in this ghost. I've always been open-minded, but Ireland was expanding my perspective further to allow for ever-more unorthodox ideas, including the possibility that we were sharing our home with a spirit. Or, well, she was sharing her house with us. When I allowed the idea to fully form, I realized I liked it.

Jackson addressed his ghost most often in the back hallway that ran from the kitchen to the entry hall and living room, specifically in front of the big paneled window that looked out onto the hill behind the house where we'd planted the kitchen garden. I didn't know what Jackson thought he saw or heard, but I had to admit that I'd sometimes sensed a presence in that spot in the house as well. Passing through, I'd feel compelled to pause by the window. I'd want to reach out and touch the shutter or the sill for a moment, as if to connect with some attracting force I couldn't see. Kaitlin, my mother, and my father said they had also felt something in that hallway they couldn't name. Lief said he thought the back hallway was creepy but only because it was a dark back hallway. He didn't perceive anything otherworldly in that or any other part of the house and doubted my mother and Kaitlin when they insisted that they also heard music from the piano in the living room when no one was playing it.

My writer's imagination concocted a theory. The ghost Jackson spoke with was the daughter of Lord Waterford attempting to communicate with the new owners of the house her father had built for her on the eve of her wedding. We were only caretakers of a property with an enchanting past. Lahardan House would live on long after we'd come and gone. I appreciated that the original and rightful owner seemed happy to share it with us during our period of stewardship. I hoped she was pleased with our efforts to restore it to its original glory.

XXVIII
Weekend In Bantry

We passed another Christmas in Lahardan House, then winter turned to early spring. The daffodil bulbs Jackson and I had planted the autumn before pushed through the cold, wet earth, and we began checking every day for buds. I suggested we name the first one to flower, like Jefferson did at Monticello each season, and Jackson ran proudly into the kitchen one finally sunny Saturday afternoon holding a yellow bloom. "Roisin," he declared, after his best friend at daycare. As I was filling a vase with water so we could display Roisin on the dining room table, the phone rang. It was my mother, calling to say she and my father were looking at dates for their next visit and she had a suggestion.

"Your father," she said, "would like to plan a few days in Bantry. He says he's wanted to see it since he heard the song 'Bantry Bay' when he was a boy. He listens to the Irish Tenors sing it almost every day now, over and over. He bought their CD when you moved to Ireland. What do you think? Would you all have time to make the trip with us?"

Hearing that my father had found a way to make Ireland a part of his life back in Baltimore made me feel more connected to him. I still missed him so, and he had a point. Over the two years my parents had been visiting us in Waterford, we'd spent all our time together on home-improvement projects. Lief and I hadn't allowed ourselves to be tourists in Ireland since our visits together before we were married. We'd been fully consumed building the business and resurrecting Lahardan House. I'd arrived on the scene with the romantic notion that our lives would be a steady feast of ancient castles, formal gardens, and thatched-roofed pubs. We'd kept meaning to go in search of some, but since taking up residence, we'd yet to venture much beyond County Waterford. A relaxed family getaway seemed much deserved and long overdue.

"Yes, we'd love to go to Bantry Bay with you and Dad." I said with enthusiasm.

My parents arrived in Waterford six weeks later. After a few nights at Lahardan House so they could recover from their jet lag, we took off for Bantry.

Located in the parish of Kilmocomoge on the coast of County Cork about three hours west of Waterford City, Bantry is a picture-perfect Irish harbor village. My guidebook recommended Bantry House as the best place to stay, so I'd booked three rooms for three nights. We set out early Friday morning for the drive along the coast from Waterford through Dungarvan and then Cork until we reached the Wild Atlantic Way, the longest and arguably the most dramatically beautiful oceanside drive in the world.

Like in the northwest of the country at Sligo, this southwestern shoreline has been molded over millennia by tides and storms roaring and raging constantly against the earth to form towering cliffs and deep bays. The icy Atlantic batters the harbors of Bantry and the other traditional villages along the coast. The sea crashes and booms, but just inland all is quiet and calm. Narrow lanes lead to whitewashed houses with thatched roofs and pubs with red and yellow front doors.

We stopped for lunch in Youghal. This port town was one of the most significant maritime centers of medieval Ireland, with ships coming and going along trading routes to northern and western Europe. Youghal's most famous resident, according to the back of the menu in the pub where we ordered shepherd's pie all around, was Sir Walter Raleigh. Queen Elizabeth gave him a house and forty-thousand acres here on this coast, which he used to introduce potato crops to the island, changing the course of Irish history.

Ordinarily, Bantry may be three hours west of Waterford, but, with our unhurried stop for lunch and another an hour later for ice cream, it took us closer to six hours to make the trip. Ireland was doing what she did when I gave her the chance, slowing everything down, and, as was increasingly the case, I didn't mind. My brain was quieting, my shoulders relaxing. I was letting go, allowing myself to become part of the Irish landscape.

I knew from the instant Bantry came into view that this mini-getaway idea of my father's had been inspired. We saw the lake before we arrived to the town. It rolled out before us and sparkled in the sun. A dozen sailboats approached the harbor, returning from their days out. Nowhere is the air as fresh as it is along the Irish coast. I rolled down my window to breathe it in. A great flock of seagulls squawked overhead then darted toward the water. Kaitlin screeched and Jackson laughed. Kaitlin had always been afraid of birds; Jackson was always wanting to catch one.

"This was the site," my father began, as we approached the bay, "of the French expedition to Ireland in 1798, known to the French as the Expédition d'Irlande." Kaitlin giggled at his attempt at a French accent.

"The French were trying to help the outlawed rebel group known as the Society of United Irishmen with their planned rebellion against the British," continued my father, sticking his tongue out in Kaitlin's direction in response to her continued giggling.

"Key in this important battle was a fellow named Wolfe Tone, one of the founding members of the United Irishmen. He was the one to enlist the help of the French with the Irish rebel cause. Unfortunately, when insurrection broke out, a storm kept the French troops from landing here at Bantry, as had been the plan, and it would be another one-hundred-and-twenty years before the Irish were finally able to free themselves from English rule."

"And they haven't forgotten a single day of any of those one-hundred-and-twenty years," I said.

"Wolfe's efforts failed," he continued, ignoring my smart-aleck interruption, "but they raised a statue to him here in Bantry. Named the square after him, too. Maybe after we check into our rooms, we can walk over to see it."

"Great idea," I said. I couldn't wait to get out and explore.

A white-gloved bellman gave us keys to our three rooms, each attached to a big green tassel for a fob. *Ah, yes*, I thought. *This will be a lovely break.*

"Take note when of the furniture, art, and objects in the public rooms. Each is a small museum," the bellman said. "The eighteenth-century manor home known as Bantry House, where you'll be spending your weekend was built by a family of wealthy merchants from Limerick that eventually amassed eighty-thousand acres overlooking our Bay of Bantry."

As we walked, we could see the lake shimmering through every window we passed.

"The second Earl of Bantry," our bellman continued, "expanded and aggrandized both the house and the formal gardens to transform the property into a palazzo like the ones he'd seen during his Grand Tour of the Continent. His descendants continue to occupy the house but opened it as a hotel in the 1980s."

So the current owners were in residence? I wondered what it'd be like to have strangers traipsing through your family home. I didn't think I'd like it. Lahardan House was nowhere near as big or as grand as this place, but thinking about random people coming and going from her bedrooms made me sad and protective. On the other hand, if opening your doors to paying customers was what you had to do to keep a legacy property like this one in the family, well, it was what you did. Better that than risk losing something you could never replace.

"Now, here you are," he said, opening the door to the first of our three rooms. "The fireplaces in the public rooms are kept stoked day and night. If you'd like, we can keep the fires burning in your rooms, as well."

"No need during the day, but in the late afternoons and evenings, yes, that would be nice," I said. It was our third summer on this island. We knew "summer" was a misnomer. We'd be lucky if the sun shone warm enough for us to go without jackets, and I'd look forward to returning to a room warmed by an open fire after our outings each day.

Two hours later, we'd walked Wolfe Tone's square, admired his statue, and visited the French Armada Center with its scaled model of one of the French ships that tried but were unable to land at Bantry when the town really needed them.

"Let's head back to the hotel," I called out to Kaitlin up ahead. "Time to get ready for dinner."

I slowed my gait so the distance between me and the others could expand. I was enjoying the view from behind. Kaitlin was walking alongside her grandfather. She and he were engrossed in a private conversation, as they often were. Jackson was between his dad and his grandmother, holding both their hands, his little legs working double time to keep up.

The approach to Bantry House was a wide, gravel-covered lane up the hill overlooking the bay bordered on both sides by thick forest that created a canopy overhead. It was June, so we still had hours of daylight ahead of us, but it was chilly, as expected. I pulled my jacket closer.

"I'll race you, Jackson!" Kaitlin called out suddenly, and she and her little brother took off running ahead. Three-year-old Jackson didn't stand a chance, but he wasn't bothered. Kaitlin ran until she reached the fork in the drive then turned and asked which way to go—to the house or could we stop in the gardens first?

"Back to the house," I called to her. "It's late. We need to change for dinner. We can come back out to walk in the gardens again after we've eaten." The azaleas and rhododendron were in full bloom, and I understood Kaitlin wanting to stop to enjoy them. We never made time for indulgences like that. But we'd make time later tonight.

The next morning, we rose early and made our way downstairs to the dining room for breakfast. I ate quickly, thinking I'd return to the room to boot up my laptop and check emails from overnight before heading out for our day, but Lief got up to go ask the valet to bring our car around and Kaitlin, Jackson, and my parents were already on their way out the front door. Emails can wait, I thought, as I pulled on my jacket and hurried to catch up with everyone.

We planned to spend the day hiking in Glengarriff, twenty minutes away on the other side of the bay. Every August when I was a kid, we'd spend two weeks at a lodge in western Maryland. What I remember most from those summer vacations are the walks, my father in front with a red bandana tied around his bald head to keep the sun and the flies off, my mother walking behind him, then we four children following single file, youngest to oldest, meaning I brought up the rear. We each carried a walking stick and choosing one was the first order of business the day we arrived. Now my dad led us again, around the hills of Glengarriff, with a red bandana on his head, then my mother, followed by Kaitlin, Jackson, Lief, and me. Lief and I took turns carrying Jackson when his legs gave out, and, by lunchtime, we'd all found suitable walking sticks. We hiked along the sea, then inland, by rivers, streams, and lakes, the fragrance of heather everywhere and the hills all around carpeted in every shade of green.

"Can we take our walking sticks home with us?" Kaitlin asked.

"Yes, of course," I told her. "They'll be great souvenirs from this great trip with Gammy and Poppy."

"I'm hungry," Lief announced, and we all agreed we'd worked up big appetites and turned back in the direction of town for lunch, feeling relaxed and happy, and I realized, that, for the first time in as long as I could remember, I hadn't been thinking about work at all.

WEEKEND IN BANTRY

"We need more weekends like this one," I said to Lief, putting my arm through his and leaning up to kiss him on the cheek.

"You're the one who insists we can't ever take a day off from the office and who's always adding to the to-do list for the house," he said. "You're the one who's still so torn between our life here and the life you left back in Baltimore."

As a rule, Lief kept his feelings to himself, but I knew my close relationships with Bill, Mark, and others at Agora continued to bother him. Every time I prioritized work over family, he took it personally, as though I were treating him like the stepchild and maybe I was. "What if I'm not enough for you?" he'd asked me one night during our honeymoon trip in Turkey. I'd laughed off the idea, dismissed it out of hand, but shouldn't have. I should have made it clear that Lief was everything I wanted from life—and not only that late night in Istanbul. I should have been making the point clearly every day since, as well.

"Yes, yes, I know. You're right," I admitted. "I'll try to ease up. I'll slow down. Can you believe we've been living here more than four years already? It's going by so quickly."

In that moment, watching my family among the rolling green Irish hills, I wanted nothing more than lots more days like this one, and my promises to Lief to cut back on work were sincere.

As much as I'd treasured the time away at Bantry Bay with my family, though, on the long drive home my mind did what it did and reverted to business. By the time we'd arrived back home at Lahardan House, the enchanting weekend had been fully set aside. I'd returned to auto-pilot and, as I carried Jackson through the mud room door, I was already running my to-do lists in my head—both for the immediate term and the week ahead. I raced through Jackson's bedtime, unpacked in a rush, threw Kaitlin and Jackson's dirty clothes in the washing machine, and then I did something that no Irish woman I knew would have done. While Lief, Kaitlin, my mother, and my father assembled in the family room to consider which movie to watch, I sat down at the kitchen table to boot up my laptop. I couldn't help myself. I hadn't had time to download emails all weekend, and I wanted a jump on my Monday. Agora Ireland had turned a corner. We were growing by a good clip, and profits were where we'd been trying to get them all along. Bill, Mark, and Agora's Executive Committee were due for another visit in two weeks, and, for the first time since we'd moved to Ireland, I wasn't dreading the experience at any level. Bring on your worst, dear Executive Committee. I've got good news to share.

"Kath, why don't you come join us?" my father called over to me from the family room. "It's 9:00 o'clock on a Sunday night. What are you doing?"

"Go ahead and start the movie," I said without looking up. "I'll just be a minute. I'm checking my email." *Maybe I'll also take another quick look at my marketing reports*, I thought, *and create a top-line summary...*

XXIX
Irish Pubs

Two weeks later, Bill, Mark, and three other members of Agora's Executive Committee flew from Baltimore to Waterford to spend two days reviewing financial statements for the prior year, our fourth full year of operations in Ireland. I'd been counting down the days, expecting that Bill and Mark would be pleased with my progress. Finally, the members of the Executive Committee would have nothing to harass me about.

Our two days together went as I'd hoped, with Bill and Mark offering congratulatory comments and brainstorming big ideas for future growth. Now that the publishing business had been established and brought to profitability, we could focus on building the real estate marketing business we'd always wanted to connect to it. Our readers were looking for options for living, retiring, and investing overseas, and their number-one investment interest was real estate, both for personal use and for portfolio diversification—"for fun and for profit," as we put it. But how could we set ourselves up to identify the best choices for would-be American retiree investors? During our discussions, Mark made a recommendation.

"To take the business to a next level," he said, "you're going to need to put permanent boots on the ground in the markets on your short list. What if you opened local offices in the places you're reporting on most regularly? I think this would bring greater depth to your editorial coverage and also be as the first step to building the real estate business we've been imagining for so long."

It was a big idea with big implications. If we were going to have representatives working for us in different countries, we'd have to invest in infrastructure in those countries. And, if we were going to take on staff and overheads like office space, Lief and I would have visit regularly, to train, manage growth, and continually evaluate the return on our investments. That'd mean more time on the road, and, between travel to meet with Bill, Mark, and the Executive Committee in Baltimore and elsewhere and research trips, we—especially Lief—were already traveling a lot. I realized all of that in a flash and, just as quickly, just as I'd done in response to every other idea Bill and Mark had suggested in all the years I'd known them, I embraced every aspect of this one without hesitation. Nothing got me more excited than a new chance for travel and discovery except maybe an opportunity for a new business.

Mark had rolled all those things into one shiny new brass ring. It'd mean more work, but I'd never been afraid of that.

Lief and I made a short list of the countries where we believed having local offices should translate to better editorial content and more real estate marketing opportunities, targeting Ecuador, Panama, Nicaragua, and Honduras to start. If we were going to open offices in these countries, we would have to find people to run them. Mark suggested a job fair, and we considered dates for scheduling one in Baltimore as soon as possible. Another trip.

At the end of the two days of meetings, we celebrated Agora Ireland's most successful year yet with dinner at Emilianos, the best restaurant in Waterford. I took the evening as a chance for Bill and Mark to get to know our management staff. The Chianti helped get the conversation going, and when we'd finished the meal and Mark complimented me on my choice of restaurant, I was so pleased with how the night out was going that I wanted to keep it going and suggested we walk across town to T&H Doolans.

T&H Doolans, the oldest pub in Waterford, is famous for its traditional Irish music. Sinead O'Connor performed here. Officially, Doolans dates to the early 1700s, but Waterfordians insist sections of the structure are from the fifteenth century and some say a wall in the lounge was part of the original city walls built by the Normans in the 1200s. I wanted to give Bill and Mark an authentic night out in the Auld Sod. With its half-timbered façade, ancient wooden bar with Guinness on big brass taps, and live music sessions, Doolans seemed just the ticket. It didn't disappoint. Bill struck up a conversation with a local. A few minutes in, the tall Irishman he was talking to leaned over in Bill's direction and then suddenly he was on the ground. He'd lost his balance—but not his pint, which remained upright in his hand. He held his glass steady, spilling not a drop, as he returned to his feet and resumed the conversation. Bill was getting a real glimpse of life among the Irish.

Within six months Bill and Mark's visit, we'd launched operations in Quito, Panama City, Granada, and Roatan. Now, in addition to the publishing house in Waterford, we were also building businesses with very different operational models in four other cities in four other countries on another continent. This meant more staff in more time zones, more emails, more management challenges, and longer days. We had a hard deadline for leaving the office every day because, unlike in Baltimore when Kaitlin was little, I didn't have my parents for backup. We had to be out of the office by 5:40 p.m. at the latest to pick up Jackson from daycare by 6:00. We were fined for every minute we were late, but that wasn't really the problem. I hated Jackson being the last kid to be picked up. The staff was more cheerful about our perpetual tardiness than the staff at Kaitlin's daycare in New Freedom had been, but they made the point in their Irish way. "Our staff have families to get home to," the director of Waterford Childcare Centre Martha reminded me every time I rushed through the door past 6:00. "We really don't want to keep them from getting home, now do we?" she'd say, causing me to blush and look away in shame.

Our tour and conference businesses were expanding, too. Before the move to Ireland, I'd been hosting two or three events a year. Now we were offering twice that many, some in the States, others in markets of interest from Belize and Costa Rica to Argentina and Uruguay. Lief was the MC for every program, meaning he was taking five or six trips a year to host events and at least eight trips a year to check in on the local offices. He was on the road three weeks out of four. Sometimes, when I needed to travel with him, my parents would come to watch Kaitlin and Jackson for us. Other times, Kaitlin would stay with Sophia, and Jackson would come along with me. By the time he was four years old, Jackson had traveled to Paris, London, Bonn, and Baltimore for business meetings and to Panama, Belize, Costa Rica, and Nicaragua for scouting expeditions.

Lief and I both were exhausted and stressed, but Lief was struggling in another way, too. He'd never recovered from not having launched his own business in Ireland. I'd always wanted to believe that the resentment Lief felt would fade, but I'd watched—at annual Agora management conferences where Lief went out of his way to remain separate from the group and at every meeting with the Executive Committee—as Lief had grown more embittered, not less. More than once he'd raised his voice in discussions with Myles and other members of the Executive Committee, and, on one particularly memorable occasion at a three-day corporate retreat in France, he'd left the room in a huff, walked out of the building without a word or a glance in my direction, and driven off in our rental car. I'd been eight months pregnant with Jackson at the time, and, when Bill and Mark asked where Lief had gone in such a hurry, I told them I was having a craving and had asked Lief to run into town and bring me back something sweet. They knew me too well to believe that, I figured—I'm not that high maintenance—but I knew them too well to worry they'd make more of an issue of Lief's behavior, and they didn't. Maybe they or I should have, but I counted blindly on my ability to make things work, with Agora, with Lief, and in general. I didn't even ask Lief where he'd gone when he returned to the retreat center two hours later.

Lief was slow to believe anyone and rarely let his guard down, but, with Bill, Mark, Myles, and the other members of the Executive Committee—the Agora collective he referred to as "The Man"—he was especially reticent. "Lief acts as though we don't trust him," Bill had told me once, "but it's the other way around." Bill was right. Lief resented Executive Committee authority over him, as he'd always resented my relationships with Bill and Mark. For Lief, his role at Agora Ireland was a job. For me, Agora was my central driving force. I wanted so badly to be taken seriously within the Agora universe that whenever anyone there suggested I jump my only thought was, how high? More than that, I found the work, the travel, and the business development exciting. I liked the rush of being part of this constantly growing global team on the move.

In the beginning, I would have described Lief's feelings about how things had fallen apart with his Pouldrew House business plan as disappointment. Six years into our move, I could no longer deny that they'd been developing slowly into what could only be called rage. I also finally had to admit that, while Bill and Mark were on the receiving end of most of Lief's bitterness, some of it was aimed in my direction. I'd become expert at deflecting Lief's rancor and had been confident we were strong enough to survive it, but it was harder all the time not to acknowledge his increasingly bad attitude. My optimist's defenses were wearing thin.

On paper, we were living the Irish country life we'd come in search of, but beneath the surface, we were struggling, especially now that we'd doubled down on work. I was being pulled like a slingshot between family and Agora, taut in one direction and then the other, and Lief was under enormous pressure. I began to wonder how long I could continue to keep a lid on things.

XXX
Family Vacation

It was Lief's idea.

"Let's take a trip," he said one Sunday morning as we were cleaning up from breakfast. Every Sunday that we were home together we had an Irish fry-up—fried eggs, rashers, tomatoes, beans, mushrooms, and hash browns. It wasn't technically a full Irish breakfast. For that you need black pudding, the traditional blood sausage the Irish make from pork blood and beef suet. We'd given up trying to acquire a taste for it.

Kaitlin and Jackson had gone out to the barn to clean Chesapeake's stall, and Lief was covering the remaining rashers with aluminum foil.

"Not a business trip," he said as he put the plate of leftovers in the refrigerator. "I want to take a trip that has nothing to do with work. A vacation. Let's take a family vacation."

A vacation? A trip just for fun with no business agenda? We

FAMILY VACATION

hadn't taken one of those since our honeymoon trip to Turkey.

"That's a great idea," I said, meaning it. "We really could use a break, couldn't we. Do you have a destination in mind?" I began running across the world map in my head. *If we could go anywhere*, I thought, *where should we go...*

"Argentina," Lief said. "You have never been there. I'd like to show it to you."

Lief had lived in northern Argentina shortly after grad school with his first wife. He'd loved it, but Monica was lonely and bored in the remote little town where the drilling company Lief was working for had placed them and had insisted they return to the States. Lief had been to Argentina several times since for conferences and to research the property markets, but we'd never been able to travel there together, and I'd wanted to see where he'd lived with the wife before me. I also wanted to see Buenos Aires. Paris was my favorite city, and BA is made out to be the Paris of Latin America with the added appeal of tango on the street corners. Plus, Lief and I had been toying with the idea of investing in a small vineyard property. Well, we rationalized it as an investment. Really, we were infatuated with the thought of growing our own grapes and making our own wine. We'd even begun drawing designs for a label. This purchase would definitely be more about the fun than the profit, and we'd been thinking that San Raphael, Mendoza, where we had *International Living* connections, would be the place to make it. I began putting together an itinerary in my mind. We'd spend a few days in Buenos Aires, then take off to tour wine country. Kaitlin wouldn't be able to miss school, but she'd enjoy the chance for an extended stay with Gerri and Sophia…

"We could fly from Buenos Aires to Mendoza and then rent a car," Lief said, interrupting my thoughts and reading my mind. "Then we could explore as we liked."

"No meetings and no schedule," I said, drying my hands on the dish towel so I could give Lief a hug and a kiss on the cheek. "What a thing!"

"Right?" Lief said, smiling. "Just imagine it. No work agenda of any kind. Just us, coming and going when and where we want. And who knows. Maybe we'll find the vineyard property we've been talking about. I'll write to Paul Reynolds to ask if he has any small vineyards near San Raphael we could look at." Paul was our friend in Argentina who ran his family's real estate agency in Buenos Aires.

Lief emailed Paul the next day, and Paul responded right away with details of two small vineyards—one ten hectares, the other fourteen. The first was fully planted with vines, the second partially so, but the second also had a hacienda. Exactly what we'd been hoping to find.

I'd scheduled a conference call with Agora house attorney Matt Turner later that week to discuss a contract with a potential new advertiser. Matt and I had been friends in Baltimore, as well

FAMILY VACATION

as colleagues, and Matt had been one of the few supporters of the Agora Ireland expansion plan from the start. He'd traveled to Dublin during our first month in Ireland to spend a few days with Lief and me and Therese Rochford, finalizing our incorporation documentation and IDA paperwork. Matt was also the one member of the Executive Committee who Lief got along with. The two had formed a friendship, based on their shared love of travel and interest in property investing. I was glad for this, because it meant at least one person at Agora Lief and I could hang out with without tension. After Matt and I had finished reviewing the advertiser contract, I mentioned the trip Lief and I were planning to Argentina.

"You're going to look at vineyards in Mendoza?" Matt said. "That's a dream of mine, too. A vineyard in Argentina. Boy. Wouldn't that be something.

"Did you know," Matt continued, "that Agora is considering partnering in a property development in Argentina? Near Cafayate. With Doug Casey.

"In fact," Matt said, "Bill has asked me to review the development plan and make a recommendation. To do that properly, I'll need to travel to see the site. Maybe we could coordinate our trips?"

"Yes!" I said. Traveling with Matt would add another layer of interest to the trip. I was always all in on things like reconnoitering property for development in some far-away place with a friend. "Great idea. We'd love to have the time with you. Plus, it'd give us a chance to get to know Mary better." I'd met Mary a few times before she and Matt had gotten married, and I'd liked her. She was bright and cheerful, a good conversationalist. Just the kind of person you wanted for company.

"I'll speak with Lief," I said. "He'll love the idea."

"This was supposed to be a family vacation," Lief said when told him about my conversation with Matt. He sat back from his laptop and looked directly at me, frowning and sad. "You, me, and Jackson. I understand that Kaitlin can't come, but the idea was for us to spend time together as a family. Just relaxing. Now you want Matt and Mary to come? We barely know Mary."

"Well, that's part of the idea," I said, surprised by his response. I really hadn't imagined that he'd mind. "I thought you like hanging out with Matt."

"Yes, I like hanging out with Matt, but this was supposed to be a family vacation."

"It'll still be a family vacation," I said, realizing that really it wouldn't be, but how could I uninvite Matt and Mary? I couldn't. I'd just have to give Lief time to process things. He'd come around.

A few days later, as I was shutting down my laptop and Lief and I were preparing to leave the office to collect Jackson from daycare, Matt called.

"I've spoken with Doug's people," he said. "And they can coordinate for us to tour the development property in three weeks. I'm

FAMILY VACATION

thinking we fly to Buenos Aires two weeks from Friday. Could that work for you guys?"

"Sounds like a plan to me. I'll confirm with Lief." Lief and I hadn't spoken much about the trip since I'd shared the news that I'd agreed to hook our family vacation up with Matt's due diligence expedition. This would give me a reason to broach the subject again and get a read on Lief's state of mind.

But Matt wasn't finished sharing news.

"Bill would like Myles to come along, too," he said, "to help with financial projections. Myles is on board and wants to bring his wife."

Uh, oh. Lief liked hanging out with Matt but not so much with Myles and, though he and I had been friendly in Baltimore, the way Myles had treated Lief over the years had changed my view of him. Lief and Myles had reached an unspoken détente and had lately been civil with each other during meetings and conference calls, but no way did Lief want Myles along for our family vacation and, frankly, neither did I. Nothing to do but take a deep breath and go tell Lief right away. I walked over to his desk.

"Hey," I started. "I just got off the phone with Matt. He's suggesting we travel two weeks from Friday, which I told him should be fine. He also mentioned that Bill has asked Myles to join us, so Myles can help review the numbers for the Doug Casey deal. Myles is going to bring his wife."

Lief sat silent for a moment staring down at his desk then

he got up from his chair and, without a word, walked out of the room. It was a better reaction than I'd expected. I'd been prepared for shouting.

The next day, Matt called again.

"Plans are coming together for our trip," he said. "I'll email you our flight details and the itinerary we've put together."

"Okay, great," I said. I'd explained to Lief that Doug's development property was near Cafayate. So we'd extend the trip. We'd spend three days in Buenos Aires, four days in San Raphael, then two days in Cafayate looking at Doug's land. "It'll give us a chance to see a different part of the country," I'd told him.

"We're going to have to cut out the time in San Raphael," Matt was saying. "Myles and I can't afford more than a week for the trip in total. There are vineyards near Cafayate, too, so I thought we could just look at those. Save us trying to squeeze in San Raphael, which is much farther south."

This wasn't good. How would I tell Lief that not only had our family vacation morphed into another business trip but now it wouldn't even include the part of the trip that mattered to him most?

"Also," Matt continued, "David Galland is going to travel with us. He'll be along as Doug's representative."

This was worse than not good. This was really bad. Lief and David didn't get along at all. I'd never understood why, but they just didn't like each other. I didn't mind the further expansion of our tour group. Being invited to travel with Matt, Myles, and David made me feel like part of Agora's inner circle, the place I'd long craved to be. But how in the world would I sell this piece of news to Lief?

After I'd hung up from the call with Matt, I took a deep breath, put on a big smile, and walked over to Lief's desk. I needed to get this out before I lost my nerve.

"That was Matt," I said. "He's going to email the final itinerary and everyone else's travel details so we can coordinate our flights. He doesn't think there's time to go to San Raphael. So we'll have our time in Buenos Aires and then go straight to Cafayate. That's wine country, too, so we'll still be able to look at vineyards."

Lief didn't respond.

"Oh, also, Matt mentioned that Doug has asked David Galland to come along, to help show us around."

For the second time in as many days, my husband walked angrily out of the office. I felt mildly panicked. He had a right to be upset. I'd done what I always do. Not wanting to say no to Matt—just as I never wanted to say no to anyone or anything—I'd agreed and agreed and agreed. My absolute openness—to people, to ideas—made Lief crazy sometimes. "You move too quickly," he was always telling me. "You should consider the consequences of a thing before leaping into it. You're like a bull in a china closet." It wasn't the most flattering metaphor for a husband to use to describe his wife, but it wasn't wrong either. Every time he offered the caution, though, I wondered if Lief recognized the irony of it. I certainly hadn't taken much time to consider the consequences of marrying a man I'd known for three months and then moving with him to another country to start a business, had I?

Lief came back to the office an hour later.

"We're getting our own rental car," he said. "For the drive to Cafayate. We'll have our own car. I'll drive us." As he tried to do whenever possible, Lief was separating us from the Agora group. In this case, the small act of rebellion was understandable.

"Okay, no problem," I said, relieved if that was the extent of Lief's response to all the changes from our original program. "You're right. It'll be better if we drive ourselves. That way, we can pull over whenever we need to for Jackson." Jackson had gotten car sick whenever we drove long distances since he was a baby, and I was worried about how he'd fare on the long mountain drive.

Over the next week-and-a-half, as we booked tickets, arranged to be away from the office, and read up on things to do in Buenos Aires and Cafayate, I focused, when we spoke about the trip, on us alone. I tried to reassure Lief that this was still a family vacation. Yes, Myles and his wife had invited yet another couple to come along, as well, friends of theirs from Baltimore, meaning we were now a group of ten, but, as far as Lief and I were concerned, I tried to reinforce, we were a party of three. Just a happy family.

How bad could it be?

FAMILY VACATION

Our time in Buenos Aires passed quickly. I barely noticed the city. I was so preoccupied trying to keep Lief as far away from Myles and David as possible. Mary asked me if I wanted to go shopping with her our first afternoon in the city, and I declined. I didn't dare leave Lief alone with the rest of the group. Each night at dinner, I made sure Jackson and I were seated on either side of Lief, creating a buffer zone. When we went to the open-air antiques market in San Telmo, Lief walked off hotly until he was well ahead of the group and I let him. Jackson and I wandered from stall to stall with Mary and Matt, and I bought a hundred-year-old map of Ireland, thinking how nice it'd look on the wall in the home office Lief and I had set up in the fifth bedroom at Lahardan House and doing my best not to let Lief spoil the experience entirely.

After our three days in the capital, we took off early for the flight to Tucumán, where we rented two cars and set out, Lief driving Jackson and me and following behind David driving the van carrying everyone else. It turned out Jackson wasn't the only one who got car sick. Mary did, too. We had to drive slowly along the hairpin, switchback roads to accommodate their sensitive stomachs and to stop every fifteen or twenty minutes so they could get out either for a breath of fresh air or to throw up. The three-hour drive took six.

Despite all my Pollyanna efforts, Lief had arrived in Buenos Aires predicting that the trip was going to be a disaster. By the time we'd finally made it to Cafayete, Jackson and Mary sick and all of us tired, he was sure he'd already been proven right. In fact, that miserable six-hour mountain drive turned out to be the best part of the trip.

We spent the next couple of nights at Patios de Cafayate Hotel and Spa, a beautiful property in a wonderful mountain setting. Our room had a four-poster bed and a dramatic view; our bathroom had a big tub and soft, thick towels. It could have been a lovely getaway, but Lief seethed. I laid awake for hours each night, watching him, and I could feel his stress, even in his sleep. One day we went hiking through the mountains, another we were off to explore the nearby vineyards. All the while, Lief smoldered.

Then it was time to go to see Doug's property. Another long drive punctuated by regular roadside stops, some triggered by Jackson's crying that he was going to be sick... right now! "Pull over, pull over, pull over!" he'd cry. Sometimes Mary would join him looking pale and weak on the side of the road. I did my best to comfort Jackson during each emergency stop and to keep up light-hearted conversation when we were back on the road.

We arrived at the property late, long after dark. We were to be the guests of one of the sellers, coincidentally also the local mayor, who had invited all ten of us to stay in houses already built on the piece of land Doug was considering developing.

FAMILY VACATION

It had been raining for hours in advance of our arrival that night. The dirt roads were muddy, the grassy areas swamps. We each were driven to our respective houses by a member of the mayor's staff and dropped off with the suggestion that we all meet back at the main house for dinner.

Lief, Jackson, and I plodded through the mud of the yard and into our house. Jackson, usually a chatterbox, was so worn out from being so sick that he could hardly hold his head up. I considered putting him straight to bed, but he really should eat something before I put him to sleep, I thought. I wanted to wash his face and my own before rejoining the group for dinner and so went straight to the bathroom and turned on the taps in the wash basin. No hot water. The water wasn't the only thing that was cold. I was, too.

"Lief, would you please see if you can find the control for the heat?" I asked.

Lief walked room to room but could find no temperature control, because, it turned out, there wasn't one. The house not only had no hot water; it also had no central heating. Not the best development, but not the end of the world, at least not for me. I knew though that for Lief this was one more chip on his already weighted shoulders.

"Okay, let's just go back to the main house and have something to eat so we can call and end to this day and come back for some sleep," I suggested. "Which room do you want to put Jackson in?"

Lief and I walked through the three bedrooms, considering the situation. Then we started looking inside cabinets and under beds. We came up with two pillows and no blankets. It was June. It gets cold at night in this part of Argentina in June. Yet we had neither heat nor blankets.

I could feel Lief's blood pressure rising from across the room.

"Maybe the best thing," I offered, "would be for the three of us to sleep together, to help keep each other warm. We can decide where exactly after dinner. Let's just go over now to the main house. We'll all feel better after we've had something to eat."

We walked through the dark, through the mud, the fifteen minutes from the house where we were staying to the one where our host and the rest of our party were waiting for us.

It was after 10:00 p.m. when we walked in, and dinner was nowhere in sight. This isn't uncommon in Argentina, where 11:00 p.m. is a reasonable family dinner hour, but Jackson wasn't accustomed to eating after 10:00 at night. Lief asked about dinner, and our host assured us it was coming. Could he possibly make something sooner rather than later for Jackson, Lief wondered. At this suggestion, Jackson perked up and asked if he could have a hamburger.

"Could you make a hamburger for my son?" Lief asked our host, translating Jackson's English to Spanish. "*Sí, sí,*" our host replied, "No problem."

An hour later there was still no sign of any dinner.

Lief asked again if something could be brought out for Jackson.

FAMILY VACATION

And, then, finally, a plate appeared and was put before Jackson on the coffee table. But the plate didn't contain a hamburger. It was a plate of chicken.

Jackson looked at the plate with the chicken on the table in front of him and began to cry. Not loudly but definitely. He looked up, pale and small, at Lief and me and said, "But I didn't want chicken. I asked for a hamburger. The man said I could have a hamburger. Do I have to eat the chicken?"

Ordinarily, a child in this situation should do the polite thing and eat what he's been served without complaint. But these weren't ordinary circumstances, and Jackson had long before this moment been pushed past his breaking point. I take full responsibility for what followed. I should have put Jackson straight to bed. If I hadn't chosen to bring him to the main house for dinner, the rest of the evening's events might have been avoided.

I leaned down to cut off a few pieces of chicken, thinking that I'd try to get Jackson to put two or three bites in his stomach and then excuse him and me for the night. But, as I bent down, I heard Lief, behind me, shouting. He wasn't speaking sternly. He wasn't speaking loudly. He was shouting. I was at a loss. What does a wife do when her husband begins to shout at their host amidst a living room full of business associates?

Lief continued to shout, at the host, at the group, at the room. The rest of our travel party, our host, the cook, the other house staff, all stood around the big stone fireplace in the big, high-ceilinged, wood-paneled living room silent and still and staring at Jackson and his plate of chicken and at me cutting pieces of chicken. But Jackson wasn't interested in the chicken. The more I cut, the more he cried. But I couldn't stop cutting. What else was I going to do?

Finally, I picked up Jackson, grabbed our coats, and headed for the door. As I pushed past him, I noticed Lief, still shouting, reaching toward the sofa and picking up two cushions. He put one cushion under one arm and the other cushion under his other arm as he stood back up.

"There aren't enough pillows in the house where you've put us," he shouted at our host, the mayor. "So I'm taking these."

With that we three walked out into the rain and the mud to make our way back to our little unheated house. I was cold, hungry, and exhausted. I held Jackson close and tried to cover his head with my jacket, so he wouldn't get too wet. I considered crying but didn't have it in me. I walked faster to keep up with Lief, afraid that if I didn't I might lose my way in the dark. What must Matt and Myles be thinking, I wondered, then realized I was beyond caring. They'd think what they'd think. I couldn't worry about it anymore. The only question that mattered for me now was how in the world would Lief and I ever get past this disastrous evening.

XXXI
Shell-shocked

Maybe the craziest thing about Lief's blow up at the mayor's house in Cafayete was that we dealt with it by not dealing with it. We didn't speak about the dinner, not that night, not the next day, not the day after that, and not the day after that. I was in shock, unable to sleep, and so often on the brink of tears that I resorted to wearing dark glasses to hide my red puffy eyes. Lief carried on raging, going to bed angry and waking up sullen, but neither of us mentioned what had happened. I was afraid that addressing the situation directly might lead us to a place I didn't want to visit and wasn't sure we'd be able to find our way back from.

Fortunately and kindly, our travel companions didn't poke that bear either, but the final three days of the trip were miserable. Lief, Jackson, and I ate meals on our own because no one else would sit at the table with Lief. Back in Buenos Aires the night before our return flight to Ireland, Matt called our hotel room to extend an olive branch. He asked Lief if we wanted to share a car to the airport in the morning with him and Mary. The two of them ended up arguing over which car service would be cheaper, and, the next day, Lief, Jackson, and I left our hotel in Buenos Aires alone.

Lief and I didn't speak about anything during the long trip home beyond "Would you please hold Jackson while I load the luggage in the car?" and "Could we please pull over at the next gas station so I can use the bathroom?" Back in Waterford, we relied on routine to get us from one day to the next. The ground had fallen away from beneath my feet. Agora had been the place I went to escape the rest of my life, but now I was too embarrassed to reach out to my Agora support system. At the same time, I couldn't look to Lief for comfort. I needed to be the one to find a way to comfort him. My years of ignoring the tension between Lief and Agora had finally caught up with us. Nothing had changed in the short time we'd been away, but everything was different, and now that our difficulties were out in the open, they'd be denied no longer. How could we go on? Seriously, how would we put all this back in a box?

The stress I felt caught in the middle between my husband and my family in Ireland and my long connections to Bill, Mark, and others at Agora in Baltimore became overwhelming. Lief and I couldn't have a conversation, personal or professional, without it devolving into an argument. I was losing something big. The question was what. It'd never occurred to me that I couldn't have both my new life in Ireland with Lief and my old one with Agora in Baltimore, but now I faced a reckoning.

The Saturday after we'd returned from Argentina, as we were cleaning up the dishes from another tense meal, I tried to approach Lief.

"Maybe today we could hang the map of Ireland that I bought at the market in San Telmo," I suggested. "Maybe we could find a place for it in the office. What do you think?"

"I think you should do what you want with your map. You always do what you want anyway. What I want is irrelevant."

There it was. I'd seen my move to Ireland as a chance to prove to the powers that were at Agora and to myself that I could compete at their level. I was infatuated with the romantic idea of Irish country life, but, much more than that, I was consumed by a quest for approval and respect from Agora's highest ranks. For so long, that had been my holy grail. If they saw me as their peer, I'd have made it. So I'd hurtled through the days, weeks, months, and years in Waterford, building a life but taking every aspect of it for granted, including the place where I happened to be basing it. I'd been treating Lief as a member of my staff and Ireland as a footnote.

It was time for me to open my eyes and acknowledge that our life was fundamentally flawed and would be until I finally made a choice between career and family. I could return to my old ways and work as obsessively as I'd done for more than two decades. Or I could finally let go and slow down.

What would that even mean? What would a family-first life look like? I had to admit to myself that I'd never before imagined the idea directly. I have trouble sitting still. I feel unsettled unless I'm doing something productive. I could fill my days for a while with home-improvement projects, but that didn't seem like a rest-of-my-life plan. I'd welcome more time with Kaitlin and Jackson if I slowed down at work, but I knew myself well enough to realize that I'd be restless without ever-expanding to-do lists and constant deadlines. What did someone do all day if she wasn't working?

I sat at my desk one afternoon a few weeks after our return from Buenos Aires, trying again to process how Lief and I might move forward, when Deirdre buzzed my phone.

"A couple of readers have stopped by," she said. "They're visiting from New York to do research for a move to Ireland."

This wasn't unusual. In our publications, we invited readers to stop by if ever they found themselves in our neighborhood. We published our address and had an open-door policy. It was a small service for our readers and a way for us to get real-world feedback from people who were actually following through on the recommendations we were making and looking to make moves overseas. I wasn't always able to speak with readers who came to visit, but, when I was available, I enjoyed the chance.

"They would like to chat with you about your experiences living and running a business here," Deirdre continued. "They don't have an appointment but would appreciate a few minutes if you can spare them."

My experiences living and running a business in Ireland? Ha. I could give them an earful, sure I could.

Then, to Deirdre, "Yes, okay. I'm not busy at the moment." Just trying to figure out how to save my marriage. "Show them into the conference room. I'll meet them there."

I sat back in my chair and stared out my window at the bright red, green, blue, and yellow front doors of the Georgian townhouses along Catherine Street. My experiences living and running a business in Ireland? Where should I begin…

XXXII
One Nice Young Couple From New York

When I opened the door to the conference room, the couple seated next to each other on the other side of the round leather-topped table looked up and smiled. They were so young. Our *International Living* readers were typically in their fifties and older. These two looked barely thirty. They were wearing matching white Aran sweaters and had hung their Mackintosh rain coats over the backs of her chairs. They probably didn't pack warm enough clothes, I thought, and had to buy sweaters and jackets here when they realized June in Ireland isn't the same as June in New York… just like I'd done my first trip to Ireland.

"Hello. I'm Kathleen Peddicord," I said.

"I'm Robert and this is Kiara, and we're so happy to meet you," the young man offered in earnest. "We've been reading your maga-

ONE NICE YOUNG COUPLE FROM NEW YORK

zine forever. We're looking to start a tech company here in Ireland based on your recommendations over the years, and we really appreciate you meeting with us. We won't take up much of your time. We just thought you might have some tips on running a business in this country. We're flexible and could start our company anywhere in the world, but Ireland's investor and tax incentive programs, as you've explained them, sound very appealing to us. Plus, the economy is booming. We believe this could be the ideal place to base our software business, but we'd really like to know what you think." Robert blurted it all out in a rush, as though he was afraid I might not be willing to stick around long before wanting to get back to my busy life. I stood there before them, unmoving, for a long minute. Robert and Kiara leaned forward in their chairs. They were literally on the edges of their seats in anticipation of the pearls of wisdom to come.

It wasn't that long ago that Lief and I were on the other side of this table, asking for help and advice as we set out to start our business in Ireland. Suddenly I felt old. And tired.

"Have you spent much time in Ireland?" I asked, as I extended my hand to shake each of theirs in turn.

"No, this is our first visit," the young woman said. "We arrived three days ago."

I sat down in the green leather arm chair across from them and paused to gather my thoughts. These two had no idea what was in front of them. How much reality should I dose out? I didn't want to scare the two off their plan altogether, but, boy, wouldn't Lief and I have appreciated speaking with another American willing to share war stories when we were at the start of our Ireland adventures.

I sat back and looked directly across the table at the nice young couple so eager for guidance. If we had had someone to turn to for honest perspective when we first came to Ireland, what would I have wanted that voice of experience to tell us? What would have benefitted us most?

"In Dublin we met with two attorneys and a representative from Ireland's Investment and Development Agency," Robert was saying, trying to fill the extended gap since he'd last spoken, I guess.

"The man from the IDA told us he believes we'll qualify for their program and that now we need to decide where we want to base our business. We told him that we think Waterford might be the right location for us. After all, it's where you chose! So, after our meetings in Dublin, we took the train down here. We'd like to look at office space for rent and houses for sale, too, but we have been having trouble finding an agent who can help us. The ones we've spoken with don't seem to understand what we're asking for."

I smiled.

"We found this office by asking a lady in line behind us at the grocery store," I said.

Robert and Kiara looked puzzled. It hadn't occurred to them, I guess, that the best way to find office space in Waterford might be to ask a stranger while buying groceries.

ONE NICE YOUNG COUPLE FROM NEW YORK

"What is your plan for the rest of your time in the country?" I said.

"We're staying at the Granville Hotel for another week. We're scheduled to meet with another real estate agent. We also want to stop by the bank to see about opening a corporate account. And we'd like to meet with a recruiter to ask some questions about the local labor market."

Good luck finding a recruiter, I thought. They don't exist. And good luck at the bank. I hope you have more patience than my husband. You're going to need it. Ha, good luck with all of it!

Wow, had I really grown that cynical? I looked up again at the eager young couple seated across from me. No, it wasn't cynicism I was feeling, I realized. It was envy. They had all those misadventures ahead of them.

"I wouldn't worry about any of those things," I said. "Not your house hunt or the bank or finding staff. I'd set all that aside for now. Instead, I'd recommend you guys take this chance to get to know Ireland."

"What do you mean?" Robert asked.

"Well, get out to see the countryside. You could rent a car and drive to Lismore Castle, for example. It's about an hour west of here. The drive is lovely, and the castle gardens are glorious this time of year, everything in full bloom. We spent a Sunday afternoon there last month. My husband and I sat in the outdoor tea room watching our children play on the garden paths…"

Robert and Kiara looked more than puzzled. The way they were staring back at me, mouths half-open, I could have been speaking Chinese. What do castle gardens and tea rooms have to do with setting up a successful software company, I could almost hear them thinking. I ignored their reactions and carried on.

"Or you could travel in the other direction, to the east, to Kilkenny," I said. "Kilkenny Castle is one of the oldest and best preserved in the country. Its gardens aren't as elaborate or colorful as those at Lismore, but the castle really is worth seeing. It dates to the twelfth century. We've gone to visit once or twice a year every year we've lived here. It's the kind of place you can return to again and again.

"Our favorite place to visit, though," I continued, "is Bantry Bay. That's a half-day drive away, along the Wild Atlantic Way. Guidebooks say it's one of the most beautiful coastal drives in the world, and I'd say the guidebooks are right. We spent a weekend at Bantry House, overlooking the bay, with my family a few years ago, and it was one of the nicest trips of my life."

Robert and Kiara looked at each other and then back at me. I'd lost my audience. They weren't interested in hearing about Ireland's country houses and coastal drives. They wanted to know what they'd need to do to qualify for the IDA investor incentives, where to find office space, and how to hire employees. I was waxing poetic about Ireland's charms. They wanted to talk business.

"That all sounds nice," Robert said, "but we've got just a week more in the country to try to formulate a plan for moving here. Do you agree that Waterford would be a good choice for where to make our base?"

"In fact," I said, smiling and feeling more envious of them all the time, "I'd say Waterford is a ridiculous place to base a business. Honestly, I'd say that Ireland in general is not a place to come as an entrepreneur." I knew that what I was saying directly contradicted recommendations we'd been making in *International Living* articles for years, but I wasn't going to let that get in my way. I was seeing Ireland clearly for the first time and didn't want to hold myself back.

"The Irish," I continued, "they're not businesspeople. Trying to do business with them has been a maddening experience. They don't value efficiency, and they don't do overtime. They do take tea breaks. Tea breaks are actually *required* in employment contracts. And they like to chat, the Irish do," I added.

"If your agenda is business, you have better options than Ireland, investor incentives and low corporate tax rates aside."

I felt as though I'd stepped out of myself, like I was standing alongside myself speaking back at me, setting myself straight.

"My husband and I came to Ireland seven years ago," I told Robert and Kiara, "with a straight-up business objective, just like you two. We roared into Ireland." I shook my head slowly. "And we held fiercely to our plan. We were going to make a success of our publishing business, by golly, no matter what obstacles Ireland put in our way. We'd overcome them. We were certain that Ireland was no match for us.

"We bought a house that turned out to have rising damp. Have you ever heard of 'rising damp'? Neither had we. It leads to rot, and the house we bought had had rising damp for years so it was full of it. Rot, I mean. Every piece of wood on the first floor was rotted through. We found a rising dap guy and pushed ahead with the renovation even though it turned out we had to tear the house apart completely and then put it back together piece by piece. We had a baby and brought him home at the height of the renovation work. My husband, my daughter, the baby, and I ate our meals together in the master bedroom for months because it was the only habitable room.

"We couldn't find staff with experience in our industry because our industry didn't exist in Waterford or anywhere in Ireland. Still doesn't. We hired stable hands and hotel front desk clerks and tried to teach them the publishing business. We had to teach the bankers, too, as well as our attorney and the auditors that the Irish Revenue Commission insisted on sending to review our books each year. None of them had ever encountered a business like ours, not before and not since."

I paused to look squarely at Robert and Kiara and burst out laughing. They were sitting straight up in their chairs, like a jolt was passing through them, and they'd gone pale. Maybe they felt misled. We had, after all, been writing for years about the business

ONE NICE YOUNG COUPLE FROM NEW YORK

opportunities on offer in Ireland. Strictly speaking, those opportunities existed and did have a financial upside. Now that Agora Ireland was turning a profit, Bill sure was enjoying the tax breaks we'd qualified for by moving here.

"But none of that's the point," I said, still speaking as much to myself as to the poor confused couple from New York.

What was the point, I wondered, as I swiveled my chair slightly so I could see beyond Robert and Kiara. From the window to the left of them, I had a view of Michael's shop on the corner, the place where we'd gone for lunch three or four times a week since we'd moved into this office. When Jackson was born, Michael and his wife had sent a small gift, even though they'd barely known us then.

A couple of years later, Michael had finally admitted that, when we'd first shown up in Waterford, everyone thought we were Jehovah's Witnesses. "We'd watch the three of ye'," he'd said, "dressed all in black, walking up and down the streets day after day for weeks. We couldn't imagine what ye' were getting up to." Back in Baltimore and Chicago, our black coats and boots were chic. Here they'd had us pegged as evangelists. "We had no choice but to walk everywhere," I'd told Michael, "because we were having so much trouble shopping for a car."

I laughed again remembering the day we'd asked the taxi driver if he'd take us out to the car dealerships on the Cork Road and how he'd told us he couldn't because it was Saturday. How daft were these Americans, he must have been thinking, not to know that you can't buy a car on a Saturday? Car salesmen weren't at work on a Saturday. They were at home with their families, right where they ought to be.

Now Robert and Kiara were looking at me as though they'd grown a little afraid. *What was wrong with this woman?* They seemed to be wondering. *Was she having some kind of attack?* Maybe I was. I couldn't stop giggling as the memories kept coming.

I recalled the first auction we'd attended at Rody's and how I'd snatched the bid card out of Lief's lap to buy a chair that two days later I had to ask Rody to resell for me. I thought about all the auctions and visits to Rody's shop since and remembered the silver dollar Rody had dropped into Jackson's stroller the first time Lief and I had stopped in with our new baby.

I thought of the day the woman in the carvery line at Reginald's Pub had piled Lief's plate with a mountain of potatoes that he kept insisting he didn't want and wouldn't pay for.

I thought about Kaitlin's evolution. Hard as she'd fought against the idea in the beginning, she'd finally created a life for herself on this island. She and Sophia were inseparable and for her birthday recently she'd hosted a half-dozen girls for a sleepover. She had hurling and ballet. And Chesapeake. How she loves her horse, I thought. I could see her and Jackson atop Chesapeake together, Kaitlin holding her little brother tightly around his middle as she trotted with him through our fields.

ONE NICE YOUNG COUPLE FROM NEW YORK

I thought of sitting on the window bench in Morette's kitchen, watching her bustle around. I should call Morette. I hadn't been over to visit since we'd gotten back from Argentina.

The thought of Argentina snapped me sharply back to the present. How long had I been lost inside my head? Robert and Kiara were looking at me now as though they were trying to come up with an excuse for a quick exit. I felt bad for them. This could hardly have been what they'd hoped for when they'd decided to stop by to meet with me.

We're a pair, Ireland and I, I thought, ignoring the looks on Robert and Kiara's faces. When we arrived on this Emerald Isle, I, like Ireland, was obsessed with being taken seriously, determined to prove myself competitive in ways that didn't matter and to earn the respect of people who didn't appreciate what I had to offer. Like Ireland, I was so driven in my quest for more that I'd become expert at ignoring what'd been right in front of me all along.

Lief and I had come to Ireland as strangers. Seven years here had shown us the best of ourselves and of each other. Ireland had given us the time and space to deconstruct the lives we'd brought with us to her shores. The question was what would we do now with all the pieces so splintered and scattered?

Looking over at Robert and Kiara, the answer to that question was clear. The thing to do was to reassemble the parts, now laid bare, of the two lives we'd brought with us into one unified new one. And the way to do that was to show Lief that I was ready to prioritize him and our family over Agora and my work. I'd ignored that challenge all along because I'd known that any attempts to convince Lief he and our family were the most important things in my life would have come off as hollow. Because, until this moment, they would have been. But thanks to that absurd dinner party in Argentina and now this trip down memory lane courtesy of this nice young couple from New York, I realized I was finally ready to step from the world of Agora fully and firmly into the new world that Lief and I had built together.

Yes, boy, how I envied these two, Robert and Kiara. What adventures they had to look forward to.

"We've taken up enough of your time," Robert was saying. "We should let you get back to work."

"No worries," I said. "I'm in no rush. I don't think I've given you what you came for. You'll never know how glad I am that you stopped by, but you don't need me. Come to Ireland with your dream. Ireland will take care of the rest. Just give her the chance."

I shook hands with Robert and Kiara as they thanked me again then walked out. I stood at the window watching them. I was glad I hadn't tried harder to dissuade them of their game plan. I wouldn't have wanted anyone to rob Lief and me of the chance to let Ireland work her magic on us in her own good time. Our experiences over the past seven years had threatened to break us, but here we were still. We'd earned the right to call Ireland home, and I couldn't think of anything that made me prouder.

XXXIII
Settled

A month after our return to Waterford, Lief and I still hadn't addressed the train wreck that had been our family vacation in Argentina. He'd taken to staying up late, playing video games on his computer in the office. I'd rise before him, to ready Jackson for daycare. "What would you like me to take out of the freezer for dinner?" I'd ask. "Whatever you want," was his regular reply. Ordinarily, Lief keeping separate because he was clearly unhappy would have distracted and stressed me. I'd want to force the issue until we'd talked through and resolved the problem. But that was the old me. The new me was more patient because I was more certain. My conversation with Robert and Kiara had shifted something inside me and refreshed my perspective. I wanted to put the tension I'd felt all the years I'd been caught in the middle between Agora and Lief and the craziness that that stress had led to in Argentina behind us and move forward with my focus fixed on my family and the home we'd worked so hard to make on the Emerald Isle. I was prepared to wait for Lief to come around. I knew that he would. We were forged steel.

I was right. It wasn't long before the day-to-day of our Irish country life pushed aside the memories of the blowup in Argentina and everything that had led up to it. Lief had always been fully pledged. It was my loyalty that had seemed in doubt. Now I was all in, too. Agora and the office were no longer my laser focus. Lief and our family were my steady priority.

No sooner had I resolved to settle into our fully fledged life in Waterford and to be open to where it might lead us than my commitment was put to the test.

In Ireland, most kids take what they call a Gap Year after the equivalent of their sophomore year of high school. They go on year-long adventures, studying, traveling, or working abroad. When Kaitlin's friends at school began discussing their plans for their Gap Years, she devised one of her own.

"I'd like to study in Paris," she told Lief and me unceremoniously on the drive home from school one afternoon.

What was this? Kaitlin, who I'd had to drag kicking and screaming to Ireland seven years before, now wanted to make another international move? My little girl wanted to go to Paris… on her own!

SETTLED

Kaitlin's reluctance to open up to Ireland had been one of the most difficult things about the move. When finally I'd allowed myself to believe that she'd made the leap to accepting Ireland as home, the sense of relief was enormous. Now she not only was no longer talking about going back to Baltimore, but she was proposing a bold going-forward plan of her own devising. Maybe I could stop worrying that me having torn her from her family in Baltimore to create a new one in Waterford might lead to years of therapy—for her and for me. My daughter was brave enough and strong enough to imagine yet another new start. It was one more triumph that I added to the list of bounties Ireland had brought us.

My first months at Agora, I'd been a fish out of water. Everyone else was so well traveled. I'd gone to Bermuda for spring break my senior year of high school, but other than that I'd never used my passport. I'd always wanted to see Paris. I'd been captivated by Hemingway and Fitzgerald's wine-soaked exploits in the City of Light since I'd read about them for the first time in English lit class freshman year of high school.

A year after I'd started at Agora, Bill had agreed to my request for an extended vacation. My college roommate and I planned a three-week-long Eurail Pass adventure across the Continent that included three days in Paris. We drank champagne at the Deux Magots, took each other's photos in front of the Shakespeare and Company bookstore, and generally followed in the footsteps of my City of Light writer heroes. Paris was every bit as beautiful and romantic as I'd expected her to be, and I knew I'd be back.

I'd returned many times for business meetings but each time for just a few days. Now here was a chance to spend extended time in Paris visiting my daughter. Kaitlin definitely had my attention. I didn't like having to admit it, but she was growing up and, my, what a young lady she was showing herself to be, capable of thinking big and being brave. Lief had the same reaction I did. It was hard to think about Kaitlin taking such an independent step but what an opportunity for her.

She and I made a reconnaissance trip to visit potential homestay families, but the accommodations on offer were so awkward and uncomfortable that I couldn't imagine placing Kaitlin in them. But she was set on the idea of spending a year in Paris and I didn't want to disappoint her. On the plane ride back to Waterford, I contemplated a big new plan. I didn't like the idea of Kaitlin being away from us and on her own in another country, and I didn't want our little family, now finally made whole, to be separated. But maybe Kaitlin didn't have to go off to Paris by herself. What if we all went along with her…

Like the suggestion set out by Bill years before that I move to Ireland, this notion, once it struck me, that Kaitlin shouldn't move alone but we should all reposition to Paris together, didn't seem dramatic. It was an organic next step. It'd be a fresh start that had nothing to do with Agora, the kind of clean slate I now wished we'd had years before.

SETTLED

Lief was an easier sell even than I expected. Like me, he had been infatuated with Paris from an early age. He'd even been married to his first wife in Paris, with wedding photos at the Jardin de Luxembourg to prove it. Now he and I would have a chance to make a home in Paris ourselves.

There was just one catch, but it was a big one. I'd decided to take this turning point as the chance to make my break from Agora. I could have spoken with Bill about reinventing my role. Maybe I could have continued managing Agora Ireland from Paris. Agora had lots of experience with those kinds of cross-border arrangements, and Bill would have been infinitely flexible. But I'd straddled two worlds for too long.

The thought of leaving Agora was paralyzing. It had been the center of my universe for more than two decades. My work there and my relationship with Bill had gotten me through my divorce from Rick and had literally opened the world up to me. On the other hand, the deep and complicated connections I felt to Agora had nearly cost me my marriage. It'd taken the absurdity of our trip to Argentina to shake me out of my denial about the tension my conflict of loyalties had created. I finally had to admit that I was well past the point of being able to keep my relationship with Agora and my marriage, too. I allowed myself several days for the enormity of that idea to settle in.

Lief had already decided to resign and was planning a next project, developing a piece of property on the Pacific coast of Panama.

He would finally have the business of his own he'd been wanting since the day I'd met him. This was my chance to show Lief that his agenda was now my priority. With my newfound clarity, I understood what I stood to lose. I had no choice but to choose family over work and to cut my Agora ties, and I was ready.

Bill didn't let me quit easily. When I called to tell him Lief and I were moving our family to Paris and that I wanted to take the transition as an opportunity for a whole new beginning, he responded as I thought he might.

"Now, hold on," Bill said. "Don't make any rash decisions. I'll come to Waterford so we can talk this through."

"No, Bill," I said, pretending strength. "I've spent enough years trying to prove myself in the business world. It's time for me to focus on my family." I wasn't sure what that meant exactly. I had no idea what my new life would look like. What in the world would I do with myself? Fortunately, I didn't have to actually come up with an answer to that question. I was clear on one thing only. I wanted the life I'd built with Lief, Kaitlin, and Jackson, and I was ready to do whatever I needed to do to deserve it, starting with moving on from the thing that had cost me so much time with my children and nearly driven Lief away.

"Okay," Bill said finally, reluctantly, after extended back and forth. "You've earned a break. You take all the time you need. We'll call it a sabbatical. When you're ready to come back, Mark and I will be here waiting for you. This is a temporary thing."

I wasn't so sure about that, but it didn't matter. I'd made the cut.

I'd persuaded Bill not to come to Waterford to try to talk me out of quitting, but I did want to meet to say good-bye in person. I thought about organizing a meeting with Bill when the opportunity presented itself without telling Lief and felt instantly ashamed. That had been my mistake all along—failing to connect Lief, who represented my new life, with Bill, from my old one. Enough of that behavior.

"I'd like to arrange to see Bill to kind of wrap things up before I go," I told Lief one night after Kaitlin and Jackson were both asleep. "Do what you want," was all he said, showing me beyond any shadow of doubt that leaving Agora was the right choice.

A few weeks later, when Bill and I were both scheduled to be in Paris, we met at a café on the river where we'd met dozens of times before over the years, for business and for fun. Bill tried to make small talk, asking how our plans for the move were coming along and what I would do with all the free time I'd have on my hands.

"I'll be busy for several months with the logistics of the move, I figure," I told him. "After that, I'll be a non-working mother in Paris. If I'm going to see what doing nothing is like, I figure Paris is a good place for it. I'll finally have time to visit some museums,"

I added wryly, trying to lighten the mood.

Then I had to stop talking because I was afraid that if I didn't I'd start crying. I was saying good-bye to the man I'd come to count on the way I counted on my father and to a life that I'd worked years to build. It was a lot of letting go. By the time Bill motioned for the check, reached for his homburg hat, and pulled out my chair for me, I could no longer restrain the tears.

On the sidewalk out front, standing with the river and the Louvre behind him, Bill took me by my shoulders, kissed me on both cheeks, smiled, and said, "It won't be forever. You let me know when you want to come back. And you stay in touch." Then he turned and walked off down the *quai*. I wasn't sure I'd be able to move from the spot where he'd left me. These would be the first steps I'd take as an adult without Agora driving me. I felt disoriented and slightly queasy. Bill turned the corner out of view. I stood a moment longer staring after where he'd been, then looked over in the direction of the Louvre and the Tuileries Gardens. Just take one step, I told myself. One step. You have places to be.

We still had one thing to do. We needed to sell Lahardan House.

When Lief and I arrived in Ireland, we were convinced the property market was at its peak. Values had been rising for years for no reason we could understand, with Irishman selling to Irishman for more at every transaction in what seemed to us to be a giant Ponzi scheme. Surely, that couldn't continue. We'd purchased Lahardan House because we needed a place to live. We weren't thinking about appreciation potential. Over the years since, every time we'd checked, property values in Ireland had continued to go up—at a rate of twenty percent or more per year. Sleepy little Waterford saw some of the slowest growth countrywide. Still, by the time Kaitlin came to us to say she'd like to leave Ireland, our Irish home looked to be worth maybe considerably more than what we'd invested in it.

We'd gone to see John Rohan, who'd told us he'd be delighted to sell Lahardan House.

"You've done her up nicely, haven't ye'," he'd said when we met. "Rody Keighery tells me the place has been fully restored and decorated beautifully." Nothing was private in Waterford.

"To get top value, given the prime condition of the property," John said, "we should sell at auction."

Since we'd stopped in to Morette's law office on Parnell Street all those years ago, Lief and I had attended several other property auctions. Real estate was our hobby. Sitting in the back of an estate agent's auction room watching how high bidders were willing to go for a particular piece of property was entertainment of the highest sort. The idea of hosting our own auction to sell our Lahardan House was exciting.

John Rohan scheduled a date and ran ads in the local papers. Then, on the morning of the auction, he installed Lief and me in a hidden, windowless room off to the side of the auction room that we'd never known existed. We sat at a small table positioned so we could watch the goings-on in the next room on a video monitor attached to the opposite wall. It was like reality TV except it was our actual reality. My stomach did loops as I watched people trickle in. Would we find a buyer? The room was filling, but we knew most of the crowd would be bystanders there just to see if the house sold and, if so, for what price.

The action got under way. It was soon clear we had five serious bidders. Three pulled out quickly, leaving a gentleman from Cork and a gentleman from Dublin. They went back and forth, first in the main auction room and then, eventually, from two separate, private rooms where John Rohan had escorted each in turn, for more than thirty minutes.

"I've told the buyer from Dublin that the gentleman from Cork is considering by how much he'd be willing to increase his offer," John Rohan said in a rush as he burst through the door into the little room where Lief and I sat waiting.

"However, the other buyer, the one from Cork, he's gone. He said he'd reached his limit and excused himself from the bidding. He's left the building. Our buyer from Dublin doesn't know this, but it won't be long before he figures it out. This is your chance. If you're selling, you're selling today, now. I believe I can push the Dublin bidder up another 50,000 euro, but that's all I'm going to get out of him."

Lief and I looked at each other and then down at the table.

SETTLED

Neither one of us seemed to want to respond. John Rohan's projected selling price had us returning our investment fourfold. Why were we hesitating to accept it?

I knew the answer to that question, of course. Lahardan House was a symbol of our life in Ireland. We didn't buy it as an investment. While the return on capital would give us the seed money we needed to launch the next phase of our lives together, it was hardly the point. We'd charged headlong into the purchase of Lahardan House, just as we'd pushed headstrong into every aspect of our move to Ireland. Then Lahardan House, like so many things about this place, had forced us to slow down. We'd had to dismantle not only an old Georgian country house but ourselves and our relationship to find the life we hadn't even realized we'd come to Ireland in search of. Ireland had taken the transients who'd shown up in a rush on her shores and settled them. I'd poured my soul into the hard work of restoring Lahardan House, and she was part of mine, but it was time to let her go.

We told John Rohan to push the bidder from Dublin as far as he could and then to accept the offer. We were selling Lahardan House.

The next morning, when we passed Rody on the street outside his auction house, he looked at us with a frown that let us know he'd heard the news. Word spreads quickly in little Waterford.

"So ye' are leaving us, are ye'?" he said. "And it's to Paris ye' are headed, is it now?"

"Yes, it was Kaitlin's idea," I said. "She decided she'd like to go for her Gap Year. Lief and I decided we'd take Jackson and tag along with her, why not?"

"Why not indeed," Rody said. "But, before you go, you must allow Anne and me to stand you a drink at J&K's. Please do us the honor. Then, after, we'll go for dinner at Henry's Downes. I'll ring Morette. She and David will want to join us, sure they will." It was Lief and I who were honored. Outsiders weren't invited to share a drink at J&K's. The Victorian pub, one of the oldest in the city, was locals only. And now, just as we were about to depart, that included us.

Two months later, we'd closed on the sale of Lahardan House, sold most of its contents, and packed the rest into a container headed for Paris.

The morning of our departure, after we'd loaded the suitcases into the car and Lief was buckling Jackson into his car seat, I went back inside the house on my own. I walked through the big red Georgian front door, through the entry, past the stairs where the little bent Irishman had plunged his screwdriver, and to the back hallway where Jackson had most often seen his ghost and where

SETTLED

I'd lingered at the big shuttered window every time I'd passed to enjoy the view of the kitchen garden at the top of the hill with its yellow picket fence and arched trellis. I stood before the window now, looking up and down the hall, to the French doors of the living room and the cypress beyond where Kaitlin and Jackson liked to play then, in the other direction, to the Stanley stove in the kitchen and the spot where my father had positioned the box containing our dishwasher so we'd have a table while the renovation work was under way. It was early spring and through the kitchen window I saw the daffodils that Jackson and I had planted, the first signs of life this season in the cottage garden Ian, Gerri, and I had made. I reached out to touch the wooden shutter of the hall window, wanting to be physically connected to this place. "Good-bye… and thank you," I said out loud, pushing back the heartbreak of knowing I'd never walk these floors again to make room for the flood of joy replacing it as I thought of the new adventure my family and I would now be chasing together. Then I marched back to the front entry and out the red front door, my chin high, my eyes smiling, to join Lief and the kids in the car.

It was time to move on. Ireland had given me one of the greatest gifts I could imagine by showing me that the life she'd help me to build was about as good as any life gets. Ireland had gotten my priorities straight. I wasn't sad leaving her now, because I knew we weren't really. She'd be coming along, grounding me wherever life took us from here, starting with Paris.

Would You Like To Stay In Touch With Kathleen?

Follow Her Global Adventures Here...

The world's savviest, most experienced, and most trusted source for information on living, retiring, and investing overseas

Kathleen Peddicord's Live And Invest Overseas has helped countless readers take advantage of the world's best opportunities for living better, retiring well, and chasing adventure. She shares her ongoing experiences around the world both through the www.liveandinvestoverseas.com website… and also through email. Kathleen's *Overseas Opportunity Letter* is a daily dispatch from her, with contributions from her far-flung network of editors, experts, friends, and advisors. Each day you'll find out about the best opportunities for international living, retiring overseas, and investing in real estate around the world.

Overseas Opportunity Letter is a completely free service. You can find out more at www.liveandinvestoverseas.com.

Made in the USA
Coppell, TX
06 June 2023